The Road through the Rust Belt

The Road through the Rust Belt

From Preeminence to Decline to Prosperity

William M. Bowen
Editor

2014

W.E. Upjohn Institute for Employment Research
Kalamazoo, Michigan

Library of Congress Cataloging-in-Publication Data

The road through the Rust Belt : from preeminence to decline to prosperity / William
M. Bowen, editor.
    pages cm
    Includes bibliographical references and index.
    ISBN-13: 978-0-88099-475-0 (pbk. : alk. paper)
    ISBN-10: 0-88099-475-4 (pbk. : alk. paper)
    ISBN-13: 978-0-88099-476-7 (hardcover : alk. paper)
    ISBN-10: 0-88099-476-2 (hardcover : alk. paper)
    1. Middle West—Economic conditions. 2. Middle West—Economic policy. I. Bowen,
William M.
    HC107.A14R63 2014
    330.977—dc23
                                    2013046745

The facts presented in this study and the observations and viewpoints expressed are
the sole responsibility of the authors. They do not necessarily represent positions of
the W.E. Upjohn Institute for Employment Research.

Cover design by Alcorn Publication Design.
Index prepared by Diane Worden.
Printed in the United States of America.
Printed on recycled paper.

Contents

1
Introduction

Edward W. (Ned) Hill
Cleveland State University

For many years, members of the faculty and research staff in the Maxine Goodman Levin College of Urban Affairs at Cleveland State University have paid keen attention to the problems and issues faced by midwestern industrial cities. As part of a university community, we joined with colleagues across campus to think about how to respond to disruptive change in the regional economies of twentieth century industrial cities and regions.

There is no one, simple recipe for renewing prosperity in midwestern industrial cities. But virtually all of the partial answers that emerged from our investigations recognize in one way or another that the greatest hopes and assets in these cities reside in the talent and energy of the people who live and work within them. In times of difficulty, individuals and groups discover unsuspected strengths and reveal qualities and capabilities that had not previously been seen. How can the huge reserve of human possibilities within midwestern industrial cities be released?

The chapters in this book do not contain a single, complete, and satisfying answer to the question of how to rekindle prosperity in these cities. They contain no silver bullets, but together they may be silver buckshot. They provide valuable ideas to generate prosperity.

We commissioned chapters in which each author looks at the prospects of renewal through the lens of his or her own specialty and experience. The chapters are all scholarly in nature, but they have been written for an audience that appreciates a style that is less formal than is usually found in purely academic writing. Some of the chapters are predicated upon the commonly shared point of view that the role of markets in these cities is often either misunderstood or insufficiently understood. Most share the perspective that one of the keys to renewed prosperity is

1

found in an increased appreciation of markets and the institutions that enable, support, and constrain them.

Historically, most city leaders work in the here and now and with the expectation that change will be gradual. Today's reality is vastly different; the pace of change has vastly accelerated. Changes that range from shorter product cycles and globalization of markets to the impact of transportation systems on sprawl require ideas and continual efforts to promote prosperity.

The next chapter, by William M. Bowen and Kelly Kinahan, provides an overview of the book's theme that we are in a time of economic transition. The world order that prevailed in the early-to-mid-twentieth century, during which time midwestern industrial cities were in their heyday, has been replaced by a different kind of global economy, one that is continuing to change. As the influence of China and India continues to grow, the U.S. economic system in general, and the regional economic systems of midwestern industrial cities in particular, will play a less dominant role. At the same time, however, much of the anxiety this transition brings about is unnecessary. While the global market dominance of midwestern cities has eclipsed, new opportunities await. Urban and regional economies can attain high levels of prosperity without economic dominance.

This is followed by a chapter written by Benjamin Y. Clark, in which he asks the question: Why do some older industrial cities continue to thrive economically while others sputter and decline? In this context, are success and failure dependent on luck, or is there something more profound at play? While there are many ways to address the issue, and certainly many factors that contribute to the success or failure of cities, this chapter examines one part of that question: Can tax expenditures play a role in stimulating the growth of these cities? The focus is on how and why state and local governments use tax expenditures to attempt to improve the conditions of their communities. The chapter seeks to demonstrate that tax expenditure policy is highly inconsistent. Local governments are at the mercy of a macroeconomic environment over which they have little influence. This lack of control leaves local governments with few tools at their disposal to create positive change in their communities. The devices that these governments often turn to are tax expenditures. Unfortunately, tax expenditures play little or no role in positive economic development. Despite the evidence, politicians continue to see tax expenditures as one of the most important options available to them. To understand this, and to act accordingly, is an important step in renewing prosperity in midwestern industrial cities.

Haifeng Qian, in Chapter 4, starts by surveying the literature on the evolution of industrial clusters and explores its implications for the revival of U.S. cities such as Detroit, Michigan, and Cleveland, Ohio. These old industrial cities feature declining or declined clusters and are struggling to invigorate their economies. The chapter reviews various definitions and typologies of clusters. Next, it summarizes four streams of literature discussing the evolution of clusters, in the process identifying some major forces behind the dynamics of clusters based on the limited research available. The chapter does not solely address clusters manifested in old industrial cities, since one type of cluster may evolve into another type. It examines cluster development in the industrial Midwest using Cleveland as an example, and explores the implications of clusters' evolution paths for the restoration of old industrial cities.

In the fifth chapter, Joel A. Elvery begins by describing a "bucket" or "shoveling" analogy for the labor force. The labor market for each skill group is a bucket. The bucket for the lowest skills is large, but it is completely full *and* shrinking relative to the other buckets. Elvery suggests that workforce development policy over the last 45 years has been analogous to efforts to keep shoveling people into the lowest-skilled labor market. While a lucky few find a way to stay in that labor market segment, most spill over the side. This discourages the unlucky who remain unemployed, and it wastes public workforce training resources. Thus, workforce development policies as presently constituted have had limited success. The chapter suggests that the workforce development system needs to refocus on advancement and describes policies and programs that fit this orientation.

The sixth chapter is written by Gregory M. Sadlek and Joan Chase. Academics have not typically made a very good case that the arts and humanities have contributed tangibly to regional prosperity. This chapter attempts to help remedy this shortcoming, largely through a focus on Cleveland as an example of cities throughout the Rust Belt in which the question of how to regain lost status and former success has become fundamental. For many, prosperity is linked only to strong and vital economic activity. This chapter takes a different view. While Sadlek and Chase recognize that wealth is fundamental to civic well-being, the arts and humanities also play a vital role. Their view is based upon the recognition that the word "prosperity," derived from our verb "prosper," ultimately comes from the Latin terms *pro* and *spes*, or, literally, "for the sake of hope." It shows how the building blocks of prosperity suggest something more than just having a strong economy. Indeed, the road to prosperity for people in midwestern industrial cities may well be the path to a broad increase in hope in the prospects for a stronger regional economy, for clean, safe, and interesting places to live, for higher levels of personal fulfillment, and for a community that once again takes pride in itself and what it can offer to the world. This chapter explores how Cleveland's traditionally solid base in the arts and culture can be a major part of the journey. It argues that the road to prosperity must involve increased quality of life in all facets.

Chapter 7 is written by Andrew R. Thomas, who has for many years worked as a geophysicist and attorney in the energy arena. Thomas draws on a wide range of sources to argue that some energy policies and practices have had a material and adverse impact on cities in general and specifically on midwestern cities. Thomas argues for a range of energy policies that would help renew prosperity in these cities. Current energy policies that have had negative effects include low-cost gasoline, which has encouraged sprawl; public policies designed to encourage rural electrification, which have caused urban electric rates to be artificially high; public policies that have discouraged cogeneration and distributed generation, which have created an artificially high-cost electrical energy grid in urban areas; promotion of trucking over railroads and waterways, which has decreased the natural advantage of Great Lakes cities as centers of transportation; and failure to adjust rapidly enough to changing technologies and circumstances. The general reason given for this inertia is the mighty resistance to change put up by the trillion-dollar-a-year energy business. Alterations that may be good for society in general may not be good for this particularly influential industry. In a society where policy is set by competing advocacy groups, alignment with the status quo has a significant advantage. Energy policies that can help to renew prosperity in these cities include those that encourage distributed generation. In addition, exploitation of natural gas from shale formations will enable near-term growth and provide a bridge to renewable generation, and policies that reflect the actual costs of producing and delivering energy will encourage development of the traditional central city. Midwestern cities must also develop an energy infrastructure that makes urban life easier and more attractive, such as faster and more comfortable public transportation systems.

Chapter 8, written by Chieh-Chen Bowen, begins by recognizing that, throughout the twentieth century, no single nation or block of nations had nearly as much economic power and influence as the United States. However, in the twenty-first century, total U.S. world supremacy is ending. China is on the rise and will one day soon—probably in the next decade—become the largest economy in the world. Indeed, at current growth rates, China's economy is doubling in real terms every seven or eight years. For industry in midwestern cities, this newly emerging economic power means, among other things, that the renewal of prosperity depends in essential ways on how well American entrepreneurs and firms can penetrate Chinese markets. This effort, in turn, demands knowledge and understanding of what Bowen calls "the basic Chinese social mechanism." The old saw that one can buy in one's own language and culture but must sell in the language and culture of the buyer is especially important when contemplating doing business with Chinese customers. This chapter describes and gives practical advice regarding the environments one must know about in order to successfully export to and invest in Chinese markets. The implications of understanding these environments are illustrated by the failure of Google when it was forced to pull its operation out of mainland China in 2010, and by the success of Rupert Murdoch when the Chinese government granted him the first "landing rights" to sell foreign programs to cable system prime-time slots, then later, rights to provide media content to its mobile users.

Chapter 9, by Ziona Austrian and Merissa C. Piazza, links public policy with stimulating entrepreneurship in regions that, because of their industrial legacy, have fallen behind. Using examples, the authors discuss the role of the nonprofit and public sectors in encouraging the development of a locally based entrepreneurial culture to increase the number of private sector start-up companies that are a critical component of the economic future of any region.

In Chapter 10, William M. Bowen and Chang-Shik Song begin by defining local economic development initiatives as public policies that involve the exercise of public authority to claim and allocate taxing power for social and economic purposes. These decisions are intended to affect consumer or firm behavior, or both. Generally, the policies involve tax abatements or public expenditures in order to provide private benefits within the urban or regional economic system. They cover a range of public subsidies and direct cash aid for businesses, such as financial incentives for branch plant recruitment, capital market programs, information and education programs, export assistance, and centers for business-related research. The policies frequently consist of public financial support with the goal of increasing levels of local consumption spending on items such as tourism and art facilities, sports stadiums and teams, casinos, and outdoor recreation activities. The chapter considers some criticisms of these initiatives and the rationales behind them. The authors conclude that while it may be within the power of local governments to help stem the tide of decline in midwestern industrial cities, the automatic and uncritical use of local economic development initiatives is not necessarily always the best way to do so.

Finally, in Chapter 11, David R. Elkins investigates whether or not the widely held impression that the Great Lakes region has lost its entrepreneurial dynamic is based on any sort of empirical reality. The chapter first explores the nature of entrepreneurship and what it means for an economy. Next, it presents descriptive evidence about the hypothesis that the Great Lakes region has lost its entrepreneurial vigor. Finally, statistical tests are performed to examine whether the Great Lakes region has, indeed, lost a step. The short answer is that it largely depends on how entrepreneurship is measured. In one sense, the Great Lakes region has, indeed, lost a step. However, like many seasoned athletes, it remains in the game and competitive.

My hope is that this book can contribute to setting in motion processes for renewal and energies that have been imprisoned by outdated ideas, policies, and habits of thought.

2
Midwestern Urban and Regional Responses to Global Economic Transition

William M. Bowen
Kelly L. Kinahan
Cleveland State University

Midwestern industrial cities continue to cede ground to low-cost, overseas competitors in the increasingly global economy. Yet transitions present opportunities and Rust Belt regions can experience prosperity despite losing the market dominance in manufacturing that they once enjoyed.

Human urban and regional settlements have existed within a system of economic expansion and contraction that may be traced back continuously at least to the development of Afro-Eurasian interregional trade in the Bronze Age (Frank and Thompson 2005; Smith 2009). The characteristic structure and cycles of this system have included core-periphery divisions of labor, alternating periods of rivalry and hegemony, and economic periods of upswing and downswing. The characteristics of the total system at any given time have strongly influenced local economic activities and overall levels of prosperity (Frank 1993).

Today's midwestern industrial cities are in some ways similar to other cities throughout history. Their local economies are parts of a larger, continuous system of economic expansion and contraction. They are driven by forces of innovation and entrepreneurship, capital accumulation, division and specialization of labor, and changes in demand and market sizes. Yet they are somewhat different from many other cities in that they originated roughly during the latter part of the industrial revolution and came to economic preeminence during the first half of the twentieth century, at which time the population not only in the United

States but in the world was larger than ever. These cities developed when transportation and communication technologies were advancing to previously unimaginable power and influence. Today, midwestern industrial cities face a new economic world order, with more competition from around the globe than ever before (Bair 2005; Ducruet and Notteboom 2012; Gereffi, Humphrey, and Sturgeon 2005; Henderson and Nadvi 2011; Henderson et al. 2002; Winters and Yusuf 2007).

To understand any system, one must understand the larger one within which it is embedded. Thus, this chapter starts with a brief overview of the evolution of the economic world system within which midwestern industrial cities attained world-scale economic dominance in the late nineteenth and early twentieth centuries. This gives perspective on why these cities achieved such preeminence, and helps provide insight as to why they cannot reasonably expect to reclaim it today. Next, the chapter briefly reviews some recent scholarly literature describing the technological, industrial, and political-economic changes during the early twenty-first century. These shifts seem likely to continue and possibly even to accelerate the long-term evolutionary trends from smaller-scale, simpler sociotechnical and trade systems to larger-scale and more complex ones. The chapter then considers some of the implications of these trends for the renewal of prosperity in midwestern industrial cities. We conclude by suggesting that the idea of prosperity needs to be reframed relative to the previous concept, which was centered on economic world dominance. However, on the basis of the reframed idea, renewed prosperity is well within reach for large segments of the population in midwestern industrial cities.

MIDWESTERN INDUSTRIAL CITIES WITHIN THE ECONOMIC WORLD ORDER THROUGH THE TWENTIETH CENTURY

Trade and investment across borders began long before the rise of modern capitalism (Muller 2009). However, there is little doubt that global economic transition intensified during and after the Industrial Revolution (More 2000). Some of the major underlying factors included the use of fossil fuels, the development of textile technology, the factory system, the growth of the human population and its concentration in urban areas, and the modernization of agricultural, mining, and metallurgical production processes. Other factors driving intensification and diffusion included the expansion of transportation through newly created and developed railroads, canals, macadamized roads, steamships, and refrigerated railway cars. Much was also promoted institutionally by radically reduced tariffs, designed to induce international trade, and the practice of pegging national currencies to gold, so as to have a common unit of exchange, especially in Europe.

Industrial Growth in the Midwest

As the Industrial Revolution diffused from Great Britain and Europe to the United States, midwestern cities were well-poised to take advantage of the newly developed methods of production. By the turn of the twentieth century, advantageous locations along prominent waterways, agricultural surplus, abundant and fertile land, availability of natural resources, and high levels of immigration resulted in flourishing manufacturing sectors throughout midwestern industrial cities and helped catapult them to the first rank of worldwide competitiveness. This dominance was achieved through mass production driven by fossil fuels, blue-collar labor forces and mechanization, and national consumption of goods at historically unprecedented rates, allowing relatively large segments of the populations within midwestern industrial cities to enjoy great prosperity.

These cities continued to grow through the early twentieth century, along with the entire American economy, arguably because of previously unparalleled opportunities to achieve scale economies offered by the exceptionally large U.S. domestic market (Hannah 2008). Between 1900 and 1920, the U.S. population increased 40 percent, from 76.1 to 106.5 million, while real gross domestic product rose 63 percent, from \$422.8 to \$687.7 billion.[1] Midwestern industrial cities thrived primarily on trade with other U.S. markets, taking advantage of railroads, waterways, and Great Lakes shipping routes. Furthermore, labor needs continued to be met through great international in-migratory flows, all but guaranteeing continued economic growth and development.

The period between World War I and World War II brought further ascendency of midwestern industrial cities. Partially this was attributable to events in other parts of the world with respect to which nobody in these U.S. cities had much if any control. Russia became the Soviet Union and closed itself off economically from competing with the rest of the world. Similarly, amidst the turmoil of the Weimar Republic's efforts to recover from the devastation of World War I, the Germans sought complete economic self-reliance. At least partially in consequence of the rapidly diffusing European retreat from international trade along with the stock market crash of 1929, widespread bank failures, and a precipitous decrease in demand for manufactured and other products, the world economy went into a deep depression in the 1930s. The closing of national borders to international trade contributed to mass unemployment, social upheaval, and the rise of fascism, all of which laid the foundation for World War II. The Great Depression induced widespread protectionism in an effort to shore up national economies around the world. For example, in the United States, the Smoot-Hawley Tariff Act of 1930 was signed into law on June 17, 1930, with the purpose of raising U.S. tariffs to record levels on over 20,000 imported goods. U.S. markets were generally large enough to consume the products coming out of midwestern industrial cities, and the widespread retreat from international trade reduced supplier competition for such products, indirectly contributing to the success of these cities.

At the end of World War II, the standing of midwestern industrial cities was nearing its peak. At the same time, American policymakers and most global leaders were convinced that the protectionist policies and trade policies in place after the First World War were an economic disaster and tended to result in antagonism and conflict. This led to efforts, spearheaded by the United States, to begin laying the institutional groundwork necessary for expanding international trade (e.g., lower U.S. tariffs). The results of these initiatives were manifold: the World Bank was created to help fund infrastructure in war-ravaged Europe; the International Monetary Fund took on the task of stabilizing the currencies of troubled economies; and the General Agreement on Tariffs and Trade (GATT) was established to reduce trade barriers and provide a forum for discussion of further reductions.[2]

While the United States and most European countries were working to bolster international trade, the communist countries, led by the Soviet Union and China, remained inwardly focused and did not participate. The centrally planned and controlled Soviet government's policy was to ensure that the bulk of the country's production was traded and consumed exclusively within the Eastern European block of communist countries. International trade by the Chinese was largely precluded, not only by communist economic policies of centralized control, but because of the protracted civil war they had fought since the 1920s and the subsequent conflict with the Japanese during World War II. China had very little industry, high unemployment, and massive food shortages. In the United States in general and midwestern industrial cities in particular, widespread fear of communism stimulated industrial production for the manufactured goods and services needed to support the Cold War. The influence of communism also had the largely salutary indirect effect that communist countries did not provide supply-side economic competition for the goods produced by midwestern manufacturers.

The Impact of Globalization

Communism notwithstanding, the period between the 1950s and the 1970s brought an enormous overall increase in international trade. Perhaps most importantly, it was at this time that Japan and the "East-Asian Tigers"—Singapore, Hong Kong, Taiwan, and South Korea—began large-scale export-oriented industrialization. The rise of industrial production, especially in the Far East, created new competition for midwestern industry in downstream markets for finished goods. Japanese production, in particular, began to compete seriously in the United States, at first with small, inexpensive trinkets, toys, and baubles of low quality, and later with high-quality motorcycles and vehicles such as automobiles, as well as office machinery, scientific and optical equipment, semiconductors, and other electronic components. U.S. firms had no choice but to participate in increasingly globalized markets, either by inclusion or exclusion.

Early signs of the decline of midwestern industrial cities—the rise of the Rust Belt—began to appear in the 1960s, as both the concept and processes of globalization began to take new root. The word "globalize" began to show up in the academic literature in the 1960s and in the mainstream press in the 1980s, roughly meaning to make global in scope (Liu, Hong, and Liu 2012; Oner et al. 2010; Oswick, Jones and Lockwood 2009). Greater numbers of people than ever before started to move around the world; more places were involved in the global economy; and flows of international goods and investments increased significantly. A greater reliance on international markets occurred universally, except in the communist regimes, and competition increased acutely in markets that had been essentially dominated by midwestern industry.

U.S. Socioeconomic Trends

Economic decline beginning in the 1950s in midwestern cities was additionally caused by a mix of factors, foremost amongst which may have been the widespread preferences of individuals to move to places with mild winters, along with increased incomes that made it possible to act upon these preferences, and the mass production of affordable air-conditioning technology (Rappoport 2003). Another major contributor was the rapidly changing industrial composition of U.S. employment. At the end of World War II, service industries accounted for 10 percent of nonfarm employment compared to 38 percent for manufacturing. By 1996, service industries accounted for 29 percent of nonfarm employment compared to 15 percent for manufacturing (Meisenheimer 1998). The changing composition of industry meant a shift from heavy manufacturing of such goods as steel and automobiles, which were concentrated in midwestern cities, to service industries, which were freer to locate throughout the country. Moreover, the cost of labor in the heavily unionized northern and midwestern cities was higher than the cost of labor in the largely union-free South and West. These factors played a significant role in the massive population migrations that occurred from the North and Midwest to the South and West (Greenwood 1997; Hobbs and Stoops 2002). To make matters worse for the inner cities, a shift occurred in the population of metropolitan areas, from cities to suburbs, brought on by widespread adoption of the automobile starting during the mid-twentieth century, along with massive investment in highway and road construction. As described in Box 1.1, the result of such trends can have dire consequences.

Economic Change in China

As the twentieth century came to a close, by far the most significant systemic alteration in world markets affecting midwestern indus-

Box 1.1 Economic Decline in Formerly Preeminent Cities: Detroit's Bankruptcy

On July 18, 2013 the city of Detroit filed for Chapter 9 bankruptcy protection. As the 11th largest city in the U.S., Detroit's bankruptcy stands as a dubious marker in the urban history of a city once considered the icon of American industry. While Detroit had been suffering from severe fiscal stress since at least 2002 (Scorsone and Bateson 2012), the possibility of bankruptcy became all but imminent with the appointment of Kevyn Orr as Emergency Manager in March 2013.[a] The city's debt has been estimated to be somewhere between $18 and $20 billion (Davey and Walsh 2013), with the city's pension fund being its largest creditor (Renaud-Komiya 2013). While some pin Detroit's failures squarely on the backs of a corrupt local government that completely failed at managing the city's finances (Marotta 2013; Auslin 2013), others see the bankruptcy as an outcome of not only this financial mismanagement, but also a set of multifaceted and complex issues plaguing the city for decades, including deindustrialization; globalization; suburban sprawl, which reduced the city's tax base; fiscal stress in the form of annual operating deficits; burdensome health care and pension costs; city services stymied by outdated technology and poor service delivery; and clear race and class separation between the city and surrounding region (Florida 2013; Davey and Walsh 2013).

As the largest municipal bankruptcy in U.S. history, there is keen interest in how Detroit will navigate these somewhat uncharted waters— less than 500 municipalities have sought Chapter 9 protection since its inception in the 1930s (U.S. Courts, n.d.). Many municipalities are experiencing greater fiscal stress since the Great Recession, and legacy costs (i.e., pension and other retiree benefits) are of particular concern to many midwestern industrial cities as many of these cities face similarly steep contribution requirements (Scorsone and Bateson 2012). In a 2012 report that evaluated merits of Chapter 9 bankruptcy for the city of Detroit, Scorsone and Bateson (2012) note that the primary advantage of bankruptcy is cost containment, specifically in regard to reduction of legacy costs, as well as improvements in cash flow.

Box 1.1 (continued)

The impact on residents and the existing assets of the Detroit is also a key concern. Both residents and city workers have been assured that city services will continue uninterrupted (Davey and Walsh 2013), but certainly changes lie ahead. Furthermore, although the liquidation of local assets is not allowed under Chapter 9, creditors have still requested and received appraisals of artwork at the Detroit Institute of Art. Kevyn Orr has stated that the sale of artwork was not in the city's plans (Haskell 2013).

Florida (2013) argues that bankruptcy may be the reset Detroit needs and that it may help bolster the city's nascent revitalization efforts by stabilizing its fiscal management, spurring greater regional cooperation, and highlighting the need for more equitable and inclusive urban revitalization models. Thus, many questions remain about Detroit's fiscal and economic future, and both the Rust Belt and the nation will be keenly observing its progress through bankruptcy, whether it helps propel the city's revitalization prospects, and the impact on residents, employees, and governance structure.

[a] Fiscal stress "refers to [financial] indicators that merit further attention [and] may be indicated by budget shortfalls, decreasing cash balances, or increasing debt loads" (Scorsone and Bateson 2012, p. 2). As Emergency Manager, Orr is the primary decision-maker and has the power to remove both the Mayor and Detroit City Council, through both Orr and local officials have been working cooperatively to this point.

trial cities was the end of communist economic ideology in China. The accession to power of Deng Xiaoping upon the death of Mao Zedong in 1976 gave rise to the so-called Chinese economic miracle, and changed the future of supremacy within the economic world system (Rodriguez 2011). Whereas previously it had been feasible for a relatively wide range of midwestern industries to achieve world-level preeminence, the ascendency of China on global markets placed constraints on the options for midwestern firms. Substantial Chinese penetration began in markets that had been virtually the exclusive domain of U.S. manufacturing. China's export bundle increasingly overlapped with that of U.S.

production, and did so at progressively low relative prices. In 1972, Chinese products were present in only 9 percent of manufacturing product categories, but by 2005 they were present in 85 percent (Schott 2008). With China's huge and inexpensive labor force, high savings rates, and investment in infrastructure, its industry began to pose new and daunting levels of competition for the United States and for other countries.

The Chinese economic transformation can generally be explained by microeconomic and institutional reforms based on decentralization, privatization, and the development of markets (Lin, Cai, and Li 1996), and by newly adopted macroeconomic policies favoring openness through increased international trade, direct investment, and integration into global production networks (Chai 1998; Lardy 2003; Lie, Romilly, and Song 1997). In the big picture, the macroeconomic openness side probably has had a larger, more direct impact upon midwestern industrial cities. However, the reform side is in some ways more instructive for those interested in the renewal of these cities, in that it illustrates the tremendous economic power that can be unleashed by the proper market incentives for self-initiative and responsibility.

The reforms were born of the revival of private enterprise following massive state spending on industrialization under Mao, along with the unimaginable catastrophes brought on by the Great Leap Forward in 1957 and the Cultural Revolution in 1966. In the aftermath of Mao's death, confusion over leadership and the control of political power at the national level brought opportunities for brave regional governments, including the well-known Anhui province in eastern China, to establish some elementary private ownership arrangements. There, for the first time since the rise of centralized communist economic control, farmers were allowed to meet their quotas and to keep excess production to sell in markets. This gave farmers the incentives to take risk and to use their intelligence to improve agricultural productivity.

Optimism for a better future grew massively along with the increases in agricultural productivity. The gains in productivity in turn stimulated the development and diffusion of the township and village enterprises in Anhui province and elsewhere. These enterprises produced a wide variety of goods and services, such as clothing and other consumer items. Production decisions began to be made by local actors with information about area conditions and markets, rather than by communist party chiefs in Beijing. Although these local actors did not at first have formal property and ownership rights over their products, they continued to follow the established Anhui province model, allowing the participants in township and village enterprises to be residual claimants on the output of their labor.

Soon, people all over the country were allowed to act as if they were the owners of any products they created in excess of the minimum amount set for them by the local leadership. Individuals throughout the vast Chinese population were thereby incentivized to produce and to begin saving and investing in their land and themselves. The economic miracle was thus born of a newfound freedom for the Chinese people to respond to market incentives, which created a sense of hope for changing some of the stagnant economic conditions created by the past mistakes of communism.

Today's economic world order provides new and daunting challenges and opportunities in midwestern industrial cities. Looming large among these challenges is economic competition by the Chinese, as well as by other newly emerging global economic competitors. Households, firms, and policymakers within the region will need to recognize and to act upon the conditions of the twenty-first century, not those of the past period of midwestern industrial dominance.

MIDWESTERN INDUSTRIAL CITIES WITHIN TODAY'S CHANGING ECONOMIC WORLD ORDER

The post–World War II economy was transformed not only by systemic changes in global-level competition but also, especially of late, by a combination of population growth and advancements in information and communication technologies. Attendant increases in interdependence throughout social systems have brought new difficulties in understanding the substantive aspects of problems such as the renewal of prosperity in midwestern industrial cities. Population growth brings greater demand for food, shelter, and other resources. Starting with the Industrial Revolution in the 1700s, advanced societies have met these demands by increasing the intensity and scale of production, leading to higher levels of output, driven primarily by fossil fuels. In turn, industrialization has had major geopolitical, strategic, economic, and social implications, some of which bear directly on the prospects for mid-western industrial cities, and some of which could hamper the ability of the United States and its allies to maintain security (Jackson and Howe 2008).

To be clear, the United States and indeed the entire world is larger than ever before and still growing. At the turn of the twentieth century, when midwestern industrial cities were being formed, the population of the United States was 76 million and the world population was 1.7 billion. Today, the U.S. population is 309 million and the world population is just over 7 billion. According to midrange projections for 2050, the U.S. population will be 400 million (U.S. Census Bureau 2013) and the world population will be 9.5 billion (United Nations 2012). All the additional people will need food, water, clothing, shelter, and other subsistence items. They will want electricity and public infrastructure for sewerage and transportation. If and when they become wealthy, they will also demand luxury goods, sometimes lots of them. All of this requires resources from nature. Thus, these unprecedented population sizes pose new risks of resource depletion, problems of resource competition, and increased pressures for interregional trade. Johnson and Earle (2000, p. 301) also argue that increased population size almost invariably brings greater opportunities and pressures for increasingly centralized political and economic control of the means of subsistence, largely because of risk management, technological complexity, and trade considerations.

Population Growth, Technology, and the Exploitation of Resources

Growth in population has historically been interdependent with technological innovation. As populations have continued to increase, greater levels of industrial production have been required to meet the sustenance needs of households. This has tended to add to the demand for agricultural products and for energy and other upstream resources or inputs to production. Moreover, the way industry and the market economy have met this enlarged demand is by first exploiting the easiest-to-acquire, most immediately available, and therefore least costly resources. As these readily accessible resources have become depleted, it has become increasingly advantageous for industry to turn to less desirable and more costly alternatives. Technological innovation is one of the primary strategies with which industry has exploited these options.

Take as an illustration recent efforts to drill for oil in deep water in places such as the Gulf of Mexico. Previously the oil and gas industry exploited the relatively accessible oil resources located in shallower water and closer to land. Prior to the 1990s, most of the oil came from shallow water wells, where drilling and production platforms could stand on stilts anchored to the sea floor. As one would expect given a growing population, the demand for oil continued to increase. During the 1990s, Global Positioning Systems (GPS) navigation technology became available; this made it possible for drilling rigs and ships to stay precisely positioned over an oil well using satellite navigation and microthrusters. Drilling rigs could thus be located and kept in exact position long enough to lay the many miles of pipes required to exploit a deepwater oil resource, and without drilling and production platforms anchored to the sea floor. Deepwater drilling has thus now taken off in the Gulf. The easiest-to-acquire, immediately available, and least-costly oil resources have been largely depleted, and new technologies have made it possible to exploit previously ignored or inaccessible ones.

New technologies have enabled more people in more households to meet their sustenance needs and to enjoy their luxury goods. Further advancements in technology have made it possible for industry to exploit additional resources, facilitating increased population growth, which has posed problems that require more technological innovation, allowing even less accessible resources to be utilized. According to More (2000), this sort of positive feedback loop between population growth and technological innovation has allowed industrialization to continue to meet the sustenance needs of growing populations since the beginning of the Industrial Revolution. Johnson and Earle (2000, p. 29) argue that this has been a general tendency in human societies throughout history, leading to an "upward spiral" of political-economic integration and more powerful leaders.

The combination of population growth and technological advancement has changed the international calculus of production, consumption, and competition in a way that is unlikely to reverse itself in the lifetime of anyone alive today, and it has brought new forms of risk. Take, for instance, products that come from rare earth elements, upstream resources used, among other things, in automobile production, petroleum refining, flat panel displays in cell phones, portable digital versatile discs (DVDs) and laptops, magnets, batteries, generators, medical devices, jet fighter engines, missile guidance systems, antimissile defense, and space-based satellites and communication systems. The United States used to be self-reliant in domestically produced rare earth elements, but over the past 15 years it has become 100 percent reliant on imports, primarily from China, largely because of lower-cost operations there (Humphries 2012).[3]

Dependence on upstream resources from foreign countries entails potentially enormous economic and political vulnerabilities. Factors such as distant natural hazards and accidents, as well as possibly hostile foreign political and economic decision makers who control upstream resources, threaten the stability of the production processes upon which the well-being of segments of local populations depend. Insofar as global markets function properly, and no hostilities arise, markets will continue to solve some of these risk problems efficiently. However, the integration of local production processes into global markets means a loss of local security for the affected firms and households.

The Need for Innovation and Entrepreneurship

As long as the U.S. and world populations continue to grow, demand will continue to increase for new technologies that enable improvements in the efficiency and effectiveness with which previously inaccessible resources can be utilized. The newly accessible resources will in turn enable increasing population growth, with its attendant increases in industrial specialization and trade. This is one big reason why innovation and entrepreneurship really matter. Regardless of whether the populations of midwestern industrial cities grow, remain stable, or shrink, rising national and world populations will put greater demand on resources and cause increased competition in markets. Households and firms in these cities can innovate, bring new goods and services to market, and either successfully compete in these markets or be excluded from them. Alternatively, households or firms can migrate in search of a better set of circumstances, as many have done over the past few decades.

Innovation, which is arguably the most desirable prospect for firms and the households that depend on them, can be seen in the central

Ohio automotive cluster, which has been able to maintain a competitive advantage over alternative locations that might offer better labor or input costs by focusing on high-value-added manufacturing. As Hill, Samuel, and Stewart (2008) explain:

> The traditional ways in which manufacturers have tried to add value to products have been to offer better quality, lower cost or more speed or dependability in meeting just-in-time demands. These factors have become business necessities: Delivery reliability, quality and cost are now standard. The new value opportunities lie in customer experience, supply risk, and product and process innovation. The quality of the business relationship, the support for innovation, and the drive to minimize supply risk perhaps best explain why some OEMS [original equipment manufacturers] are succeeding and others are struggling. New domestics like Honda of America Manufacturing [located in central OH] tend to nurture a close relationship with their chosen suppliers, even providing access to the production lines in order to improve not only product but process. Tier 1 suppliers spoke favorably of customer companies that exhibited willingness to work with them on product development and pricing. This kind of close relationship has real economic benefit in that it helps reduce risk and spur innovation. (pp. 12–13)

Technology has always been a driving force for economic change, and Freeman (1989) classifies the latest shifts attributable to information and communication as the fourth major technological revolution. This fourth phase adds to the textile innovations of the late eighteenth and early nineteenth centuries, railroads in the mid to late nineteenth century, and electricity as well as the internal combustion engine during the late nineteenth and early twentieth century. The most recent transition has accelerated the development of international markets and powerful multinational and global corporations, and has fostered a new economic climate that features the rise of the service sector, the loss of prominence for manufacturing, and widespread consumerism.

Castells (1996) notes that this latest movement has been multidimensional in nature, but that a new paradigm rooted in major advancements within information and communication technologies lies at its heart. These technological improvements have vastly increased the integration of the existing world economy and created a new globalized economy. While the previous international economy experienced capital accumulation that flowed between countries, the new global-ized economy differs in that its "core components have the institutional, organizational, and technological capacity to work as a unit in real time, or in chosen time, on a planetary scale" (p. 102).

The process of industrial globalization is characterized by connec-tions within national markets via consumers, production processes, and the expansion of market competition (Wiersema and Bowen 2008). In turn, consumers and the productive activities of firms are linked through globalized industries, which make products and services ever more stan-dardized through increasingly homogenized consumer preferences and global economies of scale in both manufacturing and research and devel-opment (Wiersema and Bowen 2008). During the latter half of the twen-tieth century, globalization was also aided by government policies favor-ing deregulation and free market principles (Castells 2000; Singh 1994); reduced trade barriers and costs of international transportation and com-munications (Hummels, Ishii, and Yi 1999; Krueger 1995); increased integration of global capital markets (Sachs et al. 1995); greater capital mobility and reduced transaction costs; and a larger number of financial instruments (Irwin 1996). All of these changes have unalterably affected the markets within which midwestern industries must compete.

The Outcomes of Globalization

By the 1990s, many developing countries had been brought into the world economy, with increases in foreign direct investment, technol-ogy transfer, and production efficiencies (McMillan and Rodrik 2011). This world market has, among other things, resulted in the breakdown of the traditional, vertically integrated "Fordist" production process, which formed the core of the U.S. manufacturing sector in the middle of the twentieth century (Feenstra 1998), and in the growth of specializa-tion by individual countries on certain phases of production (Hummels, Ishii, and Yi 1999). The outcomes of globalization have also included increased levels of regional, national, and global competition (Wiersema and Bowen 2008), cross-border mergers and acquisitions (UNCTAD 1987–1999), and the growth of multinational firms (Wiersema and Bowen 2008). Collectively, these outcomes have negatively impacted the economies of midwestern industrial cities, partially by increasing competition in product markets, and partially by concentrating the centers of financial control in fewer and fewer world cities, exacerbating the decline that began during the 1960s and 1970s. Integration of the developing countries into the world economy all but guarantees that the population and productive output of the United States in general, and of midwestern industrial cities in particular, will continue to steadily shrink as a share of the world's total (Jackson and Howe 2008).[4]

Newly structured global-scale corporations have seized upon before-unseen economies of scale in production, distribution, marketing, and management, giving way to a new level of world consumerism that was a death knell for many previously thriving midwestern firms that did not or could not operate on this scale (Levitt 1983). The global corporation is a more advanced entity than the multinational corporation, and one that "operates with resolute consistency—at a low relative cost—as if the entire world (or major regions of it) were a single entity; it sells the same things in the same way everywhere" (Levitt 1983, p. 92). While global competition has forced U.S. firms to be more productive and efficient (Hill, Samuel, and Stewart 2008), these benefits have not come without high costs, including stagnating wage rates (Lawrence and Slaughter 1993) and lost manufacturing jobs (Levitt 1983), which contributed to the decline of cities and regions that were once industrial powerhouses, such as those in the Midwest.

The "new economy" that had more or less fully emerged by the 1990s was integrated as never before in history at a global scale. It was rooted in global knowledge and ideas, with wealth and job creation tied to innovation and technology in all sectors of the economy (Acs, de Groot, and Nijkamp 2002; Atkinson and Gottlieb 2001). Electricity and the electrical engine helped bolster the industrial-based economy that allowed cities such as Cleveland and Detroit to prosper during the early and middle decades of the twentieth century. Similarly, the new knowledge-centric economy has been driven by microelectronics, computing, and digital communication advancements, including the Internet and extensive software developments, which have spurred the growth of places like Silicon Valley and the Research Triangle (Castells 1996). The infrastructure and transportation linkages that created comparative advantages for many midwestern cities during the early part of the twentieth century were crucial to the success of their manufacturing industries. But these linkages were less important to burgeoning knowledge-intensive industries that rely heavily on human capital to create a competitive advantage, and that are are primarily service- rather than production-oriented while competing at a global scale.

Another major component of this "new economy" was the momentous shift from manufacturing to the service sector, leading to a new industrial structure for many regions within the United States. The demise of the global dominance of the U.S. manufacturing sector began in the late twentieth century, during a period when developing countries experienced significant gains in technical skills and closed education gaps that previously existed with other nations, particularly in industrial and engineering fields; this was accomplished by developing infrastructure within universities, technical institutions, and vocational training schools (Singh 1994). These knowledge and infrastructure gains, coupled with rapid capital mobility, allowed U.S. manufacturing firms to exploit the regulatory, trade, wage, and environmental policies present within many developing countries by either relocating there or subcontracting through firms within those areas (Feenstra 1998). Furthermore, changes from recent technological innovations also directly affected the operations of the manufacturing sector through the expansion of new products, reduced costs, a reorganization of firms and industries, improved structure and efficiencies of large factories and firms, changes in production systems, flexible specialization, and the introduction of just-in-time production (Singh 1994).

The multidimensional forces of globalization that propelled a shift in industrial structure for many regions within the United States also helped to trigger a new, heavily bifurcated occupational structure, composed of higher-wage information technology jobs and lower-wage service sector occupations, and the decline of mid-wage, blue-collar manufacturing positions. A steady drop in both plant and firm sizes was seen in manufacturing throughout the United States and other western industrialized nations, which resulted from a combination of reduced noncore business activities and new computer-based technologies that improved productivity (Carlsson 1989).

The transition we have described means a larger-scale, more integrated, technologically intensive, knowledge-based, and service-oriented world economic order. As the influence of China, and to a lesser degree India and Brazil, continues to grow, the U.S. economic system in general, and the midwestern economic systems in particular, will surely play a less dominant role on the world stage. But we do not see this as a cause for alarm. There is no convincing evidence that the inhabitants of cities with greater economic dominance in world markets fare better than residents in cities with lesser dominance.[5] Goals, objectives, and policies oriented toward improved quality of life for residents rather than attainment or reattainment of economic dominance appear to offer greater promise for the future of midwestern industrial cities.

NEW STRATEGIES AND OPPORTUNITIES FOR PROSPERITY

In general terms, the global economic transition is driven by population growth together with technological progress, but in its details it is complex beyond human understanding. The transition is inseparable from the myriad of day-to-day decisions by unimaginably large numbers of individuals throughout the economic world order. The disconcerting and sometimes frustrating experience of uncertainty in the face of change felt within midwestern industrial cities is no doubt exacerbated by the belief that these cities will not in the twenty-first century regain the world-level preeminence they enjoyed in the twentieth century.

As a consequence, a sense of social and economic crisis and bewilderment is common today in many midwestern industrial cities and elsewhere. Within these places, there is a widespread perception of loss of past prosperity and a diminished feeling of well-being. A frequently shared view is that things used to be better, and public policies and programs must be devised and implemented to restore previous levels of affluence. Yet there is little agreement on what specific actions should be taken to this end. Public policy proposals differ vastly, not only in terms of what actions should be taken, but also who should initiate and take responsibility for them, and who should pay for them. Moreover, efforts to sort through and interpret the multitudes of inconsistent and at times even contradictory facts, rules, norms, and interests served by any given proposal tend to leave people frustrated, sometimes even those of us who have dedicated our work lives to studying cities and public policies. We are presented with a predicament in which we encounter conceptualizations and relationships among multiple interdependent variables, all of which are necessary to think coherently about the renewal of prosperity in these cities, but which when taken together exceed our unaided mental powers to meaningfully evaluate.

This book is predicated on the perspective that while midwestern industrial cities will not remain globally preeminent, they need not necessarily continue to experience diminished prosperity. Although the time and circumstances since the heyday of midwestern industrial domination have changed and sociotechnical systems have become larger scale and more complex, the foundations of renewed prosperity may stem today, much as they always have, from a vibrant market economy. Capitalistic markets are a central phenomenon of modern life. They, and the institutional frameworks that enable and sustain them, such as the U.S. Constitution, are arguably more than a little responsible for the initial rise of prosperity in industrial cities in the nineteenth and twentieth centuries.

The Importance of the Market

Capitalistic markets are in no small measure the cause of wealth and productivity increases and are the vehicle that has made a much broader array of goods and services accessible to many more people than ever before. Capitalistic markets and their institutional frameworks have been the source of technological advancements, a previously unimaginable range of choice of occupation and lifestyle, and unprecedented levels of happiness and well-being enjoyed by a relatively large percentage of the population today (Stevenson and Wolfers 2008, Nelson 1990, Ridley 2010). Perhaps most importantly, these markets, together with their enabling institutions, have arguably given rise to unprecedented access to more and better information. Consequently, examination of these markets, their institutional frameworks, and their effects on prosperity from various political and disciplinary perspectives (and from perspectives that transcend normal disciplinary boundaries) is too important to be left only to economists and public policymakers, largely because they involve a great deal more than what we typically think of as "economic" and "political" issues.

Of course, not everyone has confidence that unfettered markets and free institutions alone can or will renew prosperity in today's midwestern industrial cities, especially without exacerbating other problems, such as distributional inequities between class and race. Indeed, the concept of a capitalist market is merely a model or abstraction from reality that helps us to represent and grasp some key elements of our societies and their relationships to one another. Moreover, this model may not be an altogether adequate one. It neglects to consider a range of political and social realities that depart from premises of consumer choice and decentralized decision making. For instance, it does not provide guidance on how and when societies should regulate monopolies or provide infrastructure. It tends to come up short as to how or when societies should respond to problems of extreme income inequality and inequity. It provides no reason to have compassion for firms that go under or for individual households that have been placed at risk for homelessness and unemployment as a result of market efficiencies.

The ideal type of capitalistic market makes certain assumptions about private property, exchange between legally free individuals, and the production and distribution of goods and services through mutual understandings and agreements between transacting parties to market transactions. The assumptions about private property, in turn, presuppose the existence of governmental authority to design and establish laws and property rights, and police power for the enforcement of those laws and rights. The assumptions about exchange between legally free individuals presuppose that people possess certain rights that meaningfully distinguish them from serfs or slaves, and that labor is not forcibly extracted from them through the exercise of superior political authority or power. The assumptions about the production and distribution of goods presuppose that decisions to exchange are not made by custom or through the coercive use of power by any sort of centralized authority. In turn, all of these assumptions are open to question, if in no other way than in their applicability in any given situation or set of situations, including the renewal of prosperity in midwestern industrial cities.

The Role of Public Policy

Nevertheless, some suppositions must always be made prior to any systematic examination of a phenomenon. In this book, the assumption throughout all of the individual contributions is that while capitalistic markets provide the only tried and tested method of achieving prosperity, they have certain imperfections for which public policies are at times necessary. Furthermore, all of the contributions are consistent with the following propositions: that augmented production (rather than consumption) and exchange of goods and services within the context of free institutions offer the best long-term solution to the social and economic problems of Rust Belt regions;[6] that the development of renewed productive capacity in these regions will in the first instance require up-front investments of time, attention and energy, and in the second instance financial capital; that many of the most important resources and factors in the production of capital goods are not and will never be completely mobile with respect to space and time; and that therefore net increases in regional prosperity necessitate urban institutions, public policies, practices, and cultures willing and able to divert into enhanced production input resources that would otherwise go to goods and services that are immediately consumed.

All of the contributions assume confidence in public policies and institutions supportive of innovation, entrepreneurship, specialization, and trade as the best route to renewed regional prosperity. But just as markets have certain limitations, so do public policies. Not all public policies are conducive to renewed prosperity; indeed, as the following chapters discuss, even some of those public policies advocated in terms of their positive effects on midwestern regional economic development may do more harm than good.

We hope that the chapters in this book can avoid getting narrowly associated with labels such as "conservative" or "liberal." The focus is on how older industrial regional systems really work and what can and should be (and what cannot and should not be) done through both public institutions and private markets in efforts to improve their performance. How might urban policy be used to renew and update capitalist markets so as to put old industrial regions back on the road to prosperity? What mix of market versus nonmarket allocation mechanisms is optimal? How can and do free people in such regions, living in democratic capitalist systems, solve problems to meet the needs and wants of others, so as to turn their perceptions of scarcity and loss into ones of abundance?

Reframing Prosperity

When thinking of prosperous places, we may invoke images that translate to a high quality of life and living standards, such as vibrant artistic, musical, and literary communities; entertainment districts with a relatively high number of restaurants, bars, and cultural institutions; an environment with great parks, green spaces, and recreational activities; accessible, convenient, and affordable transportation; good schools and universities; and low rates of poverty, with high levels of employment. This is not an exhaustive list, nor are these characteristics only found in places such as New York, Chicago, or Los Angeles.

It seems to us that an important component of prosperity centers on reframing this concept. The economic dominance that was previously associated with many midwestern industrial cities is unlikely to reemerge, especially in light of the previously discussed transitions and the influence of growing economies such as China and India. However, it is important to note that prosperity need not be exclusively tied with economic dominance. Rather, the idea of a prosperous city is that most if not all of the people who live in it have good lives. In the spirit of Amartya Sen (1999), the people in a prosperous city have the freedom to live the kinds of lives they value. They see themselves as active participants in shaping their own futures and by taking initiative and accepting the responsibility for themselves and their actions, they have the opportunity to better themselves and the prospects faced by their children. There are numerous examples of urban and regional economies that have attained high levels of prosperity without economic preeminence, and there is an abundance of knowledge available to help to turn the problems currently facing midwestern industrial cities into opportunities. This book is all about such knowledge.

The concept of prosperity, which is traditionally linked to wealth and measured in terms of income, unemployment, and poverty rates, may be meaningfully and fruitfully reexamined with a more comprehensive approach, one that deemphasizes consumptive aspects and focuses on productive ones, as well as on the social, psychological, and health-related components (Bergmann 2010; Fodor 2001, 2012; Hamilton 2003; Jackson 2009; Sen 1999). In particular, the emerging policies and practices of smart decline and right-sizing are working to address the unique realities facing formerly dominant industrial cities, which include planning for fewer people, buildings, and land uses, as well as better aligning physical landscapes to meet the needs of future populations (Hollander 2011; Popper and Popper 2002; Schilling and Logan 2008). Furthermore, there is evidence that slower-growing metropolitan statistical areas (MSAs), in terms of population, outperform higher-growth MSAs on many measures of prosperity, including income and poverty rates (Fodor 2012).

Within the realm of midwestern industrial cities, achieving prosperity will require the leadership within cities and regions to broaden their focus from past models targeted at economic dominance and heavily focused on short-term economic development strategies. While the consideration of short-term strategies inclusive of business attraction, retention, and expansion is warranted, these transactions need to be linked to strengthening and improving the assets within the region's larger portfolio of products, businesses, and people.[7] Past actions of the leadership within many cities and regions have tended to be based on the overriding importance and inevitability of increasing globalization and the argument that, to be competitive in world markets, cities must compete for footloose industry not tied to any particular location or country, which can relocate in response to local economic conditions. Striving to succeed in globally competitive markets at all costs has proved less than successful for many places and has served to intensify levels of inequality among cities and among social strata within cities. Many of the economic development strategies adopted in efforts to compete for footloose investment tend to be short-term in nature and to focus on immediate needs as well as politically marketable achievements, such as job creation and growth of tax bases. While these approaches may produce some desired outcomes, they fail to address the longer-term components of a comprehensive economic development strategy, which moves beyond selling the existing assets of a region and toward improving, strengthening, and changing assets for long-term prosperity.

This book is predicated upon the assumption that renewed prosperity is feasible in midwestern industrial cities if (and only if) good decisions are made within them by individuals with influence in both the public and private sectors. Moreover, restructured public policy, especially microeconomic policy, is essential, as well as increased levels of international business exchange, especially with the Chinese.

The Industrial Revolution changed the economic world order by giving prominence to cities, regions, and nations that could adapt their governance structures and the organizational processes through which they made collective choices toward the power of free markets and private, personal industry, and innovation. By empowering the individuals within local economic systems, the Industrial Revolution empowered the cities, regions, and nations it affected. It led to a system in which nothing will improve the fortunes of firms and individuals more effectively and efficiently than public and private sector decisions that increase production of the goods and services people value and the exchange of such goods and services in free and competitive markets. This is as true for midwestern industrial cities today as it was during their inception, as it was for Chinese cities during their recent economic miracle, and as it is for cities throughout the global economic system.

Notes

1. Measured in constant 2005 dollars (http://www.measuringworth.com/datasets/usgdp/result.php).
2. GATT later became the World Trade Organization (WTO), which today sets the ground rules for international commerce.
3. Such considerations have recently given rise to the President's National Strategy for Global Supply Chain Security (http://www.whitehouse.gov/the-press-office/2012/01/25/fact-sheet-national-strategy-global-supply-chain-security).
4. The rate of growth of the U.S. population, along with the rates of growth of other advanced industrial nations such as Japan and Germany, is slowing down somewhat relative to the rate of growth of the world population overall. Partially this relative shrinkage is attributable to the high growth rates in Africa and India. Partially it is also attributable to fertility declines that have historically been found to go hand in hand with the development of wealthy and advanced industrial economies (Guinnane 2011). Various theories of fertility decline have been brought forward to explain population growth rate declines, including ones that attribute them to factors such as the availability of contraceptives, women's decisions to postpone childbirth, the relatively high cost of raising children in advanced industrial economies, and more women choosing to remain in the workforce rather than have children (Becker, Murphy, and Tamura 1990; Bryant 2007; Galor 2012; Guinnane 2011).
5. Indeed, the "global-city hypothesis" (Friedmann 1986) asserts that the most economically dominant cities are especially prone to extremes of inequality.
6. For a thoughtful, stimulating, and informative argument that far from being the path to prosperity, society's orientation toward consumption is at the heart of our social ills, see Hamilton (2003).
7. This conceptualization of a regional economic development framework stems from multiple lectures and discussions with Ned Hill.

References

Acs, Zolton J., Henri L.F. de Groot, and Peter Nijkamp, eds. 2002. *The Emergence of the Knowledge Economy: A Regional Perspective.* New York: Springer.

Atkinson, Robert D., and Paul D. Gottlieb. 2001. *The Metropolitan New Economy Index: Benchmarking Economic Transformation in the Nation's Metropolitan Areas.* Washington, DC: Progressive Policy Institute.

Auslin, Michael. 2013. "Detroit Crosses the Rubicon." *National Review Online*, July 20. http://www.aei.org/article/economics/detroit-crosses-the-rubicon/ (accessed August 10, 2013).

Bair, Jennifer. 2005. "Global Capitalism and Commodity Chains: Looking Back, Going Forward." *Competition and Change* 9(2): 153–180.

Becker, Gary S., Kevin M. Murphy, and Robert Tamura. 1990. "Human Capital, Fertility, and Economic Growth." *Journal of Political Economy* 98(5): S12–37.

Bergmann, Barbara. 2010. "Is Prosperity Possible Without Growth?" *Challenge* 53(5): 49–56

Bryant, John. 2007. "Theories of Fertility Decline and the Evidence from Development Indicators." *Population and Development Review* 33(1): 101–127.

Carlsson, Bo. 1989. "The Evolution of Manufacturing Technology and Its Impact on Industrial Structure: An International Study." *Small Business Economics* 1(1): 21–37.

Castells, Manuel. 1996. *The Rise of the Network Society, The Information Age: Economy, Society and Culture.* Malden, MA: Blackwell Publishers.

———. 2000. *The Rise of the Network Society, The Information Age: Economy, Society, and Culture*, 2nd ed. Oxford: Blackwell Publishers.

Chai, Joseph C.H. 1998. China: Transition to a Market Economy. Oxford: Oxford University Press.

Davey, Monica, and Mary Williams Walsh. 2013. "Billions in Debt, Detroit Tumbles Into Insolvency." *New York Times*, July 18. http://www.nytimes.com/2013/07/19/us/detroit-files-for-bankruptcy.html?pagewanted=all&_r=3& (accessed August 10, 2013).

Ducruet, Cesar, and Theo Notteboom. 2012. "The Worldwide Maritime Network of Container Shipping: Spatial Structure and Regional Dynamics." *Global Networks* 12(3): 395–423.

Feenstra, Robert C. 1998. "Integration of Trade and Disintegration of Production in the Global Economy." *The Journal of Economic Perspectives* 12(4): 31–50.

Florida, Richard. 2013. "Don't Let Bankruptcy Fool You: Detroit's Not Dead." *The Atlantic Cities*, July 22. http://m.theatlanticcities.com/jobs-and -economy/2013/07/dont-let-bankruptcy-fool-you-detroits-not-dead/6261/ (accessed August 10, 2013).

Fodor, Eben V. 2001. *Better, Not Bigger: How to Take Control of Urban Growth and Improve Your Community*, 2nd ed. Gabriola Island, BC,Canada: New Society Publishers.

———. 2012. "Relationship Between Growth and Prosperity in the 100 Largest U.S. Metropolitan Areas." *Economic Development Quarterly* 26(3): 220–230.

Frank, Andre Gunder. 1993. "Bronze Age World System Cycles." *Current Anthropology* 34(4): 383–429.

Frank, Andre Gunder, and William R. Thompson. 2005. "Afro-Eurasian Bronze Age Economic Expansion and Contraction Revisited." *Journal of World History* 16(2): 115–172.

Freeman, Chris. 1989. "New Technology and Catching Up." *European Journal of Development Research* 1(1): 86–99.

Friedmann, John. 1986. "The World City Hypothesis." *Development and Change* 17(1): 69–83.

Galor, Oded. 2012. "The Demographic Transition: Causes and Consequences." *Cliometrica* 6(1): 1–18.

Gereffi, Gary, John Humphrey, and Timothy Sturgeon. 2005. "The Governance of Global Value Chains." *Review of International Political Economy* 12(1): 78–104.

Greenwood, Michael J. 1997. "Internal Migration in Developed Countries." In *Handbook of Population and Family Economics*, Vol. 1B. Mark R. Rosenzweig and Oded Stark, eds. Amsterdam, New York and Oxford: Elsevier Science, North-Holland, pp. 647–720.

Guinnane, Timothy W. 2011. "The Historical Fertility Transition: A Guide for Economists." *Journal of Economic Literature* 49(3): 589–614.

Hamilton, Clive. 2003. Growth Fetish. Sterling,VA: Pluto Press.

Hannah, Leslie. 2008. "Logistics, Market Size, and Giant Plants in the Early Twentieth Century: A Global View." *Journal of Economic History* 68(1): 46–79.

Haskell, Josh. 2013. "Bankrupt Detroit Assesses Its Art Treasures." *ABC News*, August 7. http://abcnews.go.com/US/bankrupt-detroit-assesses-art -treasures/story?id=19885360 (accessed August 11, 2013).

Henderson, Jeffrey, Peter Dicken, Martin Hess, Neil Coe, and Henry Wei-Chung Yeung. 2002. "Global Production Networks and the Analysis of Economic Development." *Review of International Political Economy* 9(3): 436–464.

Henderson, Jeffrey, and Khalid Nadvi. 2011. "Greater China, the Challenges of Global Production Networks and the Dynamics of Transformation." *Global Networks* 11(3): 285–297.

Hill, Edward W., Jim Samuel, and Fran Stewart. 2008. Driving Ohio's Prosperity. Report prepared for CompeteColumbus. Cleveland, OH: Cleveland State University. http://works.bepress.com/edward_hill/8 (accessed April 8, 2013).

Hobbs, Frank, and Nicole Stoops. 2002. "Demographic Trends in the Twentieth Century." U.S. Census Bureau, Census 2000 Special Reports, Series CENSR-4, Washington, DC: U.S. Government Printing Office.

Hollander, Justin B. 2011. "Can a City Successfully Shrink? Evidence from Survey Data on Neighborhood Quality." *Urban Affairs Review* 47(1): 129–141.

Hummels David L., Jun Ishii, and Kei-Mu Yi. 1999. "The Nature and Growth of Vertical Specialization in World Trade." Staff Reports No. 72. New York: Federal Reserve Bank of New York. http://www.newyorkfed.org/research/staff_reports/sr72.pdf (accessed April 8, 2013).

Humphries, Marc. 2012. "Rare Earth Elements: The Global Supply Chain." Report to Congress. R41347. Washington, DC: Congressional Research Service.

Irwin, Douglas A. 1996. "The United States in a New Global Economy? A Century's Perspective." *American Economic Review* 86(2): 41–46.

Jackson, Richard, and Neil Howe. 2008. *The Graying of the Great Powers: Demography and Geopolitics in the 21st Century*. Washington, DC: Center for Strategic and International Studies.

Jackson, Tim. 2009. *Prosperity without Growth: Economics for a Finite Planet*. London: Earthscan.

Johnson, Allen W. and Timothy Earle. 2000. *The Evolution of Human Societies*, 2nd ed. Stanford, CA: Stanford University Press.

Krueger, Anne O. 1995. "U.S. Trade Policy and the GATT Review." In *The World Economy: Global Trade Policy*, Sven Arndt and Chris Milner, eds. Oxford: Blackwell Publishers, pp. 65–79.

Lardy, Nicholas R. 2003. "Trade Liberalization and Its Role in Chinese Economic Growth." Paper presented at the International Monetary Fund and National Council of Applied Economic Research conference, "A Tale of Two Giants: India's and China's Experience with Reform and Growth," held in New Delhi, November 14–16. Washington, DC: Institute for International Economics. http://www.imf.org/external/np/apd/seminars/2003/newdelhi/lardy.pdf (accessed April 8, 2013).

Lawrence, Robert Z., and Matthew J. Slaughter. 1993. "International Trade and American Wages in the 1980s: Giant Sucking Sound or Small Hiccup?" *Brookings Papers on Economic Activity, Microeconomics* 2: 161–226.

Levitt, Theodore. 1983. "The Globalization of Markets." *Harvard Business Review* (May-June): 92–102.

Lie, Xiaming, Peter Romilly, and Haiyan Song. 1997. "An Empirical Investigation of the Causal Relationship between Openness and Economic Growth in China." *Applied Economics* 29(12): 1679–1686.

Lin, Justin Yifu, Fang Cai, and Zhou Li. 1996. "The Lessons of China's Transition to a Market Economy." *The Cato Journal* 16(2): 201–231.

Liu, Xingjian, Song Hong, and Yaolin Liu. 2012. "A Bibliometric Analysis of 20 Years of Globalization Research: 1990–2009." *Globalizations* 9(2): 195–210.

Marotta, David John. 2013. "Detroit's Bankruptcy Doesn't 'Just Happen.'" *Forbes*, August 4. http://www.forbes.com/sites/davidmarotta/2013/08/04/detroits-bankruptcy-doesnt-just-happen/ (accessed August 10, 2013).

McMillan, Margaret S., and Dani Rodrik. 2011. "Globalization, Structural Change, and Productivity Growth." NBER Working Paper No. 17143. Cambridge, MA: National Bureau of Economic Research. http://www.nber.org/papers/w17143.pdf (accessed April 8, 2013).

Meisenheimer, Joseph R. II. 1998. "The Services Industry in the 'Good' versus 'Bad' Jobs Debate." *Monthly Labor Review* 121(2): 22–47.

More, Charles. 2000. *Understanding the Industrial Revolution*. New York: Routledge.

Muller, Jerry Z. 2009. Thinking about Capitalism. Chantilly, VA: The Great Courses. http://www.thegreatcourses.com/tgc/courses/course_detail.aspx?cid=5665 (accessed April 8, 2013).

Nelson, Richard R. 1990. "Capitalism as an Engine of Progress." *Research Policy* 19(3): 193–214.

Oner, Asli Ceylon, Diana Mitsova, David Prosperi, and Jaap Vos. 2010. "Knowledge Globalization in Urban Studies and Planning: A Network Analysis of International Co-authorships." *Journal of Knowledge Globalization* 3(1): 1–29.

Oswick, Cliff, Philip J. Jones, and Graeme Lockwood. 2009. "A Bibliometric and Tropological Analysis of Globalization." *Journal of International Business Disciplines* 3(2): 60–73.

Popper, Deborah E., and Frank J. Popper. 2002. "Small Can Be Beautiful: Coming to Terms with Decline." *Planning* 68(7): 20–23.

Rappoport, Jordan. 2003. "U.S. Urban Decline and Growth, 1950 to 2000." *Economic Review: Third Quarter*. Kansas City, MO: Federal Reserve Bank of Kansas City. http://kansascityfed.org/publicat/econrev/Pdf/3q03rapp.pdf (accessed April 8, 2013).

Renaud-Komiya, Nick. 2013. "Bankruptcy Administrators Find $1M Check in Detroit City Hall Drawer." *The Independent*, August, 10. http://www .independent.co.uk/news/world/americas/bankruptcy-administrators-find-1m-cheque-in-detroit-city-hall-drawer-8755844.html (accessed August 11, 2013).

Ridley, Matt. 2010. *The Rational Optimist: How Prosperity Evolves.* New York: HarperCollins Publishers.

Rodriguez, Peter. 2011. China, India, and the United States: The Future of Economic Supremacy. Chantilly, VA: The Great Courses. http://www .thegreatcourses.com/tgc/courses/course_detail.aspx?cid=5892 (accessed April 8, 2013).

Sachs, Jeffrey D., Andrew Warner, Anders Åslund, and Stanley Fischer. 1995 "Economic Reform and the Process of Global Integration." *Brookings Papers on Economic Activity* 1: 1–118.

Schilling, Joseph, and Jonathan Logan. 2008. "Greening the Rust Belt: A Green Infrastructure Model for Right Sizing America's Shrinking Cities." *Journal of the American Planning Association* 74(4): 451–466.

Schott, Peter K. 2008. "The Relative Sophistication of Chinese Exports." *Economic Policy* 23(53): 5–49.

Scorsone, Eric, and Nicolette Bateson. 2012. "Evaluating a Chapter 9 Bankruptcy for City of Detroit: Reality Check or Turnaround Solution?" Staff Paper No. 2012-01. East Lansing, MI: Michigan State University, Department of Agricultural, Food, and Resource Economics.

Sen, Amartya. 1999. *Development as Freedom*. New York: Alfred A. Knopf.

Singh, Ajit. 1994. "Global Economic Changes, Skills and International Competitiveness." *International Labour Review* 133(2): 167–183.

Smith, Richard L. 2009. *Premodern Trade in World History*. Abingdon, UK: Routledge.

Stevenson, Betsey, and Justin Wolfers. 2008. "Growth and Subjective Well-Being: Reassessing the Easterlin Paradox." NBER Working Paper No. 14282. Canmbridge, MA: National Bureau of Economic Research. http:// www.nber.org/papers/w14282 (accessed August 16, 2013).

UNCTAD (United Nations Conference on Trade and Development). *1987–1999. World Investment Report*. New York: United Nations.

United Nations. 2012. *World Population Prospects: The 2012 Revision*. New York: United Nations. http://esa.un.org/wpp/Excel-Data/population.htm (accessed July 23, 2013).

U.S. Census Bureau. 2013. "2012 National Population Projections: Middle Series." Washington, DC: U.S. Census Bureau. http://www.census.gov/ population/projections/data/national/2012/summarytables.html (accessed July 23, 2013).

U.S. Courts. n.d. "Chapter 9 Municipal Bankruptcy." Washington, DC: United States Courts. http://www.uscourts.gov/FederalCourts/Bankruptcy/ BankruptcyBasics/Chapter9.aspx (accessed August 11, 2013).

Wiersema, Margarethe F., and Harry P. Bowen. 2008. "Corporate Diversification: The Impact of Foreign Competition, Industry Globalization, and Product Diversification." *Strategic Management Journal* 29(2): 115–132.).

Winters L. Allan, and Shahid Yusuf, eds. 2007. *Dancing with Giants: China, India, and the Global Economy*. Washington, DC: World Bank and Singapore: Institute of Policy Studies.

3
Can Tax Expenditures Stimulate Growth in Rust Belt Cities?

Benjamin Y. Clark
Cleveland State University

An oft-used arrow in the quiver of those overseeing local and regional economic development is the incentivization of tax expenditures (public investment via tax abatements and credits, infrastructure improvements, and workforce training). Most states and communities, including those in the Rust Belt, participate in the game to some extent, leading to competition for promised jobs and economic activity. Despite the willingness to offer such incentives, there is at best scant evidence that these incentives are an efficient use of public funds.

Why do some cities thrive economically and others sputter and decline? Are success and failure dependent on luck, or is there something more profound at play? While there are many ways to address these issues, and certainly many contributing factors, this chapter will examine one part of the question: Can tax expenditures play a role in stimulating the growth of these cities? Consideration of the role of tax rates, rather than tax expenditures, is also important but is outside the scope of this chapter. Instead, the discussion will focus on how and why state and local governments use tax expenditures to attempt to improve the conditions of their communities.

This chapter seeks to demonstrate that tax expenditure policy is a highly inconsistent use of public funds. Local governments are at the mercy of a larger macroeconomic environment, over which they have little influence (Rubin and Rubin 1987). The lack of control leaves localities with few tools to create positive change in their communities. The device that these governments often turn to is tax expenditures. As will be indicated, unfortunately, tax expenditures have been demonstrated for the most part to play little-to-no role in positive economic development. Further, despite this evidence, politicians continue to see tax expenditures as one of the most important options available to them.

Using a case study of an intraregional corporate headquarters move, this chapter will investigate how competition among jurisdictions transfers wealth, yet creates few, if any, benefits. It then explores how cities, counties, and other countries are dealing with the competition for jobs that leads to tax expenditures and associated movements of wealth. Finally, there will be a brief examination of some alternative economic development tools that do not result in the large shifts of wealth associated with tax expenditures.

WHAT ARE TAX EXPENDITURES?

The bundle of tools that state and local government officials use within the tax code to try to encourage development are called tax expenditures; they may also be viewed simply as spending that has been initiated through the tax code. Surrey (1970, p. 706) describes them as "special provisions . . . which represent government expenditures made through [the tax] system to achieve various social and economic objectives." The state of Ohio's Executive Budget describes tax expenditures in the following way:

> Both tax expenditures and direct budgetary expenditures incur a cost to the state in order to accomplish public policy goals. Unlike direct budgetary expenditures, unless there is a pre-existing termination date, tax expenditures may remain in effect indefinitely with little or no scrutiny by policy makers. In most states, tax expenditures are not analyzed and reviewed as part of the budget appropriation process; Ohio is one of the relatively few states that do produce a tax expenditure report in conjunction with the state budget. It is probably safe to assume that if it were not for this report, the fiscal impact of the various Ohio tax expenditure provisions would not be systematically estimated (Testa 2011, p. 1).

Tax expenditures include tax deductions, tax abatements, and tax credits. Two examples are the federal mortgage interest deduction and hybrid car tax credits. While there is a general belief that the original goal of the mortgage deduction was to encourage homeownership, the subsidy came about largely by accident (Lowenstein 2006). Though the origin may have been accidental, the inability of opponents in Congress to rid the tax code of this tax expenditure could largely be tied to the myth that it is the backbone of increasing homeownership. The benefits generated from the mortgage interest deduction accrue to those that own homes, have mortgages, and itemize their tax returns—which ends up being about 37 million people, or about half of the individuals who own homes (Lowenstein 2006). It does not directly benefit renters or even the lower-income homeowners who do not make enough money to itemize their deductions.

In a less accidental turn of events, the early adopters of the Toyota Prius received tax credits the year they purchased the car. The size of this hybrid car credit varied from year to year, but it provided a direct subsidy, through the tax system, that encouraged the ownership of fuel-efficient automobiles. And like spending on roads or other goods and services, all tax expenditures are transfers of resources from one group to a designated priority; however, in the case of tax expenditures, the wealth transfers are manifested in lower tax payments for select groups or firms.

Tax expenditures are found at all levels of government. State and local governments have been using tax expenditures to lure and develop businesses since colonial times—in fact, Alexander Hamilton was the beneficiary of a tax expenditure by New Jersey in 1791 to locate a factory in the state (Buss 2001). Despite the long history of tax expenditures in the United States, it was not until after the end of World War II that their use gained significant traction. The changing political moods of the 1980s and 1990s further fueled the practice, leading many to see tax expenditures as "free money," by simplifying them as foregone revenues rather than a true expense.

The flawed view of tax expenditures is problematic for budgeting and makes fiscal policy evaluation exceedingly difficult. Some states, such as Ohio (where the case study in this chapter takes place), do try and estimate the budget impact of tax expenditures. Further, the evidence, even if it may not be precise, presents a story of a big budget hole, $7.4 billion in fiscal year 2012 and $7.8 billion in fiscal year 2013 of "foregone revenues" or tax expenditures for Ohio (Testa 2011, p. 9). Taken together, at more than $15 billion, Ohio would not have had a deficit to work around for the biannual budget for fiscal years 2012–2013 and would have actually been in surplus for both years. The magnitudes for local governments will clearly be much smaller, but the comparative impacts can be just as large.

States often "prefer not to evaluate tax incentive programs in any way," thus avoiding the difficult question of their effectiveness (Buss 2001, p. 93). Rigorous evaluations are often requested when direct expenditure subsidies are provided to individuals or businesses (i.e., grants, food stamps, welfare checks), but they are frequently not required when tax expenditures are being considered (Buss 2001). This results in a huge void in our understanding of their impact on the fiscal condition at all levels of government. The state of Ohio report on tax expenditures specifically states that it "offers no conclusions about the validity of those expenditures. The responsibility of evaluating the expenditure's merit with regard to public policy belongs jointly to the General Assembly and the Governor" (Testa 2011, p. 1).

Neither of the preceding parties has offered a comprehensive in-depth analysis of the effectiveness of these programs. This demonstrates that, even in a state that has made efforts to actually account for and report on the size of the tax expenditure budget, there still remains a huge hole in our understanding of how effective these policies are at achieving their goals. More broadly, however, tax expenditures decrease the transparency of government budgets. Tax expenditures "allow politicians to appear to be reducing the size of government (reducing taxes) while actually increasing it (increasing spending)" (Steuerle 2000, p. 1639).

At the local level, tax abatements are one of the most common types of tax expenditures. Tax abatements are the product of a process that is both bureaucratic and political in nature and result in lowering the property tax burden on specific parcels of land. The political aspect of tax abatements demonstrates how they are meant for more than just tax relief, to encourage redevelopment of an area or economic growth more broadly (Dalehite, Mikesell, and Zorn 2005). Finding a comprehensive study of a state's local tax expenditures is not possible. States that allow tax expenditures at the local level have "established the fiscal framework under which local governments operate, including determination of the tax options available to them and the extent to which those governments may adopt exceptions to the general structure" (Mikesell

2002, p. 41). While some states track major local taxes, "local tax expenditures are not detailed to particular local governments" (p. 41). What this all means for state and local governments is that they need to allocate more resources to investigate the effectiveness of tax expenditures if they are going to use them—something that just is not happening right now.

Why Are Tax Expenditures Being Used? Are They Effective?

Poor and rich cities alike have been employing tax expenditures to attempt to spur economic development across the country, and not just in the Rust Belt. The strategy is used to encourage development and attract new jobs, under the assumption that if net taxes (taxes minus all tax expenditures) in one city are higher than in its neighbor's, jobs will flow to the jurisdiction with the lower net tax rate.

Unfortunately, this generally accepted and overly simplistic notion is not consistent with the evidence. A firm's decision to locate in a community (leading to an inflow of jobs to that community) is far more complex than making a comparison of taxes across jurisdictions (Chi and Hoffmann 2000; Wassmer 2007). The location decision-making process falls under a much broader concept of business climate—although there is significant disagreement over how we can actually measure climate—but it typically includes the quality of life, government policies, and the quality and cost of resources (Buss 2001). Some business climate measures amount to seeking out the state with the lowest wages, taxes, and utility cost, paired with the weakest regulations, the absence of a unionized workforce, and high subsidies for capital (p. 98). However, it is clear that if that were the only possible determinant for firm location, the states with the nation's highest tax burdens, such as New Jersey, New York, and Connecticut, would be without employers, and that is clearly not the case.

What does have a clearer connection to a firm's location decision is the linkage between the levels of revenue collected and the services provided by a jurisdiction. Consequently, the bundle of features a firm seeks out, including tax rates and expenditures, involves not just the taxes, but the taxes and level of service provided (Buss 2001). As with any sort of investment, firms seek ones (in this case, in their location) that will bring the biggest "bang for their buck,"where most are willing to pay a higher tax rate if the service they are receiving is also higher quality or more comprehensive.

The Impact of Tax Expenditures

Ideally, investments yield positive returns. Similarly, the appropriate use of tax expenditures "should produce economic benefits greater than [their] costs. An even better [tax expenditure] is one that is cost-effective, meaning that it delivers more benefits for a given cost than other similarly targeted initiatives" (Weiner 2009, p. 6). Tax expenditures, particularly those targeted at large firms, have failed "to produce significant net benefits for their host communities, calling into question the high-stakes bidding war over jobs and investment" (Fox and Murray 2004, p. 78). Weiner (2009) shows that "for each dollar of credit granted, states usually collect less than one dollar in new tax revenue. Thus most credits do not appear to 'pay for themselves.' It is therefore important to understand the benefits states are gaining for the revenues they are giving up" (p. 4).

The discussion of benefits foregone is often one that is not had by states and local governments. A great deal of effort goes into crafting tax expenditure policies, for little or no payoff, while much of what affects local/regional economic growth (labor costs, skilled workers, energy cost, natural resources, or climate) is beyond the control of these governments (Bradbury, Kodrzycki, and Tannenwald 1997).

When a government entices a large firm to move to a particular jurisdiction with a host of incentives, including tax expenditures, "the location of a large company can crowd out other economic activity by shifting sales from existing firms, congesting local infrastructure, and raising prices in factor markets" (Fox and Murray 2004, p. 79). A large organization locating in an area can create a diminishing return (Fox and Murray 2004; Porter 1999). This may come about because a large firm may choose to locate in an area without other significant competition in order to dominate that place and discourage other large companies from locating there (Fox and Murray 2004); these businesses may actually be hampering further economic development, rather than encouraging it.

Examples of this can be seen in Mercedes-Benz locating in Tuscaloosa County, Alabama (where the firm claims to be the "state's largest exporter, with more than $1 billion exported each year to countries throughout the world" [MBUSI 2011]); and BMW in Spartanburg, South Carolina (where the company asserts that it is "one of several powerful engines driving the state's growth" [BMW 2011]); and Volkswagen in Chattanooga, Tennessee (where the "plant is expected to generate $12 billion in income growth and an additional 9,500 jobs related to the project" [Volkswagen Group of America 2011]); and Kia Motors locating in West Point, Georgia (where the "project is the largest in history for the State of Georgia" [KIA Motors 2011]).

The incentive packages that these firms received were substantial, but they were only a small part of the firms' decision-making process. Ultimately, the data on firm site selection show that "the location of a large firm has no measurable net economic effect on local economies" if it is examined holistically (Fox and Murray 2004, p. 79). This means that the aggressive effort to recruit firms "fails to create positive private sector gains and likely does not generate significant public revenue gains either" (p. 79). This can be interpreted to mean that the siting of a firm, often lauded as a major "win" by state and local development agents, may not actually have the great effect promised. Because "there is little evidence of positive or negative growth impacts associated with the location of large firms," local governments should instead try to make more cost-effective economic strategic moves (p. 91).

The big "win," as seen in high-profile "mega-events" like the Super Bowl and Olympics, which cities constantly fight over, also provides very little help in spurring economic development. Activities like the Super Bowl or Olympics "have no real effects on spending in host communities," a result that can in part be blamed on the "crowding-out phenomenon," where long-term economic activity and investments lose out to short-term jobs (Fox and Murray 2004, p. 79).

Distributional Issues

The intent of many property tax abatements is to draw employers to an area that might have otherwise been ignored; this can help to create conditions that improve economic equality. When the tax expenditures are constrained only to high-poverty and high-unemployment areas, research suggests that tax expenditures can provide a disproportionate benefit to minorities and low-income individuals (Bartik 2007; Peters and Fisher 2004; Wassmer 2007; Wassmer and Anderson 2001).

However, most applications of economic-development-oriented tax expenditures create an environment of inequality (Bradbury, Kodrzycki, and Tannenwald 1997; Chi and Hoffmann 2000; Goss and Phillips 1999; Greenbaum, Russell, and Petras 2010; Kocieniewski 2011; Reese 1991; Reese and Sands 2006; Wassmer 2007). Tax expenditure policies tend to exacerbate inequality across a region, rather than abate it. The wealthy jurisdictions can afford tax expenditures that the poor ones cannot, which can lead to the rich getting richer (more jobs and economic development) and the poor jurisdictions getting poorer (Dewar 1998; Goss and Phillips 1999; Reese 1991; Reese and Sands 2006). This is not to say that poor cities are not using tax expenditures, but that these expenditures often put additional stress on communities in an already difficult financial position (Rubin and Rubin 1987). For rich and poor cities alike, these incentives rarely provide the benefit they promise, and those benefits they do provide rarely exceed the costs (Reese and Sands 2006; Wassmer and Anderson 2001).

Moreover, the benefits associated with tax expenditures tend not to accumulate where policymakers state they are supposed to accummulate (which is often in economically distressed areas). Goss and Phillips (2001), for example, find that "business tax incentives have had a positive effect on economic growth in low-unemployment counties, but not in high-unemployment counties" (p. 237) and "tended to be undertaken in areas with historically higher investment activity, thus contributing to greater economic performance differences among counties in the state" (p. 217). Tax expenditures have often been "criticized because they are only effective at the margins in business location decisions" (Reese and Sands 2006, p. 72). Negative relationships have been found between some types of tax expenditures and the improvement of a jurisdiction's economic health spanning a 20-year period. While this does not mean that in all instances tax expenditures will have a negative impact on a jurisdiction, the research indicates that by not using tax expenditures jurisdictions are not hindering their growth (Reese and Sands 2006).

Tax expenditures may foster inequality by favoring one industry over another. A great number of tax expenditures concentrate exclusively on manufacturing, but in the process end up ignoring other important sectors such as business services, health care, and finance (Buss 2001).

At the federal level, the corporate tax system can rightly be considered both uneven and highly complex (Kocieniewski 2011), in large part because of tax expenditures that benefit individual firms or specific industries. The inequity can spread to an intra-industry inequality, where two companies in the same industry, producing very similar products, have different tax rates. This is often a result of the larger firm having more power and wealth, allowing it to have its effective rates reduced through new tax expenditures. At the federal level, tax expenditures that "intentionally benefit specific companies or industries, cost an estimated $100 billion more a year" (Kocieniewski 2011). However, Greenbaum, Russell, and Petras (2010) show that when controlling for the location of tax expenditures, neither distressed areas nor specific industries were seen to benefit, and that instead tax expenditures (or incentives) were distributed in a pattern that "largely reflects the local industrial mix" (p. 155). This same study did find disparities between urban and rural areas, where the benefits of tax expenditures accrued at higher rates to rural than to urban locales.

Many who support interjurisdictional competition claim that it reduces taxes for all competing jurisdictions. This assertion, however, is only valid when jurisdictions "are similarly endowed with taxable resources and face similar fiscal challenges" (Bradbury, Kodrzycki, and Tannenwald 1997, p. 12). Reality tells us that jurisdictions within a region are rarely in the same resource/fiscal position, because some "jurisdictions are continual winners and others perpetual losers in the competitive process, especially in the absence of equalizing aid from a higher level of government" (p. 12).

To make matters worse, most states do not have any written guidelines for determining how and when tax expenditures to business are offered (Chi and Hofmann 2000). This can result in inequality in the distribution of tax expenditures and make evaluation of the programs very difficult. Iowa, seeing some of the problems in Minnesota, where "tax incentives tend to be focused on those areas already primed to do well," limited its tax expenditure program to "business investment in areas of the state lagging in economic performance" (Goss and Phillips 1999, p. 226). Focusing on a particular socioeconomic group does not necessarily mean that the tax expenditures will provide a greater benefit than cost, but, in terms of creating policy aimed at alleviating inequality, Iowa at least targets communities in greatest need.

Information and Competition

If tax expenditures are only effective at the margins, as Reese and Sands (2006) indicate, a significant information asymmetry problem arises for local jurisdictions. They are faced with a task of determining which of those employers seeking the tax expenditures are the marginal cases and which are just seeking additional rents (or profit seeking) for a decision they have already made. Unfortunately, these governments have no good way to determine which cases are marginal and which are not. Traditionally, the outcome of negotiations between a firm seeking a tax expenditure and a local government depends on the relative power of the respective sides (Byrnes, Marvel, and Sridhar 1999). If a jurisdiction has little to lose if the firm leaves, it can certainly try and call the firm's bluff, wait it out, and hope for the best.

In Ohio, as the ability to offer tax abatements extends to more jurisdictions, the competition among these areas leads to larger abatements (Cassell and Turner 2010). From 1993 to 2009, nearly half of the 2,059 tax expenditures in Ohio that were approved by the state Tax Credit Authority "were terminated or canceled before completion" (Lieb 2011). The failure rate to which the state of Ohio is admitting is simply pointing out that these projects were terminated or cancelled, not that they were actually successful in creating the jobs or economic gains that they set out to attain. The current year projection puts tax expenditures approved in one year for eight northeast Ohio (the area that includes Cleveland/Akron/Canton) projects at $49.5 million over a period of 15 years (Schoenberger 2011). This results in large sums of money being promised for projects over the long term, which come with very high incompletion rates.

While these risky moves may be good for firms, the evidence that tax expenditures provide a net benefit is not very strong. Interjurisdictional competition is a zero-sum game, in which companies pit neighboring cities against one another for the best deal, and can hardly be described as good for development across jurisdictions. The consequences are the "job gains" for one city and "job losses" for its neighbor, a strategy that does not provide net benefits to the region. And, in many cases, the businesses have no intention of moving but just want to get a better tax expenditure deal in their current location (Lynch, Fishgold, and Blackwood 1996). Wohlgemuth and Kilkenny (1998) note that "acquiescing to the rent-seeking behavior of firms leads to socially suboptimal outcomes" (p. 140). The best case tax expenditures scenario, say Peters and Fisher (2004), "is that incentives work about 10 percent of the time, and are simply a waste of money the other 90 percent" (p. 32).

IF TAX EXPENDITURES ARE A LARGELY INEFFECTIVE TOOL, WHY ARE THEY USED SO FREQUENTLY?

If tax expenditures aimed at economic development have at best a 10 percent success rate, and are a waste of money the other 90 percent of the time, why do governments continue to use them? The reason appears to be political, rather than their economic value. Although nothing is inherently wrong with a strategy based on politics, tax expenditures programs are frequently sold to the public based on their effectiveness. It is time that politicians acknowledge that these are frequently political actions, not economic ones.

One reason tax expenditures are used so commonly is that politicians frequently do not view them as actual outlays of government revenues. The fight over what constitutes a tax expenditure and what constitutes a tax can pit long-time ideological allies against each other. For instance, in 2011, there was a battle over eliminating ethanol tax expenditures, which, coincidentally, were commonly referred to as subsidies in the media. Grover Norquist, iconic antitax champion and head of the group Americans for Tax Reform, was pitted against Senator Tom Coburn, an antitax conservative from Oklahoma, who was himself a signatory to Norquist's famous antitax pledge. Norquist claimed that the elimination of ethanol tax expenditures was an increase in taxes for farmers and producers. In his view, a tax expenditure was not an expenditure at all but a part of the tax rate, so that any attempt to eliminate a tax expenditure was actually a tax increase. On the other hand, Senator Coburn rightly saw tax expenditures for what they are: spending. As a result, two natural allies publicly opposed one another because they could not agree on what constitutes an expenditure. This is problematic for the government's ability to manage its finances and budget.

While two self-defined fiscal conservatives have fought over what is and is not a tax expenditure, the broader political marketplace is even murkier. Beyond the debate over the definition of tax expenditures, our political climate in recent decades has made new expenditures very difficult to justify. This has led to expenditures masquerading as tax cuts, and policymakers pushing for tax expenditures because they are more politically palatable than additional spending.

Job and industry mobility within the United States and internationally, or at least the perception of that mobility, increases the pressure to do something (Wolman and Spitzley 1996). However, it appears that the fear of relocation is not necessarily based on verifiable reality. Lee (2008) finds "a relatively small role for relocation in explaining the disparity of manufacturing employment growth rates across states" (p. 436). Also, firms moving from one jurisdiction to another, while not uncommon, cannot be explained by the incentive programs trying to keep or pull them to or from a jurisdiction. In some situations, these incentive programs are even positively correlated with a loss of jobs or shuttering of factories. This may just indicate that state and local governments are acting too late to keep firms that are moving jobs, but it may also show that tax expenditures simply are not what drives the decision to locate or relocate. A number of tax expenditures, particularly those for capital purchases, actually have a negative impact on employment because they are making the machinery and equipment that replace laborers cheaper, resulting in layoffs (Lee 2008).

Cutbacks in state and federal intergovernmental aid are putting burdens on local governments to do more with less (Wassmer 2007). At the heart of the $1.4 billion budget impasse that shut down the state of Minnesota in July 2011 was more than $400 million in cuts to local governments (Dunbar 2011). Ohio's 2011–2013 biennial budget cut its support to local governments by nearly half a billion dollars (Marshall 2011). The challenges that many local governments face are not just found in shrinking intergovernmental aid, but also in the ways and amounts of money that can be raised. Here again politics is a primary agent. State lawmakers are compelled to do *something*, which often results in the institution of property tax restrictions that further hinder the ability of local governments to raise money. These cutbacks and restrictions cause local governments to seek out alternative ways to redevelop their economic situation. The result has often been the use of tax expenditures policy, "not because it was effective but because it was a remarkably easy path to follow, one that allowed [politicians] to claim they were mounting a serious attack on the economic problems of the city" (Swanstrom 1985, p. 149). The tax expenditures allow politicians "to take a bow for causing some massive private project" or "point to towering skyscrapers downtown and say, 'without my help these never would have come about'" (pp. 149–150).

Often it appears as though "the solutions not only precede the problems, they may supersede them and provide their own motivation" (Rubin and Rubin 1987, p. 57). As a consequence, short-sighted public officials trying to maximize reelection probabilities "may offer more incentives than required. That is, the closer the negotiation with business is to an election, the less chance the government official will take in 'losing' the business, and the more likely the incentive package will be larger" (Byrnes, Marvel, and Sridhar 1999, p. 809). To counteract these self-serving political aspirations, adding citizen involvement could be beneficial in tax expenditure negotiations with firms.

Another element of the political calculation is the number of jobs the projects supported by tax expenditures will create. Both politicians and firms have a motivation to overestimate job numbers to justify spending. Gabe and Kraybill (2002) find that tax expenditure programs result in firms on average overestimating the number of jobs the tax incentives will create by 28.5 jobs with each facility's expansion. Their results "suggest that [tax expenditure] incentives do not result in the creation of more jobs than would have been created without the programs" (p. 724). Again, politicians are willing enablers of these approaches because they want to be seen doing "something" and want to be able to take credit for benefits—if any materialize. Voters are left without sufficient information to do post hoc evaluations of these programs, uncertain if the jobs were created as a result of the tax credits or not. The lack of an analysis of the promises made by the companies creates an incentive for these organizations to overestimate the benefits and to garner larger tax credits.

THE CASE OF BROOKLYN, OHIO, AND
AMERICAN GREETINGS

The case of American Greetings (AG), the largest publicly traded greeting card company in the United States, provides a real-world example of the implementation of tax expenditures at the state and local levels in an attempt to keep or lure a firm. The predicament of Brooklyn, Ohio, a Cleveland suburb and site of AG's corporate headquarters, is all too familiar. In May of 2009, Brooklyn faced the challenge of choosing between drastic cutbacks to services and a tax increase in order to balance its budget. The citizens of Brooklyn voted, albeit narrowly, to raise the local income tax rate from 2.0 to 2.5 percent (Noga 2009). Between the time that this tax levy was put onto the ballot and the time that voters approved the measure, employers Key Bank, Hugo Boss, and AG all announced layoffs from their local facilities. In response, the city's leaders pledged that they would reduce the property tax millage from 6.9 to 5.9 if the income tax rate were increased, as it eventually was (Noga 2009). The total property tax rate for a Brooklyn property owner would be 75.9 mills for those without exemptions, and considerably lower for those who qualified for exemptions.

What transpired after the voters of Brooklyn approved the tax increase is a story that many cities face every year: AG threatened to move its headquarters out of the city because of the tax increase. The company stated that although it understood Brooklyn's predicament, it was "disappointed" in the action taken by the city (Cho 2010). AG then began a search for a new headquarters to locations not just in northeast Ohio, but throughout the nation. In return, Brooklyn promised to lower its income tax rate back to the 2 percent level at which it had been prior to the voter-approved increase, with some in the government pushing for it to be reduced to 1.5 percent. The challenge for Brooklyn Mayor Richard Balbier was that "you just can't take the taxpayers' money and give it to a company" (Cho 2011b).

By November 2010, AG had narrowed its new headquarters search to 15 Ohio sites, most of which were still in the Cleveland area, and to one in Chicago. Brooklyn prepared a tax expenditure package that would be worth $6.5–$10 million over 15 years (Cho 2011b). The state of Ohio got involved by passing a special tax credit for AG to remain in Ohio, signed ceremonially at the AG headquarters by Governor John Kasich. In total, the state package prepared to encourage AG to stay in Ohio equaled $93.5 million over 15 years (Cho 2011a). Days after this tax expenditure package was signed into law, AG announced that it was staying in Ohio.

A few weeks later, on May 20, 2011, AG announced that it was moving its headquarters to Westlake, another Cleveland suburb. Coincidentally or not, the new headquarters location is part of a larger development that is owned in part by members of the Weiss family, which leads AG (McFee 2011).

The move of AG's headquarters from Brooklyn to Westlake will be a devastating blow to its former home, as 13 percent of that city's revenues, or about $3 million, are generated from AG. Westlake may have won out over Brooklyn in part because of a lower tax rate (1.5 percent rather than Brooklyn's 2.5 percent), but company officials did make it clear that the decision was much larger than taxes. AG wanted "an environment that more accurately reflects and effectively supports our creative and innovative culture" (Cho 2011a). The firm also had an aging headquarters that needed to be replaced. If one considers total tax burdens, and not just the income tax, as is often the case, Westlake actually has a substantially higher property tax millage of 9.6. The total property tax burden for city residents is 100.9 mills, which includes city, library, schools, and county taxes (City of Westlake 2011a).

IF TAXES WERE NOT THE IMPETUS FOR AG LEAVING BROOKLYN, THEN WHAT COULD IT BE?

During the search for a new headquarters, executives of AG consistently stated that "they sought a location that would allow it to recruit and retain talent in an atmosphere fostering creativity" (Bullard 2011). The firm's chief executive officer stated that the new location, Crocker Park in Westlake, would provide AG with a "lifestyle center that will be attractive to our current and future associates. You will be able to shop, dine, and find a variety of leisure activities nearby. It is easily accessible from several local freeways. The amenities and environment at Crocker Park will give our associates in every department a place to flourish, and maximize their performance, innovation and creativity" (Bullard 2011).

The benefits of having more perks and services nearby have been mastered by Silicon Valley firms like Google, which have barbers, day care, dining, laundry, and recreation facilities. These perks for employees "have the added bonus of keeping the employee workforce in the office more often. Give employees enough reasons to stick around and you'll likely see productivity go up. Why head home when everything you need is at work?" (Strickland 2008). By moving to Crocker Park in Westlake, AG will have access to far more services that could potentially entice its workers to stay around the office longer and that perhaps could lead to higher productivity. This is clearly a benefit for AG that has nothing to do with tax expenditure policy.

By further comparing Brooklyn's and Westlake's infrastructures and finances, a clearer picture of AG regarding the move will start to surface. This is not to say that any one of these factors provides the answer as to why AG moved, but together they do create a picture of the differences between these two locations.

First and foremost, Westlake is a wealthier community than Brooklyn. This can be measured with two simple metrics: median household income and median value of homes. In 2010, the median home value in Westlake was about 89 percent higher than in Brooklyn, $234,000 and $124,100, respectively (U.S. Census Bureau 2010). Westlake's median household income in 2010 was 67 percent higher than Brooklyn's ($68,091 and $40,661, respectively). Westlake has fared substantially better during the housing bust that started across the country in 2008. Brooklyn saw the average sales price of homes drop by 24.33 percent between 2005 and 2010, while Westlake saw only a 12.12 percent decline. The 10-year change in prices for the two cities also shows a disparity: Brooklyn's average change from 2001 to 2010 was a decline of 8.02 percent, while Westlake saw a modest 0.56 percent increase (*Cleveland Magazine* 2011).

The disparities between Brooklyn and Westlake can be further examined by looking at the cumulative assessed value of both cities. Since the population sizes of the cities differ substantially, Figure 3.1 controls for assessed value based on population. What is demonstrated in this chart is that Westlake's assessed value per capita consistently hovers around a value that is about three times as large as Brooklyn's.

Next, Brooklyn also has 1.6 times as many people living below the poverty line as Westlake (6.6 percent below poverty for Brooklyn and 2.5 percent for Westlake). Why might a wealthier city attract AG? It may be that AG wants to project an image of prosperity to its employees, and clearly Westlake has a substantial advantage according to those two measures of community wealth.

Third, there are substantial and measurable differences in the performance of the two cities' education systems. Each year Ohio rates all of its school districts. In 2011 it rated Brooklyn's schools as "effective," while Westlake's were rated as "excellent." Each school district was additionally given performance ratings (ranging from 0 to 120); Westlake received a score of 107.2 and met adequate yearly progress (Ohio Department of Education 2011). While Brooklyn's performance rating score was 96.8, the district did not meet adequate yearly progress. Additional information comes from *Cleveland Magazine's* annual "Rating the Suburbs" issue. While rating systems in a magazine are bound to come with some controversy, they are still read by people in the community and by those planning to move to the area. Here again we see Westlake with substantially higher scores in education, receiving a rank

Figure 3.1 Assessed Value per Capita, Brooklyn and Westlake, Ohio (2011$)

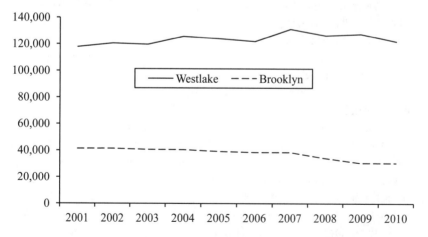

SOURCE: Assessed valuation data come from the cities' Comprehensive Annual Financial Reports. Population estimates are from the U.S. Census Bureau.

of 10 out of more than 200 communities in the Cleveland metro area, as compared to Brooklyn, with a rank of 46 (*Cleveland Magazine* 2011).

Fourth, Westlake outperforms Brooklyn on a broad range of other "lifestyle" ratings. Westlake is perceived to be a safer community than Brooklyn. Again drawing from the *Cleveland Magazine* (2011) profiles, Westlake received a rank of 20 (lower being better) and Brooklyn received a rank of 73. These scores are based upon a variety of crime statistics for all metro Cleveland jurisdictions. Westlake's "total community services" rating is 13, while Brooklyn's is 15.

Finally, the financial stability of the two cities is quite different. One very broad indicator of financial condition is bond ratings. Brooklyn's bond rating, in September 2011, by Moody's (2011), was Aa2. Westlake's rating by Moody's, from December of 2011, was Aaa. While both cities' credit ratings are excellent, Westlake's rating is as high as a rating can be, considered a prime rating, while Brooklyn's rating is two notches lower. Westlake is unique in the entire state for being "the first suburb in Ohio to have been awarded all of the Aaa/AAA ratings" (City of Westlake 2011b).

We can also look at financial stability in terms of budget balances. The fund balances of both cities are exceptional. Both carry fund balances well in excess of the best practice recommendations of the Government Finance Officers Association (2009). This is particularly relevant in recent years of stagnating revenues (the Great Recession), where both cities have been very capable of providing a cushion from which to draw down excess funds without raising taxes or cutting services.

What can we tell from looking at the perceptions of infrastructure, safety, and financial stability? The case demonstrates clearly that taxes were not the main issue in AG's deliberations. Table 3.1 summarizes the potential deciding factors in AG's move from Brooklyn to Westlake. On all nontax elements, Westlake has a clear advantage over Brooklyn. If taxes were the main driver, then AG would have stayed in Brooklyn because the city offered to lower its income tax rate to one comparable to Westlake's, in addition to a tax expenditure package worth up to $10 million and lower property tax rates. The case further demonstrates a reality for many cities; they are at a great disadvantage relative to firms, particularly large companies. If a major employer wants a new facility, perhaps even one that it has been planning for years, it can leverage the

Table 3.1 Comparison of City Advantages, Brooklyn and Westlake, Ohio

	Advantage		
	Brooklyn	Westlake	
State tax expenditures	Neutral		Ohio offered the largest package, although there were no requirements to stay in Brooklyn.
Local tax expenditures	X		Brooklyn offered a larger package of tax expenditures.
Tax rates	X		Total tax burden in Brooklyn is lower. Brooklyn income tax rate was readjusted after AG threatened to move; Brooklyn previously had a lower property tax rate than Westlake.
Community wealth		X	
Home sale price		X	
Median household income		X	
Assessed value		X	
Poverty rate		X	
Education systems		X	
"Lifestyle" ratings		X	
Financial stability		X	

system to reap, at times, huge sums of money to do something it was already going to do, with or without the funds.

In the case of AG, a triggering event (a one-half percentage point income tax increase in Brooklyn) gave the company a strong negotiating position. Without access to AG's internal communications, there is no way of knowing if the firm truly wanted to leave the area prior to this circumstance. What can be seen is a company seizing the opportunity to extract rents from different jurisdictions by threatening to leave the city, county, and state.

One can question the actions of the state in the Brooklyn-AG case. Was the rush to keep AG in Ohio actually what killed Brooklyn's chance at keeping AG? The deal (nearly $100 million) provided by the state of Ohio may have kept AG in Ohio, but for the state it did not matter where AG was located, as long as it was within the state. This creates an environment for the rich to get richer: the company got nearly $100 million and the city of Westlake got a new large employer at apparently little direct cost themselves. This also provides an environment for the poor to get poorer: the state of Ohio's revenues dropped by nearly $100 million at a time when Governor Kasich was trying to fill an $8 billion budget deficit, and Brooklyn, a poorer Cleveland suburb, lost its largest employer, creating a big hole for it to dig out of. As stated by Cuyahoga County Executive Edward FitzGerald, with AG leaving Brooklyn, "You will have a community that will be the big loser [Brooklyn], and the state will have paid for that" (Niquette 2011).

The case of AG echoes the finding in the literature that the decision to move is not simple and pits neighboring cities and states against one another, to the direct advantage of the firm. AG's actions are rational, based on its operating environment, and the company cannot be faulted for how it handled the situation. This case is not meant to be a critique of AG, but rather a critique of the political ecosystem within which it operates.

A WAY FORWARD

AG's move within Cuyahoga County from Brooklyn to Westlake is having a significant local political impact. This case is an example of a kind of interjurisdictional competition that is seen across the United States. Clearly the move will be devastating to Brooklyn, and while it may not be a net loss for the county, it again feeds more inequality into the jurisdiction in this zero-sum game. This is leading Cuyahoga County and other places nationwide to start thinking less about competition and more about cooperation.

Cooperation among Jurisdictions

One step Cuyahoga County took in the Brooklyn-AG situation was to not provide any incentives to AG. Cuyahoga County did not "want to give them any incentive to move from one city in Cuyahoga County to another," especially in this case with, as Cuyahoga County Executive

FitzGerald notes, "wealthier suburb[s] that can afford more grants and tax incentives" (Cho 2011a). In an effort to stem the tide of cities within Cuyahoga County fighting with each other to land the next big head-quarters, FitzGerald is trying to leverage his economic development budget by offering incentives to cities signing on to an antipoaching pact. Communities that commit to this will get revenue sharing and a piece of the county's $100 million economic development fund (Johnston 2011).

The fight for jobs through tax expenditures among U.S. jurisdictions is also going on elsewhere in the world. In 2003 all but one of Australia's states and territories "signed an historic pact to end interstate bidding wars for business investment and major events" (State of Victoria 2003). The pact, which was renewed in 2006 (State of Victoria 2006) and set for another renewal vote in 2011, came about as a result of a bidding war for a A$430 million News Corporation/Fox movie studio. Similar to the approach being taken by FitzGerald in Cuyahoga County, the Australian pact "includes protocols to avoid offering financial and other investment incentives to companies relocating from elsewhere in Australia—a situation where there is no national economic benefit." Australian subnational officials have found the pact to be very valuable in reducing the firms' rent extractions, because the businesses try to overstate "the incentives offered by the potential 'rival' location" (State of Victoria 2003).

One of the keys to the Australian and Cuyahoga County programs is the explicit goal of sharing information among governments. By doing so, these programs reduce the information asymmetry that exists when firms attempt to play one jurisdiction against another. At heart, the challenge for these potentially rival jurisdictions is a prisoner's dilemma, in which cooperation will yield a better outcome for both government parties, but with informational barriers present, one or both of the jurisdictions will tend to defect, resulting in a race to the bottom (Oates 1972, 1999).

The race to the bottom creates a fear in community officials of "losing local business and jobs [which] thus leads to suboptimal levels of state and local public goods" (Oates 1999, p. 1135). Alice Rivlin (1992), the first to head the Congressional Budget Office and a recent member of the Obama Administration's Debt Commission, sees the competition between neighboring jurisdictions as a fight that produces inadequate levels of public service delivery because the competition drives revenues too low. She has proposed a revenue-sharing scheme that would alleviate some of jurisdictions' worries about losing business (Rivlin 1992).

While Cuyahoga County strives to create a system in which its cities share information, the state of Ohio appears to be going in the opposite direction. It has privatized its development activities, which constrains access to information and citizen involvement. The limits that Ohio Governor Kasich seeks are thought by some people to be an economic advantage for the state, as it competes with its neighbors for companies. Site brokers, the agents working for firms trying to relocate, counsel governments to keep all bids secret. These consultants essentially threaten to blackball states and site brokers if they do not comply with the secrecy pacts (Markusen and Nesse 2007, p. 22). The firms benefit from having information asymmetry on their side, which keeps the fear of losing a deal alive by leaving cities and states in the dark. But it is obvious that cities and states may not be going in the same direction on this issue.

Jurisdictions are left in a quandary: they want to improve their fiscal and economic situations without being taken advantage of by firms or decimating neighboring jurisdictions. Rivlin (1992) suggests that

> States might provide higher-quality services if they shared some taxes and did not have to worry so much about losing businesses to neighboring states with lower tax rates. They would then have more incentives to compete on the basis of excellence of their services. They would have to attract businesses and residents with good schools, parks and transportation, rather than with tax breaks. The common taxes would also simplify the tax structure and lower the compliance costs facing companies that operate in many states, as well as reducing the enforcement costs of the tax collectors. (p. 142)

The Importance of Evaluating Results

We know that tax expenditures will continue to be used. It is also clear that under certain circumstances tax expenditures can be marginally effective policy tools, but only if the jurisdictions employing them take the time to analyze their use. Unfortunately, research suggests that "few municipalities place conditions on [tax expenditures], most never evaluate the performance of firms . . . and abatement requests are seldom or never rejected" (Sands, Reese, and Khan 2006, p. 44). When data are collected, the information is often not appropriate to help in evaluation of programs, nor is it timely (Buss 2001). One-third of governments place few, if any, conditions on who gets tax expenditure benefits, and 88 percent of governments reject virtually no one (Sands, Reese, and Khan 2006). Because most jurisdictions do not bother to evaluate the outcomes of tax expenditures, it is little wonder that this tool is so ineffective. The shotgun approach clearly is not working; targeting tax expenditures to distressed areas and evaluating the programs could turn tax expenditures from a 10 percent to a 90 percent success rate (Peters and Fisher 2004).

Further thought needs to be put into what types of firms are getting the benefits as well. Does the tax expenditure create negative externalities for a community (sweatshop work environments or major environmental burdens)? If so, does this really help to develop the community? Clear goals for development are necessary, rather than a mechanism "to provide political cover for the decision to grant an abatement" (Sands, Reese, and Khan 2006, p. 53); not rejecting any firm's applications for tax expenditures provides just such a situation. However, in most programs the evidence of targeting simply does not exist (Greenbaum, Russell, and Petras 2010).

In addition to a lack of actual evaluation of the tax expenditure policies, there is also some difficulty in defining the problem that is being addressed. How is growth defined? Is it growth of GDP, or employment, or some other factor? Why a company decides to move its headquarters to the Rust Belt, or out of it, is not a simple question. Trying to model this decision-making process is even more difficult. For example, Phillips and Goss (1995) note that "studies that use investment or income growth as the dependent variable find that taxes have a larger influence on growth than do studies using aggregate employment or individual firm data" (p. 325). Both income growth and employment would presumably measure the economic health of a region, but if they are leading to contrary conclusions, then modeling this question will be problematic, at best.

Decisions made in the past can haunt a city for years, even when the conditions are not the same today (see Box 2.1). If a large part of

Box 2.1 Minicase of Atlanta, Georgia

Atlanta's rapid growth has resulted in "traffic congestion so bad it threatens the region's vitality" (Hart 2011, p. A:1). No definitive plan has been developed, but Georgia's and Atlanta's leaders want to ensure that the area can continue to grow. A proposed new sales tax could be one way to fund a "balanced" approach (roads and public transit), but "fierce debate is under way over what that balance should be" (p. A:1).

Some leaders in the region are starting to recognize that, while "tax cuts may favorably tilt the cost-benefit analysis of investors pondering whether to build a manufacturing plant in Georgia," those benefits "may be quickly reduced if the end product is trucked through Atlanta, as plant owners incur the indirect, yet real cost of tractor-trailers slogging inefficiently across" the city (*Atlanta Journal-Constitution* 2010). The Atlanta metro area has been described as being a "region at odds with itself," as it contains cities poaching firms from one another in the same zero-sum game that the Rust Belt faces. Leaders in the region do recognize the inconsistencies, as Atlanta residents hate the traffic problems but also hate the idea of raising taxes to the level necessary to fix those problems. The prospect of resolving these issues is complicated by a lack of cooperation among governments in the metro area, "which makes it more difficult to create a thriving region and compete with our peer cities around the country and world" (Chapman 2011).

Atlanta's future hinges on its ability to solve not just its traffic challenges, but also its water problem. The state of Georgia has been in protracted disputes with Tennessee, Florida, and Alabama for access to river waters, and the Atlanta area constantly fights with south Georgia for waters within the state. Droughts in recent years have made access to water perhaps even more important than transit to Atlanta's future, and this debate is more complicated because of rainfall, something no one can control.

why a company stays or leaves a particular location is based on "softer" issues like quality of life, which are even harder to measure than economic growth, the subjectivity of the potential answers will bias study results. Some good first steps will be to collect data, make sure the data being collected can actually measure the outcome, and have that data collected and analyzed in a timely manner.

One of the basic themes of this book is that free trade in unfettered markets and the production of things people value, rather than tax expenditures and other forms of government intervention into local economies, offer the greatest promise for economic prosperity. The tools that surface time and again in the tax expenditure literature are investments in physical and human capital. These topics could necessitate entire chapters or books to cover their depth, but will be touched upon briefly here to illustrate alternative approaches.

Other Ways to Promote Industrial Development

Shifting the tax burden from businesses to residents often creates an environment that reduces the quality of services that are provided (Markusen and Nesse 2007). As has been mentioned earlier in this chapter, taxes and tax expenditures are only a small part of the decision-making process for firm location. The results of a higher tax rate or lower tax expenditures may actually be welcomed by companies because many of them place a high value on government services that benefit the firms directly or indirectly (Bradbury, Kodrzycki, and Tannenwald 1997; Wassmer 2007). For example, good school or university systems will provide quality workers to firms, and good transportation systems will allow for easier and cheaper shipping of goods to market. In the case of Brooklyn-AG, Brooklyn's infrastructure and schools were seen as insufficient (or even deteriorating), while Westlake's were viewed as some of the best in the region (and improving). This disparity provided yet another reason why AG would want to move its headquarters out of an area with inferior services to one with superior services.

Mathur (1999) provides evidence that investment in the development and accumulation of human capital is a more productive and prudent strategy to help support growth than are programs that focus on other aspects of developing an economy. An overreliance on simply luring companies based on tax rates or expenditures puts a region at risk in the long term; if a company locates somewhere simply because of the low rates, it is likely to jump ship as soon as another jurisdiction can offer a better rate. However, if a company has made a choice because of a region's broader set of advantages, then small changes in a tax rate or tax expenditures will be little noticed, given all of the other factors that brought the firm to its present location. As Mathur (1999) points out, "public policy that encourages human capital stock and R&D is in the long-term interest of a region, and the threat of interregional spillovers should not distract regional policy makers from initiatives that promote human capital stock of the region" (p. 214).

Investing effectively in physical or human capital infrastructure requires actual outlays of funds, which is why the tax expenditure route is taken so frequently—it offers much less resistance and conflict. Each city, county, or region has its own special needs, and there is no one-size-fits-all approach available for economic development. But it is clear that investing in physical and human capital can be an alternative to tax expenditures that has a more predictable and lasting effect on the local economy. The mayor of Westlake, for one, does not want to be faulted for the investments his city has made in infrastructure. He states that "Westlake put a lot of money into its infrastructure and quality of life. . . . Why shouldn't we reap the dividends on that investment?" (Miller 2011). In the case of AG, clearly Westlake is reaping the dividends of its investment. Broadly speaking, one of the best things a city can do to ensure its future is to "take care of the basics, like infrastructure and education" (Talbot 2012, p. 74). This is particularly important when resources are idle during a recession, when building materials, capital, and labor are much cheaper, and will enable a city to prepare for its next industry or employer.

CONCLUSION

The challenges that Rust Belt communities face are substantial. Let us reconsider the question raised at the start of this chapter: Why do some of these cities thrive, as others decline? Clearly, special attention should be paid to the lessons that can be learned from the use of tax expenditures in economic development programs. The fiscal stresses that the region faces are substantial and reinforce the problems. Much of the political rhetoric surrounding the demise of the area and the rise of the South and Southwest tends to focus only on taxes, essentially ignoring all other relocation factors.

At the same time one needs to consider that these southern states were also very far behind economically when compared to northern states, so some of the geographical southern shift can be attributed to the equalization of regions rather than an outright flight. This is, of course, no comfort to the residents of Flint, Michigan, who have lived through decades of economic struggle, or to those of Cleveland, which once had among the greatest concentrations of corporate headquarters in the country, and is now frequently seen as an also-ran.

The problems facing Rust Belt communities are not isolated. Booming cities in the South, such as Atlanta, which were once the beneficiaries of the southern shift, are now facing the same challenges: companies leaving for greener pastures.

References

Atlanta Journal-Constitution. 2010. "Georgia's Post-election Priorities. Atlanta Forward: Turn Promises into a Map to Prosperity." *ajc.com.* November 8. http://www.ajc.com/opinion/georgias-post-election-priorities-724706.html (accessed April 8, 2013).

Bartik, Timothy J. 2007. "Solving the Problems of Economic Development Incentives." In *Reining in the Competition for Capital*, Ann Markusen, ed. Kalamazoo, MI: W.E. Upjohn Institute for Employment Research, pp. 103–139.

BMW. 2011. "Economic Impact." Greer, SC: BMW Manufacturing Company. http://www.bmwusfactory.com/news-center/economic-impact/ (accessed August 13, 2011).

Bradbury, Katherine L, Yolanda K. Kodrzycki, and Robert Tannenwald. 1997. "The Effects of State and Local Public Policies on Economic Development: An Overview." *New England Economic Review* (March/April): 1–12.

Bullard, Stan. 2011. "American Greetings to Build New Headquarters at Crocker Park in Westlake." *Crain's Cleveland Business*, May 20. http://www.crainscleveland.com/apps/pbcs.dll/article?AID=/20110520/FREE/110529980 (accessed December 22, 2011).

Buss, Terry F. 2001. "The Effect of State Tax Incentives on Economic Growth and Firm Location Decisions: An Overview of the Literature." *Economic Development Quarterly* 15(1): 90–105.

Byrnes, Patricia, Mary K. Marvel, and Kala Sridhar. 1999. "An Equilibrium Model of Tax Abatement." *Urban Affairs Review* 34(6): 805–819.

Cassell, Mark K., and Robert C. Turner. 2010. "Racing to the Bottom?" *State and Local Government Review* 42(3): 195–209.

Chapman, Dan. 2011. "1 Region, Many Voices." *Atlanta Journal Constitution*, August 3, A:1.

Chi, Keon S., and Daniel J. Hofmann. 2000. *State Business Incentives: Trends and Options for the Future.* Lexington, KY: Council of State Governments.

Cho, Janet. 2010. "American Greetings May Pull Its World Headquarters Out of Brooklyn, Ohio." *cleveland.com*, January 7. http://www.cleveland.com/business/index.ssf/2010/01/american_greetings_may_pull_it.html (accessed June 13, 2011).

———. 2011a. "American Greetings Won't Get County Money for New Headquarters, Ed FitzGerald Says." *cleveland.com*, March 11. http://www.cleveland.com/business/index.ssf/2011/03/american_greetings_wont_get_co.html (accessed June 13, 2011).

———. 2011b. "How Brooklyn Tried to Keep American Greetings." *cleveland.com*, June 12. http://www.cleveland.com/business/index.ssf/2011/06/how_brooklyn_tried_to_keep_american_greetings.html (accessed June 13, 2011).

City of Westlake, Ohio. 2011a. "2011 Annual Budget." Westlake, OH: City of Westlake Ohio. http://www.cityofwestlake.org/pdfs/Finance/Budgets/2011Budget.pdf (accessed June 13, 2011).

———. 2011b. "City of Westlake, Ohio Comprehensive Annual Financial Report for the Year Ended December 31, 2010." Westlake, OH: City of Westlake Ohio. http://www.auditor.state.oh.us/auditsearch/Reports/2011/City_of_Westlake_10-Cuyahoga.pdf (accessed December 14, 2011).

Cleveland Magazine. 2011. "Rating the Suburbs." *Cleveland Magazine.* June.

Dalehite, Esteban G., John L. Mikesell, and C. Kurt Zorn. 2005. "Variation in Property Tax Abatement Programs Among States." *Economic Development Quarterly* 19(2): 157–173.

Dewar, Margaret E. 1998. "Why State and Local Economic Development Programs Cause So Little Economic Development." *Economic Development Quarterly* 12(1): 68–87.

Dunbar, Elizabeth. 2011. "What's the Budget Fight About? $1.4 Billion and Much More." *MPR News*, July 11. St. Paul, MN: Minnesota Public Radio News. http://minnesota.publicradio.org/display/web/2011/07/11/minnesota-budget-fight-is-over-policy-differences/ (accessed July 11, 2011).

Fox, William F., and Matthew N. Murray. 2004. "Do Economic Effects Justify the Use of Fiscal Incentives?" *Southern Economic Journal* 71(1): 78–92.

Gabe, Todd M., and David S. Kraybill. 2002. "The Effect of State Economic Development Incentives on Employment Growth of Establishments." *Journal of Regional Science* 42(4): 703–730.

Goss, Ernest P., and Joseph M. Phillips. 1999. "Do Business Tax Incentives Contribute to a Divergence in Economic Growth?" *Economic Development Quarterly* 13(3): 217–228.

———. 2001. "The Impact of Tax Incentives: Do Initial Economic Conditions Matter?" *Growth and Change* 32(2): 236–250.

Government Finance Officers Association. 2009. "Best Practice: Appropriate Level of Unrestricted Fund Balance in the General Fund (2002 and 2009) (Budget and CAFR)." Chicago: GFOA. http://www.gfoa.org/downloads/ AppropriateLevelUnrestrictedFundBalanceGeneralFund_BestPractice.pdf (accessed April 8, 2013).

Greenbaum, Robert T., Blair D. Russell, and Tricia L. Petras. 2010. "Measuring the Distribution of Economic Development Tax Incentive Intensity." *Economic Development Quarterly* 24(2): 154–168.

Hart, Ariel. 2011. "Denver's Lessons for Metro Atlanta: Our Gridlock Propelled Colo. Region's 2004 Tax." *Atlanta Journal Constitution*, July 24, A:1.

Johnston, Laura. 2011. "Cuyahoga County Executive Ed FitzGerald Proposes Business No-poaching Agreement for Communities." *cleveland.com*, June 9. http://www.cleveland.com/cuyahoga-county/index .ssf/2011/06/cuyahoga_county_proposes_no-poaching_agreement.html (accessed June 13, 2011).

KIA Motors. 2011. "Our Company." West Point, GA: KIA Motors Manufacturing Georgia. http://www.kmmgusa.com/about-kmmg/our-company/ (accessed August 13, 2011).

Kocieniewski, David. 2011. "U.S. Business Has High Tax Rates but Pays Less." *New York Times*, May 2. https://www.nytimes.com/2011/05/03/business/ economy/03rates.html (accessed July 11, 2011).

Lee, Yoonsoo. 2008. "Geographic Redistribution of U.S. Manufacturing and the Role of State Development Policy." *Journal of Urban Economics* 64(2): 436–450.

Lieb, David A. 2011. "Job Creation Tax Credits Falling Short in States." *BloombergBusinessweek*, December 1. http://www.businessweek.com/ap/ financialnews/D9RC1LSG1.htm (accessed April 9, 2013).

Lowenstein, Roger. 2006. "Who Needs the Mortgage-Interest Deduction?" *New York Times*, March 5. http://www.nytimes.com/2006/03/05/ magazine/305deduction.1.html (accessed November 11, 2011).

Lynch, Robert G., Gunther Fishgold, and Dona L. Blackwood. 1996. "The Effectiveness of Firm-Specific State Tax Incentives in Promoting Economic Development: Evidence from New York State's Industrial Development Agencies." *Economic Development Quarterly* 10(1): 57–68.

Markusen, Ann, and Katherine Nesse. 2007. "Institutional and Political Determinants of Incentive Competition." In *Reining in the Competition for Capi-

tal, Ann Markusen, ed. Kalamazoo, Michigan: W.E. Upjohn Institute for Employment Research, pp. 1–41.

Marshall, Aaron. 2011. "Ohio Senate Passes Budget Deal on Near Party-line Vote." *cleveland.com*, June 28. http://www.cleveland.com/open/index.ssf/2011/06/senate_passes_budget_deal_on_n.html (accessed July 11, 2011).

Mathur, Vijay K. 1999. "Human Capital-Based Strategy for Regional Economic Development." *Economic Development Quarterly* 13(3): 203–216.

MBUSI. 2011. "MBUSI Corporate Info." Vance, AL: Mercedes-Benz U.S. International, Inc. http://mbusi.com/pages/corporate_home.asp (accessed April 9, 2013).

McFee, Michelle Jarboe. 2011. "American Greetings to Move Headquarters to Crocker Park in Westlake in 2014." *cleveland.com*, May 20. http://www.cleveland.com/business/index.ssf/2011/05/american_greetings_moving_its_world_headquarters.html (accessed April 9, 2013).

Mikesell, John L. 2002. "Tax Expenditure Budgets, Budget Policy, and Tax Policy: Confusion in the States." *Public Budgeting & Finance* 22(4): 34–51.

Miller, Jay. 2011. "FitzGerald, Mayors to Address Poaching." *Crain's Cleveland Business*, June 6. http://www.crainscleveland.com/article/20110606/FREE/306069964 (accessed December 22, 2011).

Moody's. 2011. "Brooklyn (City of) OH Credit Rating." New York: Moody's. http://www.moodys.com/credit-ratings/Brooklyn-City-of-OH-credit-rating-600027721 (accessed December 14, 2011).

Niquette, Mark. 2011. "States Use Tax Breaks in War for Jobs." *Bloomberg Businessweek* May 4. http://www.businessweek.com/magazine/content/11_20/b4228029534552.htm (accessed April 9, 2013).

Noga, Joe. 2009. "Brooklyn Voters Adopt 0.5 Percent Income Tax Increase by a Narrow Margin." *Sun News*, May 6. http://blog.cleveland.com/brooklyn sunjournal/2009/05/brooklyn_voters_adopt_05_perce.html (accessed June 13, 2011).

Oates, Wallace E. 1972. *Fiscal Federalism*. New York: Harcourt Brace Jovanovich.

———. 1999. "An Essay on Fiscal Federalism." *Journal of Economic Literature* 37(3): 1120–1149.

Ohio Department of Education. 2011. "Interactive Local Report Card." Columbus, OH: Ohio Department of Education. http://ilrc.ode.state.oh.us/ (accessed December 20, 2011).

Peters, Alan, and Peter Fisher. 2004. "The Failures of Economic Development Incentives." *Journal of the American Planning Association* 70(1): 27–37. http://dx.doi.org/10.1080/01944360408976336 (accessed August 8, 2013).

Phillips, Joseph M., and Ernest P. Goss. 1995. "The Effect of State and Local

Taxes on Economic Development: A Meta-Analysis." *Southern Economic Journal* 62(2): 320–333.

Porter, Philip K. 1999. "Mega-Sports Events as Municipal Investments: A Critique of Impact Analysis." In *Sports Economics: Current Research*, John L. Fizel, Elizabeth Gustafson, and Lawrence Hadley, eds. Westport, CT: Praeger, pp. 61–74.

Reese, Laura A. 1991. "Municipal Fiscal Health and Tax Abatement Policy." *Economic Development Quarterly* 5(1): 23 –32.

Reese, Laura A., and Gary Sands. 2006. "The Equity Impacts of Municipal Tax Incentives: Leveling or Tilting the Playing Field?" *Review of Policy Research* 23(1): 71–94.

Rivlin, Alice M. 1992. *Reviving the American Dream: The Economy, the States and the Federal Government*. Washington, DC: Brookings Institution Press.

Rubin, Irene S., and Herbert J. Rubin. 1987. "Economic Development Incentives." *Urban Affairs Review* 23(1): 37–62.

Sands, Gary, Laura A. Reese, and Heather L. Khan. 2006. "Implementing Tax Abatements in Michigan: A Study of Best Practices." *Economic Development Quarterly* 20(1): 44–58.

Schoenberger, Robert. 2011. "Ohio Offers Tax Breaks to 30 Companies including Ford, Timken." *cleveland.com*, December 5. http://www.cleveland.com/business/index.ssf/2011/12/ohio_offers_tax_breaks_to_30_c.html (accessed December 20, 2011).

State of Victoria, Office of the Treasurer. 2003. "States Agree to End Investment Bidding Wars." Melbourne, Australia. Media Release, September.

———. 2006. "Historic Anti-Bidding War Agreement Renewed." Melbourne, Australia: State of Victoria. Media Release, March.

Steuerle, Eugene C. 2000. "Summers on Social Tax Expenditures Part Two: Where He's Wrong . . . or at Least Incomplete." *Tax Notes* 89: 1639.

Strickland, Jonathan. 2008. "How the Googleplex Works." HowStuffWorks.com. http://computer.howstuffworks.com/googleplex3.htm (accessed December 22, 2011).

Surrey, Stanley S. 1970. "Tax Incentives as a Device for Implementing Government Policy: A Comparison with Direct Government Expenditures." *Harvard Law Review* 83(4): 705–738.

Swanstrom, Todd. 1985. *The Crisis of Growth Politics: Cleveland, Kucinich, and the Challenge of Urban Populism*. Philadelphia: Temple University Press.

Talbot, David. 2012. "Tectonic Shifts in Employment." *Technology Review* January/February: 72–74.

Testa, Joe. 2011. "Book Two: The Tax Expenditure Report." Columbus, OH: State of Ohio, Office of the Tax Commissioner. http://www.tax.ohio.gov/

portals/0/communications/publications/fy%202012-2013%20ter%20-%20 final.pdf (Accessed July 16, 2013).

U.S. Census Bureau. 2010. *American Community Survey, 2010*. Washington, DC: U.S. Census Bureau. http://www.census.gov/acs/www (accessed October 29, 2013).

Volkswagen Group of America. 2011. "Volkswagen Chattanooga Hires 2,000th Employee." Press Release, July 29. Chattanooga, TN: Volkswagen Group of America. http://www.volkswagengroupamerica.com/ newsroom/2011/07/29_vw_chattanooga_hires_2000th_employee.html (Accessed August 13, 2011).

Wassmer, Robert W. 2007. "The Increasing Use of Property Tax Abatement as a Means of Promoting Sub-National Economic Activity in the United States." SSRN eLibrary. http://papers.ssrn.com/sol3/papers.cfm?abstract_ id=1088482 (accessed June 29, 2011).

Wassmer, Robert W., and John E. Anderson. 2001. "Bidding for Business: New Evidence on the Effect of Locally Offered Economic Development Incentives in a Metropolitan Area." *Economic Development Quarterly* 15(2): 132–148.

Weiner, J. 2009. "State Business Tax Incentives: Examining Evidence of their Effectiveness." New England Public Policy Center Discussion Paper 09-3. Boston: Federal Reserve Bank of Boston. http://www.bostonfed.org/ economic/neppc/dp/2009/neppcdp0903.pdf (accessed April 9, 2013).

Wohlgemuth, Darin, and Maureen Kilkenny. 1998. "Firm Relocation Threats and Copy Cat Costs." *International Regional Science Review* 21(2): 139– 162.

Wolman, Harold, and David Spitzley. 1996. "The Politics of Local Economic Development." *Economic Development Quarterly* 10(2): 115–150.

4

The Evolution of Clusters and Implications for the Revival of Old Industrial Cities

Haifeng Qian
Cleveland State University

It has long been thought that firms cluster to gain shared economic benefits related to scale, access to skilled labor forces, and transportation costs. Over time the concept of clusters has evolved, no more so than in the Rust Belt cities of the Midwest.

The study of industrial or regional clusters has a long history. Alfred Marshall (1920) discussed the localization of firms within the same area to pursue a shared labor pool, local provision of industrial inputs, and spillovers of knowledge and information. The neoclassical tradition emphasizes the impact of transportation costs and economies of scale on shaping the location of firms (Hoover 1937; Isard 1951; Krugman 1991). Following the economic transformation from Fordist capitalism to post-Fordist capitalism in the developed world, there has been renewed attention on agglomeration and clusters for the past three decades. Scholars with a variety of backgrounds, including economics, regional science, geography, planning, and business management, have sought the reasons for clustering or agglomeration economies. These researchers have pursued new perspectives, including increasing returns, flexible production, innovation, entrepreneurship, knowledge spillovers, and networks (Acs and Varga 2005; Gordon and McCann 2000; Jacobs 1969; Markusen 1996; Porter 1998; Scott 1988).

Witnessing the success of U.S. high-technology clusters, such as Silicon Valley in California; Austin, Texas; and Research Triangle Park in North Carolina, policymakers have increasingly considered clusters as an effective tool for economic development. President Obama, for instance, supported a federal initiative to bolster regional innovation clusters, with $100 million requested in his proposed fiscal year 2010 budget. This has been especially inspired by the work of Harvard Business School Professor Michael Porter (1998, 2003), who has sought to operationalize the identification of clusters. Professor Porter was invited to speak on clusters at the 2011 annual meeting of the National Governors Association. Meanwhile, as of July 2011, 7 of the 10 most read articles in *Economic Development Quarterly*, a journal focusing on economic development policy and practice, included "cluster" in their titles.[1]

The purpose of this chapter is to survey the literature on the evolution of clusters and explore its implications for the revival of old industrial or Rust Belt cities. Many old industrial cities feature declining or declined clusters and are struggling to revitalize their economies. The chapter starts with a review of definitions and typologies of clusters. It then summarizes four streams of literature discussing the evolution of clusters and endeavors to identify some major forces behind the dynamics of clusters, based on the limited research available. It does not solely address clusters manifested in old industrial cities (e.g., the industrial complexes identified by Iammarino and McCann [2006]), since one type of cluster may evolve into another type. The chapter further examines cluster development in the U.S. Rust Belt, using Cleveland as an example, and explores the implications of clusters' evolution paths for the revival of old industrial cities.

CLUSTERS: DEFINITIONS AND TYPOLOGIES

There are several terms associated with clusters, which have been increasingly used in an interchangeable fashion, including "agglomeration," "new industrial districts/places," and "regional/industrial/business clusters," among others. The first wave of cluster research was primarily propelled by the seminal work of Marshall (1920), who popularized an agglomeration approach to understanding the phenomenon. This perspective was carried forward in the work of Hoover (1937, 1948), Mills (1972), and Krugman (1991). Together with Isard's industrial complex approach (e.g., Isard and Vietorisz 1955), the agglomeration view explored the benefits of spatial or geographical clusters in terms of transportation costs, economies of scale, shared labor and industry-specific inputs, and to a lesser extent, knowledge spillovers. Hoover (1937, 1948) classified agglomeration as consisting of firms' internal expansion, localization economies, and urbanization economies. Internal expansion represents a firm's economies of scale; localization economies address cost reductions as a result of the spatial concentration of businesses from the same sector; and urbanization economies consider the benefits of agglomeration irrespective of sectors.

Clusters regained scholarly attention in the early 1980s among not only economists but geographers, planners, regional scientists, and management scholars. This second wave commenced from several case studies of the artisanal and design industries in the "Third Italy" (e.g., Brusco 1982) and was later extended to the film industry in Los Angeles (Storper and Christopherson 1987) and to high technology, particularly in Silicon Valley (Saxenian 1994; Scott and Angel 1987).[2] Scott (1988) terms these places "new industrial spaces," which are characterized by flexible production, social division of labor, formation of external economies, dissolution of labor market rigidities, and reagglomeration of production. These industrial districts feature "a congeries of inter-connected producers and associated local labour markets" (Scott 1988, p. 182).

Markusen (1996) provides an influential typology of the industrial district, which she defines as "a sizable and spatially delimited area of trade-oriented economic activity which has a distinctive economic specialization" (p. 296). She argues that there are other types of "sticky" industrial districts beyond Scott's new industrial places that have demonstrated resilience, and proposes four types of industrial districts.

The first type, called "Marshallian industrial districts," features a business structure dominated by small and locally owned firms. In these districts, there is a substantial amount of trade among locally embedded suppliers and buyers, which is generally secured by long-term contracts, and a flexible labor pool internal to the district instead of to any specific firms. Compared with the classic Marshallian industrial district, its Italianate extension is more innovative, cooperative, embedded, and government led.

The second type of industrial district, the "hub-and-spoke," is one in which one or several large firm headquarters play a pivotal role in local business. These firms are vertically integrated, surrounded by local suppliers, and embedded nonlocally. They are also globally oriented in terms of their input, products or services, and investment decision making.

The third type is coined "satellite industrial platforms" and has a business structure dominated by large branch facilities that are externally owned and headquartered. These branches can range in the nature of production from routinized assembly plants to research facilities, as long as they are able to "stand alone." Because the facility is controlled by its remote headquarters, its cooperation with other local facilities is generally low.

The last type, named "state-anchored industrial districts," involves a business scenario dominated by the local presence of state or national capitals, large government institutions, or big public universities.

Porter (1998) proposes the most influential framework of clusters. He defines clusters as "geographic concentrations of interconnected companies and institutions in a particular field" (p. 78). He considers clusters to be a strategy for regions to build competitive advantage. Consistent with his diamond model (Porter 1990), clusters involve other industries connected with the core industry via both backward linkages (i.e., suppliers) and forward linkages (i.e., channels and customers), and supporting institutions such as governments, universities, and trade associations.

Porter argues that clusters encourage both competition and co-operation and promote innovation, entrepreneurship, and productivity. He further operationalized his concept of clusters, using a combination of location quotient analysis, locational correlation analysis, and input-output models to identify the clusters of traded industries in a specific region (Porter 2003). The Porter school of cluster theory soon gained popularity among not only scholars but also planners, practitioners, and policymakers. This occurred despite the seemingly traditional policy instruments Porter has proposed, such as improving human capital, infrastructure, and intellectual property protection (Porter 1998). However, Martin and Sunley (2003) suggest cautious use of clusters as a development strategy.

Porter's concept of clusters is extended by Hill and Brennan (2000), who define a "competitive industry cluster" as "a geographic concentration of competitive firms or establishments in the same industry that either have close buy-sell relationships with other industries in the region, use common technologies, or share a specialized labor pool that provides firms with a competitive advantage over the same industry in other places" (pp. 67–68). This idea advances the research by providing a methodology based primarily on cluster analysis and discriminant analysis to identify the clusters with competitive advantages in a region.

Gordon and McCann (2000) and Iammarino and McCann (2006) develop a typology of industrial clusters in terms of transaction costs. Under their deductive approach, categories of industrial clusters include "pure agglomeration" following the tradition of Marshall (1920); "the industrial complex" following the perspective of Isard (Isard 1951; Isard and Kuenne 1953; Isard and Vietorisz 1955); and the "social network" following the work of Granovetter (1973). The first type, echoing Marshallian industrial districts in Markusen's typology, is structured by atomistic firms with unstable trading relations. Industrial complexes, with one or several large firms surrounded by local suppliers, represent identifiable and stable trading relations, and are structurally consistent with the hub-and-spoke model. And the social-network model is characterized by the role of trust and social capital in forming business relations and is "essentially aspatial" (Iammarino and McCann 2006).

The aspatial nature of the social-network model discussed by Iammarino and McCann (2006) suggests that the geographic unit for clusters is indeed flexible. Although every cluster has a geographic scope, what matters for a cluster is interconnectedness of economic agents (Porter 1998). The geographic unit of a cluster can be very small or very large, depending on the spatial extent to which economic activities interact. By the same token, the geographic boundary of a cluster is rarely consistent with any administrative boundaries and may even be transnational (e.g., the Seattle-Vancouver technology corridor). The unclear geographical scope of clusters has incurred criticism, such as from Martin and Sunley (2003).

It should also be noted that, within the same region, different types of clusters might coexist. An example is Silicon Valley, which, as Markusen (1996) points out, hosts all of the four types of clusters she identifies. According to Scott and Angel (1987) and Saxenian (1994), Silicon Valley is a typical Marshallian district. However, it also features the hub-and-spoke model with the presence of major hubs such as Stanford University and Hewlett-Packard, the satellite industrial platform with the presence of branches of IBM, Oki, NTK Ceramics, Hyundai, and Samsung, and the state-anchored model with the presence of a strong defense electronics and communications sector (Markusen 1996).

THE EVOLUTION OF INDUSTRIAL CLUSTERS

To date, the literature on clusters' evolution has been relatively insufficient for at least two reasons. First, clusters did not regain scholarly attention until the 1980s, and the most influential studies to date are concerned with definitional and typological issues in the context of post-Fordism and generally consider clusters to be static (e.g., Markusen 1996). Second, different types of clusters (and even those within the same type) may exhibit diverse paths of evolution, which make it difficult to find commonalities. Efforts to explain the evolution of industrial clusters have been made for some specific cases (e.g., Feldman, Francis, and Bercovitz 2005; Huggins 2008). Despite the difficulties of generalization, a few scholars have discussed cluster evolution, and the resulting literature may be categorized into four streams: 1) an industrial cluster evolves following the product cycle of its core industry, 2) technical changes lead to new industrial composition of a cluster, 3) an industrial cluster transforms itself from one type to another, and 4) an existing cluster or even an incumbent firm may incubate a new cluster. Each stream is discussed in detail in this section.

The Product Life Cycle Approach

The product life cycle theory, introduced by Vernon (1966) in the context of international trade, describes the evolution of products, which can be applied to the evolution of the associated industries. A typical product life cycle can be decomposed into four stages: introduction, growth, maturity, and decline. In the first stage, a new product is introduced to the market and produced locally. As it is increasingly accepted by consumers both locally and from outside the region, the industry experiences a rapid expansion in the second stage, and production starts to move to other areas seeking lower costs, especially in terms of land and labor. At the third stage, the market demand for this product is stable or even starts to fall, the production process is mature, and production facilities are primarily located in areas with low costs. Last, new products emerge as better substitutes, and the industry declines. Jacobs (1969) finds that large diversified cities are cradles of innovation and are thus the natural environment for the first stage of the product life cycle. Duranton and Puga (2001) further reveal that innovations generally occur in diversified cities, but production may relocate to specialized cities with lower costs once the production process becomes standardized.

In his seminal paper, Porter (1998) also addresses the evolution of clusters in a way similar to the product life cycle approach. He lists some forces behind the birth, growth, and decline of a cluster, arguing that a cluster may emerge simply by a chance event, or as a result of historical circumstances or new demand. An incumbent cluster or large firms may also serve as the incubator of a new cluster. Once a cluster starts emerging, according to Porter, its growth and expansion are characterized by a self-reinforcing process, in which opportunities in the new cluster will bring dynamic, collective actions of talent, specialized suppliers and forward channels, service providers, and related government agencies. A vigorous local business climate and supportive institutions provide jurisdictional advantages for the region, facilitate the growth of clusters, and enable long-term prosperity for the region and the cluster. The decline of a cluster, as Porter argues, generally comes with technological discontinuities, failure to meet consumers' changing demand, and internal rigidities.

Change of Industrial Composition

In addition to the product/industry/cluster life cycle approach, some quantitative scholars trace cluster changes over time in terms of their industrial composition. A cluster in the Porter school involves not only one or more traded industries but also linked industries as suppliers and channels or consumers. These interindustry linkages can be identified through the input-output model. Industries may also be interconnected through shared labor pools and knowledge spillovers, as suggested by Marshall (1920) and Hill and Brennan (2000), but these flows are much less measurable than interindustry trade.

The industrial makeup of a cluster may be altered over time, reflecting technical developments occurring during that period. Montana and Nenide (2008) adopt this approach and examine evolving clusters in California's central San Joaquin Valley and northeast Indiana from 1997 to 2002. The business and innovation services cluster in northeast Indiana, for instance, was composed of five four-digit North American Industrial Classification System (NAICS) industries in 1997: 1) printing and related support activities (3231); 2) other financial investment activities (5239); 3) agencies, brokerages, and other insurance-related activities (5242); 4) insurance and employee benefit funds (5251); and 5) employment services (5612). By 2002, this cluster had evolved by adding five newly related industries: 1) Internet publishing and broadcasting (5161); 2) securities and commodity contracts, intermediation and brokerage (5231); 3) management, scientific, and technical consulting services (5416); 4) office administrative services (5611); and 5) facilities support services (5613).

Cluster Transformation between Different Types

As the third evolutionary approach, a cluster can be transformed from one type to another under a given typology. Historically, regions hosting the automobile cluster, e.g., Detroit, were transformed from Marshallian industrial districts in the early decades of the twentieth century to hub-and-spoke districts (Markusen 1996), or from the pure agglomeration model to the industrial complex model (Iammarino and McCann 2006). Today, there are only a few oligopolistic producers dominating the local business structure in these regions. The financial market in London, the fashion cluster in New York, and the semiconductor and electronics sector in Silicon Valley evolved from the social network type to pure agglomeration (Iammarino and McCann 2006). As Iammarino and McCann (2006) point out, even for the high-tech industrial sector, its cluster type and evolution path may vary from case to case: Unlike its counterpart in Silicon Valley, the electronics industry in Scotland has remained an industrial complex cluster for the past 40 years.

New Cluster Born out of Incumbent Clusters and Firms

The fourth type of evolution focuses on the role of one or several incumbent clusters in incubating new clusters. Southern California's aerospace cluster, which has attracted talent and suppliers specialized in castings and advanced materials, was associated with the birth of the golf equipment cluster in San Diego (Porter 1998). Gray, Golob, and Markusen (1996) and Markusen (1996) report that the aircraft/spacecraft cluster in Seattle anchored by the giant company Boeing contributed to the formation of other clusters such as port-related activities, software, and biotechnology. Sometimes, several clusters may jointly foster the formation of a new cluster. Porter (1998) finds that a cluster producing built-in kitchens and appliances was developed at the intersection of the home appliances and household furniture clusters in Germany.

Alternatively, the "incubator" may not be existing clusters but simply large and innovative firms or institutions. A new cluster may emerge as a result of massive spin-offs from an incumbent firm in a region. For instance, Fairchild Semiconductor played a critical role in shaping the semiconductor cluster in Silicon Valley, spinning off a large number of new entries, including major players such as AMD, Intel, and National. According to Klepper (2011), a majority of the top performers in the semiconductor industry were located in Silicon Valley and descended from Fairchild Semiconductor, directly or indirectly. Klepper also reports that the influence of B.F. Goodrich is associated with the creation of Diamond Rubber, Kelly-Springfield, Goodyear Tire & Rubber, and Firestone Tire & Rubber, which collectively underpinned the tire cluster in Akron, Ohio. Similarly, America Online and MCI were the hubs that facilitated the formation of the telecommunications cluster in the Washington, D.C., metropolitan area (Porter 1998).

CLUSTER DEVELOPMENT: THE CASE OF CLEVELAND

This chapter seeks implications of the evolution of clusters for the revival of old industrial cities. This is a challenging task, because there have been various evolutionary paths and because the diversity among

old industrial cities implies different cluster-based economic revitalization strategies. The old U.S. industrial cities in the Rust Belt, such as
Chicago, Cleveland, Detroit, and Pittsburgh, differ from each other in
terms of their industrial base and industrial organization, as well as the
extent of their progress toward renewal. As a result, it is inappropriate
to discuss cluster development in the general context of old industrial
cities.

This chapter's focus is on the Cleveland-Elyria-Mentor metropolitan area. Cleveland has been declining for the past several decades,
suffering both population loss and stagnant economic performance. The
2010 census data show that Cleveland was still among the top 30 largest
metropolitan areas, with a population slightly above 2 million, down
3.3 percent from 2000. Economically speaking, employment had a 14
percent drop for the period of 1998–2009, as indicated by the census
metropolitan statistical area (MSA) business pattern data. This section
presents the pattern of cluster development in the Cleveland metropolitan area, and the next section will discuss the implications of the cluster
evolution literature for the revitalization of this region.

Given the emphasis on cluster evolution, examining the longitudinal data is critical. Longitudinal cluster development in Cleveland will
be described using two sets of data. One is from the Cluster Mapping
Project led by Porter, which identifies clusters for each metropolitan
area using a combination of location quotient, locational correlation,
and input-output analysis (Porter 2003). At the core of each cluster is
one four-digit Standard Industrial Classification (SIC) code industry
that exports products, with a group of local industries supplying inputs.
The size of each cluster is measured by total employment in both the
traded and supplier industries.

There are two interrelated problems in using this data set for
this research. First, it covers only the time period of 1998–2008 (as
of March 2011). When looking at the evolution of clusters, long-term
historical data are needed, since it generally takes decades for clusters
to evolve (Sallet, Paisley, and Masterman 2009). Data for one decade
shed little light on the long-term evolution of clusters. Second, because
Cleveland started to lose its competitive advantage in the 1960s, data
for only the latest decade may not provide insights into the sources of
the decline. Technically, as long as employment data by industry are
available, it is possible to extend Porter's methodology into earlier peri-

ods. However, input-output relationships among industries, which are needed to identify clusters, are not stable in the long term. The industrial composition of the same cluster hence could be very different over a long time period due to technical changes in production. As a consequence, it is almost impossible to examine the growth and decline of a cluster defined in terms of a static industrial composition. However, if changes in input-output relationships are accounted for, as in Montana and Nenide (2008), a cluster could change significantly in its structure over a long time period, making the temporal data less comparable at different times. This approach might be feasible for investigating one or a few clusters based on the case study methodology, which allows for reporting details of cluster structural changes along time, but might not be appropriate for studying all clusters in a region.

As complementary information, long-term employment changes of Cleveland's leading traded industries, without considering intraindustry linkages, will also be studied. Traded or export industries are identified using the methodology introduced by Porter (2003) and the 2002 employment data by industry (four-digit NAICS code).[3] The industry data used in this chapter are from Moody's Analytics Web site, (2013) economy .com. The advantages of this site are that its data reach back to 1970 and address the suppressed data problem that appears in the federal data source—the County Business Patterns (CBP). In the latter case, industry employment data are occasionally suppressed to avoid disclosing information of individual businesses. These leading traded industries are likely to be the core of major clusters and thus can be used to track their evolution in Cleveland to some extent.

Table 4.1 presents the national ranking of major clusters in the Cleveland metropolitan area based on Porter's Cluster Mapping Project. A cluster is considered "major" and included in the table if its employment size in Cleveland was among the nation's top 20 either in 1998, the earliest year with available data in the Cluster Mapping Project, or in 2008, the latest year with available data (as of March 2011 [Porter 2011]). The table also shows the percentage change in employment during this decade. It can be seen that major clusters in Cleveland are all in manufacturing, reflecting the historical economic base of the city. In terms of employment size, the three largest among these clusters are metal manufacturing (the largest both in 1998 and in 2008), production technology (the third largest in 1998 and the second largest in

Table 4.1   National Rankings (by Employment) of Major Clusters in Cleveland, Ohio, 1998 and 2008

Cluster name	Ranking 1998	Ranking 2008	% change in employment (1998–2008)
Automotive	4	7	−44
Lighting and electrical equipment	4	10	−51
Metal manufacturing	**4**	**3**	**−29**
Production technology	**5**	**3**	**−21**
Motor driven products	8	>40	n/a
Building fixtures, equipment, and services	**10**	**5**	**62**
Plastics	10	11	−23
Chemical products	12	14	−25
Medical devices	13	26	−33
Power generation and transmission	14	21	−31
Biopharmaceuticals	16	20	−28
Aerospace engines	**17**	**13**	**−3**
Construction materials	**19**	**12**	**−2**
Heavy machinery	**29**	**11**	**81**

NOTE: Bold type indicates a rise in ranking.

2008), and automotive (the second largest in 1998 and the third largest in 2008), as the Cluster Mapping Project data show. In terms of national rankings, which provide insights into regional competitive advantage, Cleveland placed in the top five nationally in employment in the automotive, lighting and electrical equipment, metal manufacturing, and production technology clusters in 1998. In 2008, the leading clusters were metal manufacturing and production technology. Cleveland was among the nation's top three in these two clusters. In addition, Cleveland had the nation's fifth-largest building fixtures, equipment and services cluster in 2008.

As for changes between 1998 and 2008, Cleveland gained competitive advantage, as evidenced by rising national rankings, in 6 out of the 14 listed clusters: 10 metal manufacturing; 2) production technology; 3) building fixtures, equipment and services; 4) aerospace engines; 5) construction materials; and 6) heavy machinery. Among them, the heavy machinery cluster marked the most significant improvement, jumping from number 29 to number 11. Following that, Cleveland moved up by at least four spots in the construction materials, aerospace engines, and building fixtures, equipment, and services clusters. It is worth noting that, although Cleveland had a higher rank in 6 out of 14 clusters in 2008, only two clusters—heavy machinery and building fixtures, equipment, and services—experienced employment growth in this decade.

In comparison, Cleveland's rank in 8 of the 14 clusters worsened during the period. Among them, Cleveland's motor driven products cluster was number 8 in the nation in 1998, but dropped below number 40 in 2008. Other significant declines occurred for the medical devices, power generation and transmission, and lighting and electrical equipment clusters, each moving down in the ranking by at least six spots.

Now we turn to industry data for the time period of 1970–2009, which provide better information for studying evolution trajectories. Figure 4.1 demonstrates the longitudinal change of Cleveland's top-10 traded industries as ranked by their 1970 employment. Only 2 out of these 10 industries—wired telecommunications carriers and insurance carriers—are not manufacturing based. In 1970, the dominant traded industry was motor vehicle parts manufacturing (with total employment of roughly 30,000), which shrank tremendously in the ensuing 39 years through 2009. Likewise, other top-traded industries in Cleveland also declined during this period, although not as significantly. One exception was the insurance carriers industry, which grew by 60 percent, thanks to the expansion of a few large insurance companies based in Cleveland, such as Medical Mutual of Ohio and Progressive.

Figure 4.2 exhibits the industrial evolution of the 10 most specialized traded industries in Cleveland as ranked by their 1970 location quotient;these are all in manufacturing, except interurban and rural bus transportation.[4] Using the location quotient instead of employment size can control for the national growth trend of industries (i.e., product/industry life cycles) and thus can better represent the dynamics of Cleveland's economy relative to the nation or other regions. Four manufacturing industries also appear in Figure 4.1 among the largest traded industries: 1) foundries; 2) machine shops, turned product, and screw, nut, and bolt manufacturing; 3) metalworking machinery manufacturing; and 4) motor vehicle parts manufacturing. Changes in the

Figure 4.1   Employment of Top 10 Traded Industries, 1970–2009, as Ranked by 1970 Employment, Cleveland MSA, Ohio

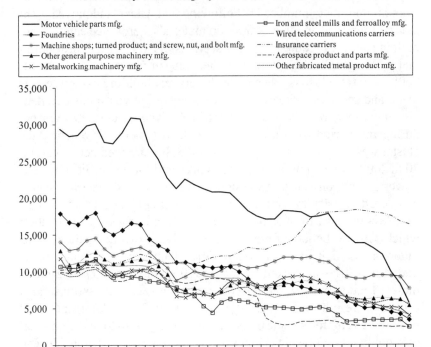

SOURCE: Moody's Analytics (2013).

location quotient of these most specialized traded industries exhibit more diversified patterns than does the employment change in the major traded industries listed in Figure 4.1. The location quotient of the electric lighting equipment manufacturing industry, in which Cleveland was most specialized in 1970, dropped from 6.5 to 1.8 from 1970 to 2009. Significant drops also occurred in the other transportation equipment manufacturing industry, the motor vehicle parts manufacturing industry, and the interurban and rural bus transportation industry. By contrast, specialization in the forging and stamping industry intensified during the same period. The longitudinal location quotient for the electrical equipment manufacturing industry shows an interesting U-shaped

Figure 4.2 Location Quotients of Top 10 Traded Industries, 1970–2009, as Ranked by 1970 Location Quotient, Cleveland MSA, Ohio

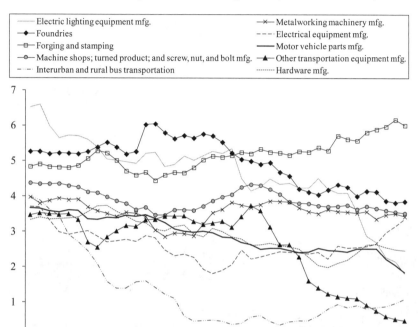

SOURCE: Moody's Analytics (2013).

curve, first becoming less specialized and after the 1990s regaining its proportion relative to the national level. Changes in other traded industries were moderate.

Figures 4.3 and 4.4 replicate Figures 4.1 and 4.2, respectively, except that the industries are identified based on the 2009 data. A comparison between industries included in Figure 4.3 with those included in Figure 3.1 suggests major shifts of leading traded industries between 1970 and 2009. In 2009, the top five largest traded industries were all service based. Only 3 out of the top 10 were manufacturing industries: 1) the motor vehicle parts manufacturing industry; 2) the machine shops, turned product, and screw, nut, and bolt manufacturing industry; and 3) the other fabricated metal product manufacturing industry. As shown

Figure 4.3 Employment of Top 10 Traded Industries, 1970–2009, as Ranked by 2009 Employment, Cleveland MSA, Ohio

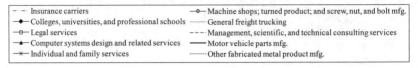

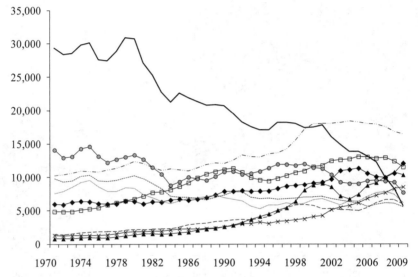

SOURCE: Moody's Analytics (2013).

in Figure 4.1, these were also among the largest traded industries in 1970 but declined since then. The "big four" traded industries—insurance carriers; colleges, universities, and professional schools; legal services; and computer systems design and related services—have expanded significantly since 1970 and each hired over 10,000 employees in 2009. Behind the high rank of the individual and family services industry was Cleveland's largest employer, the Cleveland Clinic.

In contrast to Figure 4.3, Figure 4.4 reveals that the 10 traded industries with the highest location quotients in 2009 were exclusively manufacturing industries, and 5 of them were also among the top 10 most specialized traded industries in 1970. The most remarkable change between 1970 and 2009 was in the paint, coating, and adhesive manu-

Figure 4.4 Location Quotients of Top 10 Traded Industries, 1970–2009, as Ranked by 2009 Location Quotient, Cleveland, Ohio

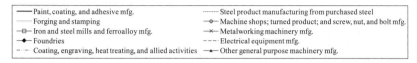

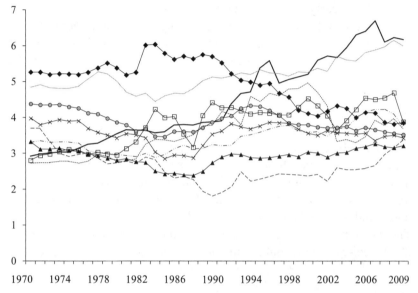

SOURCE: Moody's Analytics (2013).

facturing industry, with an increase in its location quotient from 2.9 to 6.2. Location quotient changes for other traded industries were moderate, providing evidence that Cleveland has been consistently specialized in these manufacturing industries.

What can be learned about cluster development and the evolution of traded industries in Cleveland based on these data? Three observations merit attention. To begin with, manufacturing clusters and industries are foundational to Cleveland's economy. Table 4.1 demonstrates that all clusters with a high national rank (by employment) are manufacturing based, as of 1998 or 2008. Similarly, Figures 4.2 and 4.4 show that Cleveland was consistently specialized in manufacturing industries between 1970 and 2009.

In addition, Cleveland's manufacturing clusters and industries have declined, but to a large extent due to product life cycles—the nation-wide downsizing of manufacturing employment. In the case of clusters, the decade following 1998 witnessed employment growth in 2 of the 14 leading clusters in Cleveland; however, Cleveland moved upward in the national rankings of 6 of these 14 clusters. In the case of traded industries, while nearly all of Cleveland's top-10 largest traded industries in 1970 shrank in the following decades, changes in location quotients for Cleveland's 10 most-specialized traded industries in 1970 (9 of which were manufacturing industries) were rather diversified. For example, Cleveland in 2009 lost 80 percent of its1970 employment in the found-ries industry; its location quotient by contrast went down only slightly, from 5.3 to 3.9.

Last but not least, some service-based traded industries have exhib-ited their vibrancy and have been driving job creation in Cleveland for the past four decades; however, they have yet to build standout compet-itive advantage nationally. For example, the insurance carriers indus-try had over 16,000 employees in 2009 and was Cleveland's largest traded industry, but had only a modestly high location quotient of 1.7. The location quotient for Cleveland's second-largest traded industry in 2009—colleges, universities, and professional schools—was only 1.2.

THE EVOLUTION OF CLUSTERS: IMPLICATIONS FOR CLEVELAND

How may the literature on the evolution of clusters shed light on the revitalization of a declining manufacturing city like Cleveland? The four streams of literature on cluster evolution introduced previously may have the following implications for cluster-based economic devel-opment and revival strategies.

To begin with, economic development strategies should reflect the primacy of the market in cluster development. As Porter (1998) has argued, the growth of a cluster is a self-reinforcing process in which entrepreneurs seize market opportunities embedded in the dynamics of cluster emergence. Entrepreneurship and competition are funda-mentally important for cluster development, irrespective of the cluster type. Even for the industrial complex model identified by Gordon and McCann (2000), or similarly the hub-and-spoke districts defined by Markusen (1996), the barriers to or opportunities for entrepreneurship created by one or a few large firms are critical to the performance of a cluster. While Seattle is generally considered a success (Markusen 1996), Detroit is notorious for the rigidity and inflexibility brought by the "Detroit Three" automakers.

Industrial policy, represented by tax incentives and government subsidies specific to certain industries or firms, has been a popular practice. One of the latest cases of this kind of policy in Cleveland was a 15-year, $93.5 million incentive package put together by the state government in 2011 to retain the headquarters of American Greetings, a Fortune 1000 company, in northeast Ohio.[5] This case is discussed in Chapter 3 of this book. Industrial policy, which reflects the preference of the government and not necessarily competitiveness in the market, may distort competition, discourage new entries, and create opportunities for rent seeking and destructive entrepreneurship—not to mention the generally higher-than-minimum costs taxpayers have to bear due to information asymmetry between the government and incentive receivers. This type of policy challenges market primacy, is a threat to healthy cluster development, and thus should be abandoned.

The acceptance of market primacy and the repeal of industrial policy do not, however, mean that there is no role for government in cluster development. As Porter (1998) suggests, intellectual property protection and antitrust law enforcement at the national level and human capital development and physical infrastructure improvement at the subnational level are important aspects of cluster policy. The decline of population in Cleveland has made physical infrastructure sufficient for cluster development. The focus should be on investing and retaining human capital. Based on 2000 census data, only 23 percent of Cleveland's adult population has a bachelor's degree, a proportion that ranks as 157 among the 331 U.S. metropolitan areas. Human capital is critical to both knowledge creation and entrepreneurship (Qian and Acs 2013) and accordingly plays an important role in maintaining the vibrancy of clusters.

The second implication from the literature is that economic development strategies should take into account the path-dependent nature of cluster evolution. Cleveland, as it has been for most of its history, is still specialized in manufacturing production both for clusters and for traded industries. Nationally, most of these are declined or declining industries, constituting the major source of the stagnancy of Cleveland's economy. Despite that, any proposed cluster development strategy for Cleveland cannot simply overlook its manufacturing base. The history of the city renders its infrastructure, supply chains, business climate, and institutional setting all favorable to the manufacturing sector. The competitive advantage of Cleveland lies in its support systems for manufacturing. For the last several decades, growth has been remarkable in service areas such as insurance carriers and legal industries, yet these services are very competitive given the values of their location quotient. Policies or strategies in favor of service industries over manufacturing industries would be fundamentally wrong.

In fact, it is not "shameful" to be manufacturing based. It is good to have a specialization in "sexy" industries where that reflects genuine competitive advantage, such as within high-tech industries in Silicon Valley or Research Triangle Park, financial and fashion industries in New York City, or entertainment industries in Los Angeles, but manufacturing industries can also be drivers of economic growth. According to Markusen (1996), when the national manufacturing employment growth rate between 1970 and 1990 was almost zero, the manufacturing employment of industrial cities that grew most rapidly during this period increased by at least 50 percent. Porter (1998) states that "all industries can employ advanced technology; all industries can be knowledge intensive" (p. 80).

Consequently, cities like Cleveland should not think of abandoning manufacturing, but rather should focus on building regional capacity and jurisdictional advantages that reinforce the competitiveness of manufacturing clusters. As long as Cleveland maintains its competitive advantage, a manufacturing industry in the city may still grow by taking a higher share of this nationally shrinking industry. At the core of the competitiveness of manufacturing clusters is continuous innovation. Such changes are not specific to high-tech industries; they are fundamentally important for sustaining the growth of all industries or clusters. This imperative also calls for public policy to strengthen regional or local human capital.

The third implication from the literature is that there is a supporting role that public policy may play in facilitating the emergence of the next competitive cluster in Cleveland. As Klepper (2011), Markusen (1996), and Porter (1998) have contended, the emergence of a cluster may result from the incubation activity of existing clusters, large incumbent firms, or institutions like universities. Irrespective of industry, knowledge spillovers and entrepreneurship are critical in the formation of clusters this way. In fact, these two factors are interrelated; as Acs et al. (2009) and Qian and Acs (2013) argue, entrepreneurial activity may serve as a mechanism of transmitting knowledge spillovers. Cleveland's productivity in knowledge creation, as measured by patents per capita in year 2000, ranked 144 out of 331 metropolitan areas; by contrast, its entrepreneurial activity, as measured by new firms per capita in year 2000, ranked 224 out of 361 metropolitan areas.[6] These measures suggest that not only knowledge creation and spillovers but also entrepreneurship in Cleveland need to be strengthened to foster the development of new clusters.

Beyond human capital investment and retention, as discussed under the first implication, public efforts may be put into small business support programs, like business incubators and Small Business Development Centers. Business incubators, for example, may facilitate both knowledge spillovers (through the networking opportunities they provide) and entrepreneurship (through the various primary and professional services they offer). The publicly funded business support programs, in accord with cluster policy, should service local businesses from all industries.

Last but not least, it does not matter when a regional cluster was transformed from one type to another under a typology like Markusen's (1996) or from one industrial composition to another one as suggested by Montana and Nenide (2008), as long as the cluster maintains its competitiveness. The fall of Detroit was not because its automobile cluster evolved from a Marshallian industrial district to a hub-and-spoke district (Markusen 1996), but because, along with this transformation, the oligopolistic Detroit Three lapsed into rigidities that deferred entrepreneurial new entries (Chinitz 1961). Cleveland used to be one of the most entrepreneurial cities in the United States a century ago, and its decline was largely attributed to the loss of that spirit. Cleveland's clusters, as elsewhere, have been evolving, and today its leading clusters more or less cover all of the four types of industrial districts identified by Markusen. All these types of clusters could be competitive, or not.

Regardless of cluster type and industrial composition, the true sources of clusters' competitiveness in a region are high stocks of human capital, well-developed infrastructure, and social, business, and institutional climates that encourage learning and innovative and entrepreneurial activities. Cluster development policy in Cleveland and other old industrial cities should be made in these directions.

CONCLUDING REMARKS

This chapter focuses on the evolution of clusters and the associated implications for the revival of old industrial cities, using Cleveland as an example. It reviews the literature on the definitions, typologies, and evolution paths of clusters and also introduces some facts about Cleveland's cluster development based on the Cluster Mapping Project and Moody's economy.com data. At the core of the discussion is how cluster evolution theories may shed light on the revitalization of Cleveland. Four implications are drawn from the literature: 1) highlighting the roles of primacy of market, 2) path dependency, 3) public policy in the emergence of clusters, and 4) the irrelevance of cluster types in the context of economic development. In conclusion, human capital, innovation, and entrepreneurship should be the targets of Cleveland's focus in building competitive clusters and regaining economic vibrancy. The capacity building approach to cluster development, as Sallet, Paisley, and Masterman (2009) have noted, may mean that it will be decades before Cleveland regains its former stature in the national economy, and it may require collective leadership from both public and private sectors.

Notes

The author would like to thank Minkyu Yeom for his research assistance with the data and Srikanth Sivashankaran for his editing work.

1. See http://edq.sagepub.com/reports/most-read (accessed August 18, 2011).
2. The Third Italy refers to the central and northeast regions of Italy.
3. Porter (2003) gives three primary criteria for traded industries: 1) all states with a location quotient greater or equal to 1 account for at least half of the total employ-

ment, 2) the top five states represent an average location quotient of at least 2, and 3) the Gini index is at least 0.3. Following Porter's suggestion, we also excluded resource-based industries, in this case all four-digit NAICS industries under Agriculture, Forestry, Fishing and Hunting (NAICS code 11) and Mining, Quarrying, and Oil and Gas Extraction (NAICS code 21).

4. Location quotient is the share of employment in an industry in a region divided by the share of employment in the same industry in the nation. It reflects the extent to which the region is specialized in the industry compared with the nation as a benchmark.

5. For details, see http://www.cleveland.com/business/index.ssf/2011/03/american_ greetings_to_stay_in.html (accessed October 1, 2011).

6. Patent data and new firm formation data used the 1999 metropolitan statistical areas (MSAs) definition and the 2003 MSAs definition, respectively, leading to different total numbers of MSAs. Patent data were provided by Kevin Stolarick (University of Toronto); population data were from the 2000 census; and new firm formation data were from Business Information Tracking System of the U.S. Census Bureau.

References

Acs, Zoltan J., Pontus Braunerhjelm, David B. Audretsch, and Bo Carlsson. 2009. "The Knowledge Spillover Theory of Entrepreneurship." *Small Business Economics* 32(1): 15–30.

Acs, Zoltan J., and Attila Varga. 2005. "Entrepreneurship, Agglomeration and Technological Change." *Small Business Economics* 24(3): 323–334.

Brusco, Sebastiano. 1982. "The Emilian Model: Productive Decentralization and Social Integration." *Cambridge Journal of Economics* 18(6): 529–546.

Chinitz, Benjamin. 1961. "Contrasts in Agglomeration: New York and Pittsburgh." *American Economic Review* 51(2): 279–289.

Duranton, Gilles, and Diego Puga. 2001. "Nursery Cities: Urban Diversity, Process Innovation, and the Life Cycle of Products." *American Economic Review* 91(5): 1454–1477.

Feldman, Maryann P., Johanna Francis, and Janet Bercovitz. 2005. "Creating a Cluster while Building a Firm: Entrepreneurs and the Formation of Industrial Clusters." *Regional Studies* 39(1): 129–141.

Gordon, Ian R., and Philip McCann. 2000. "Industrial Clusters: Complexes, Agglomeration and/or Social Networks?" *Urban Studies* 37(3): 513–532.

Granovetter, Mark S. 1973. "The Strength of Weak Ties." *American Journal of Sociology* 78(6): 1360–1380.

Gray, Mia, Elyse Golob, and Ann Markusen. 1996. "Big Firms, Long Arms, Wide Shoulders: The 'Hub-and-Spoke' Industrial District in the Seattle Region." *Regional Studies* 30(7): 651–666.

Hill, Edward W., and John F. Brennan. 2000. "A Methodology for Identifying the Drivers of Industrial Clusters: The Foundation of Regional Competitive Advantage." *Economic Development Quarterly* 14(1): 65–96.

Hoover, E. M. 1937. *Location Theory and the Shoe and Leather Industries.* Cambridge, MA: Harvard University Press.

———. 1948. *The Location of Economic Activity.* New York: McGraw-Hill.

Huggins, Robert. 2008. "The Evolution of Knowledge Clusters: Progress and Policy." *Economic Development Quarterly* 22(4): 277–289.

Iammarino, Simona, and Philip McCann. 2006. "The Structure and Evolution of Industrial Clusters: Transactions, Technology and Knowledge Spillovers." *Research Policy* 35(7): 1018–1036.

Isard, Walter. 1951. "Distance Inputs and the Space Economy. Part II: The Locational Equilibrium of the Firm." *Quarterly Journal of Economics* 65(August): 373–399.

Isard, Walter, and Robert E. Kuenne. 1953. "The Impact of Steel upon the Greater New York-Philadelphia Industrial Region." *Review of Economics and Statistics* 35(4): 289–301.

Isard, Walter, and Thomas Vietorisz. 1955. "Industrial Complex Analysis, and Regional Development with Particular Reference to Puerto Rico." *Papers and Proceedings of the Regional Science Association* 1(1): 229–247.

Jacobs, Jane. 1969. *The Economy of Cities.* New York: Random House.

Klepper, Steven. 2011. "Nano-economics, Spinoffs, and the Wealth of Regions." *Small Business Economics* 37(2): 141–154.

Krugman, Paul. 1991. "Increasing Returns and Economic Geography." *Journal of Political Economy* 99(3): 483–499.

Markusen, Ann. 1996. "Sticky Places in Slippery Space: A Typology of Industrial Districts." *Economic Geography* 72(3): 293–313.

Marshall, Alfred. 1920. *Principles of Economics.* London: Macmillan.

Martin, Ron, and Peter Sunley. 2003. "Deconstructing Clusters: Chaotic Concept or Policy Panacea?" *Journal of Economic Geography* 3(1): 5–35.

Mills, Edwin S. 1972. *Urban Economics.* Glenview, IL: Scott, Foresman, and Company.

Montana, Jennifer Paige, and Boris Nenide. 2008. "The Evolution of Regional Industry Clusters and their Implications for Sustainable Economic Development." *Economic Development Quarterly* 22(4): 290–302.

Moody's Analytics. 2013. *economy.com.* West Chester, PA: Moody's Analytics. http://www.economy.com (accessed August 12, 2013).

Porter, Michael E. 1990. *The Competitive Advantage of Nations.* New York: The Free Press.

———. 1998. "Clusters and the New Economics of Competition." *Harvard Business Review,* November-December: 77–90.

————. 2003. "The Economic Performance of Regions." *Regional Studies* 37(7): 549–578.

————. 2011. Cluster Mapping Project, Institute for Strategy and Competitiveness, Harvard Business School (accessed March 6, 2011).

Qian, Haifeng, and Zoltan J. Acs. 2013. "An Absorptive Capacity Theory of Knowledge Spillover Entrepreneurship." *Small Business Economics* 40(2): 185–197.

Sallet, Jonathan, Ed Paisley, and Justin R. Masterman. 2009. "The Geography of Innovation: The Federal Government and the Growth of Regional Innovation Clusters." *Science Progress*, September. http://scienceprogress .org/2009/09/the-geography-of-innovation/ (accessed April 11, 2013).

Saxenian, Annalee. 1994. *Regional Advantages: Culture and Competition in Silicon Valley and Route 128.* Cambridge, MA: Harvard University Press.

Scott, Allen. J. 1988. "Flexible Production Systems and Regional Development: The Rise of New Industrial Spaces in North America and Western Europe." *International Journal of Urban and Regional Research* 12(2): 171–186.

Scott, Allen. J., and D. P. Angel. 1987. "The U.S. Semiconductor Industry: A Locational Analysis." *Environment and Planning A* 19(7): 875–912.

Storper, Michael, and Susan Christopherson. 1987. "Flexible Specialization and Regional Industrial Agglomeration: The Case of the U.S. Motion Picture Industry." *Annals of the Associations of American Geographers* 77(1): 104–117.

Vernon, Raymond. 1966. "International Investment and International Trade in the Product Cycle." *Quarterly Journal of Economics* 80(2): 190–207.

5
Stop Shovelling

A New Workforce Development Strategy to
Promote Regional Prosperity

Joel A. Elvery
Federal Reserve Bank of Cleveland

Workers laid off in the declining industries of Rust Belt cities are often targets of the nation's workforce development system. Additional training, it is thought, will help these workers find new jobs requiring their newly acquired skills. However, this is a "needs-based" approach; those workers perceived to have the greatest need are offered training. Perhaps, instead, the system should target displaced workers who are most likely to advance in occupations (those possessing interest and aptitude), thereby eventually creating openings for lower-skilled workers, i.e., job chains.

Workforce development policy in the United States has been driven by goals, rather than by what is achievable. The main focus has been to help people with few skills enter or reenter the labor market. The programs implemented to achieve those goals, however, have had limited success. The simple truth is that many low-skilled workers have a difficult time finding work because they cannot keep up with advances in the economy. This has been especially problematic in the manufacturing centers of the Rust Belt, where many jobs have been lost to automation and competition from other regions. Even if low-skilled workers could be trained for in-demand occupations, the number of openings at any time is much smaller than the number of people who are unemployed or working for low wages (Lafer 2002). This means that job training for the least skilled has limited ability to reduce poverty.

As an analogy, the labor market for each skill group is like a bucket. The bucket for the lowest skills is large, but it is completely full and shrinking relative to the other buckets. Workforce development organizations have historically focused on helping individuals enter this portion of the labor market. This emphasis continues today with the tiered service system of the Workforce Investment Act (WIA), where people are only eligible for intensive training if they have proven to be unable to find work at pay near that of their prior position. Consequently, training resources are targeted to people who have difficulty finding work and, except during recessions and their aftermath, these individuals are typically low skilled. The training available is generally too little to move these participants beyond entry-level positions. While a lucky few find a way to stay in the labor market, most spill over the side of the bucket. This effect discourages the many unlucky training participants who remain unemployed and wastes public resources.

It is time to stop shoveling more individuals into low-skilled markets. We must recognize that poverty reduction is only one potential goal for workforce policy; increasing the efficiency of labor markets and the level of individuals' earnings are also good objectives. The most effective way to achieve these aims is to orient our workforce system toward facilitating advancement into occupations in which the vacancies outnumber the applicants. Job training dollars should be targeted to individuals based on interest and aptitude, not need. While this strategy would not directly assist the poorest individuals, it would have the potential to create job openings for them. As people advance in their careers, their prior positions will open up, which could create a job chain that results in openings for low-skilled workers. In addition, the productivity and income increases connected to job advancement would create economic growth. This means that an advancement-centered workforce system could better achieve the goal of the current system: to increase the number of low-skilled individuals who are working.

Reorienting the workforce system to promote advancement into open positions is especially important for metropolitan areas (metros) in the Rust Belt. In the last 50 years, the growth of regions has been closely tied to the education level of their population (Shapiro 2006) and there is every reason to believe that this will remain true (Moretti 2012). The Rust Belt has suffered large, long-lived manufacturing job losses both from 1970 to 1985 and again from 1998 to 2003. These losses have generated a negative cycle that is difficult to interrupt. First, population declines; one estimate finds a metro's population declines by

1.8 people per job lost from the auto or steel industries (Feyrer, Sacerdote, and Stern 2007). The population decline reduces unemployment rates to typical levels, but it also alters the composition of the workforce. Declines in population lead to declines in housing prices and the poor, who are low-skilled on average, are disproportionately attracted to inexpensive housing (Glaeser and Gyourko 2005). As a result, Rust Belt metros, whose residents were less educated than other metros with similar income levels and house prices before the decline in manufacturing jobs, saw slower increases in education levels than regions that did not suffer catastrophic job loss.

Numerous programs have been put in place to increase state education levels, but evidence of their effectiveness is lacking (see Groen [2011] for a review of the literature). The challenge is that skilled people choose to live in regions where they can find work. As a result, for every 10 additional bachelor's degree holders a state graduates, it only gains three more degree holders than it would have otherwise (Bound et al. 2004). By focusing on the jobs that are available, programs that help people advance into open positions are likely to be an effective way for the Rust Belt to increase its skill level.

This chapter argues that we need to reorient our workforce development system to focus on advancement and describes policies and programs that fit that orientation. The first section presents an informal model for thinking about how labor markets function. Then, the discussion documents the limited success of the workforce development system created in WIA, describes the kinds of programs that would facilitate career advancement, and presents recent successful initiatives that demonstrate the value of advancement-centered workforce development.

A LABOR MARKET FRAMEWORK

A great deal of evidence shows that labor markets in industrialized countries are imperfectly competitive (well summarized in Manning [2003]). It is best to think of U.S. labor markets as made up of many submarkets, where each one covers a particular skill level and a metropolitan area or nonmetropolitan region. Due to chance, people with the same skills can earn different wages, depending on which job they find. A worker with the good fortune to find a high-paying job is less likely to leave. People can only take jobs that are available, and most submarkets have about as many open positions as job seekers. The least-skilled submarkets are the largest; the more skilled the submarket, the smaller it is. Movement between different submarkets can be done in several ways. If individuals lose a job and cannot find one at the same skill level, they eventually fall to a lower-skill submarket. People can also advance from one level to the next, but only with an investment of time and usually money.

There are two types of unemployed workers in our labor markets. Some jobless individuals have worked before or have recently completed college or other substantial training. The other group consists of people who are hoping to enter the labor market either for the first time or after a long spell of unemployment.

The degree of balance between the number of jobs and the number of people at each skill level has important ramifications. In submarkets with more people than jobs, unemployment persists and employers face little pressure to increase wages. In submarkets with more jobs than people, employers increase wages to attract the available workers. There are large differences in the numbers of jobs and people in low-skilled submarkets (where people outnumber jobs) and submarkets that require specific technical skills but not a college degree (where jobs sometimes outnumber people). This can be seen in Figure 5.1, which shows the average from May 2005 to November 2007 of the number of unemployed individuals by most recent occupation and the number of openings advertised online in the occupation.[1] The occupations where there were more than five unemployed workers for every advertised position are less skilled: farming, fishing, and forestry; construction and extraction; buildings and grounds cleaning and maintenance; food preparation and serving related; personal care and service; and production. The occupations with less than one unemployed worker per each opening are all highly skilled: computer and mathematical science; health care practitioners and technical; architecture and engineering; business and financial operations; life, physical, and social science; management; community and social services; and legal.

The least skilled submarkets have many more seekers than jobs. Most individuals enter the labor market at this stratum. Some people

Figure 5.1 Average of the Help Wanted Online Supply/Demand Rate, by Occupation, from May 2005 to November 2007

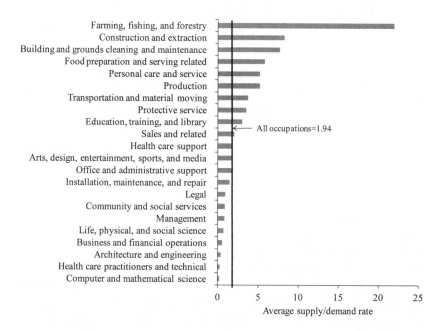

NOTE: Average supply/demand rate is the average from May 2005 through November 2007 of the number of unemployed persons divided by the number of online help-wanted ads. "All occupations" is the total number of unemployed divided by the total number of ads. The occupation-specific rates are based on unemployed persons' occupations in their prior occupations and the number of ads specific to that occupation.
SOURCE: Author's calculations from Help Wanted OnLine (Conference Board 2013), accessed through Haver Analytics on March 6, 2013.

quickly move on to more skilled work, but others stay in these submarkets for their whole career. There are two major reasons that these low-skilled markets have more participants than positions. First, workers of any skill level can compete in this market if they need to do so. Second, the demand for labor in the least skilled submarkets has been declining as a share of overall demand; as a proportion of employment, the number of workers who specialize in manual tasks or routine cognitive functions has steadily declined since 1970 (Autor, Levy, and Murnane 2003).

Many submarkets for skilled technical workers with less than a college degree have more positions than eligible job seekers. These midskilled occupations account for a large share of our labor markets (Holzer and Lerman 2009). However, the number of people pursuing skilled technical degrees and certificates is predicted to grow more slowly than the number of positions requiring those skills (Aspen Institute 2003). This is already leading to fast-rising wages for some midskilled jobs. For example, while overall real wages grew by 5 percent from 1997 to 2005, the real wages of radiological technicians rose by 23 percent, and those of electricians rose by 18 percent (Holzer and Lerman 2009). Because many such jobs require both specialized training and related experience, it takes time for people to enter these submarkets. People qualified for skilled technical jobs are less likely to migrate for a job than are people in occupations that require a college degree or higher (Borjas, Bronars, and Trejo 1992). Therefore, employers usually find themselves searching for someone with a narrowly defined set of skills within the local region, which can be difficult. This has been true even during the slow recovery from the 2007–2009 recession.

How does the workforce development system fit into this framework? In an ideal world, workforce programs would help people move from submarkets with more seekers than openings to those with more openings than seekers. This means facilitating the transition of people into skilled technical submarkets and out of the least skilled submarkets. However, the workforce development system created by WIA allocates occupational training services to people who cannot find work. Except during recessions, much of the money goes to the least skilled job seekers, who are unlikely to have the basic skills required for midskilled jobs. This means that public money is focused on training people to enter low-skilled labor submarkets. Without job growth in the least skilled submarkets, this is like adding sand to a bucket that is already full. Some of the new entrants may find jobs, but only at the cost of displacing other people who are already working or looking for work.

This is why we need to refocus workforce development toward advancement in the labor force, which would start with increasing the flow of people into skilled technical occupations. Typically, individuals with some skills and work history can move into technical work more easily than people who have been out of the labor force or in the least skilled jobs. This implies that the people most eligible for advancing into skilled technical work are those who have been or are currently employed in the next tier down. While helping such individuals would not directly assist those who are disengaged from the labor market, it could produce substantial benefits for people in less-skilled submarkets by beginning a string of advancing workers, called a job chain. Persky, Felsenstein, and Carlson (2004) estimate that 10 new jobs with hourly wages of $16.75 to $26.15 create 8.6 vacancies in lower-wage positions.[2] Job chains provide real opportunity to low-skilled individuals, in contrast to the false promise of training that does not lead to employment.

THE TRACK RECORD OF THE CURRENT WORKFORCE SYSTEM

Many readers may be disturbed by the proposition that the workforce system should abandon its almost exclusive focus on reducing poverty by assisting the least skilled. I am not arguing that we should give up the goal of assisting the poor—indeed, I believe our nation should be doing more to that end—but I do believe that the current public job training system is not a good way to achieve this mission.

It is not at all clear that the present approach to workforce development helps the poor in a meaningful way. Harry Holzer, a supporter of job training programs, acknowledges the limited success of the public job training system (2009). Unfortunately, there has not been a rigorous evaluation of the benefits of the WIA system, but the system that was in place from 1986 to 1998, created by the Job Training Partnership Act (JTPA), was evaluated using a classical randomized experiment. Holzer (2009) reports that the average annual earnings gain for disadvantaged adults found by the National JTPA Study was about $100 per month in real dollars, with these effects appearing to dissipate over time. While these programs have net benefits, the fact remains that $100 per month in gross benefit per participant is a minor gain. The results for youths are even weaker. These figures cover the program under the JTPA, when classroom-based occupational skills training was the main service individuals received from workforce agencies. Because evaluations have shown that occupational skills training have the largest and longest sustained effects, it is likely that the typical effect of WIA services on individuals' earnings is well below that of the JTPA. In 2007, only 13.6 percent of people assisted through the federal WIA received training services (Social Policy Research Associates 2010).

In his book, *The Job Training Charade*, Gordon Lafer (2002) makes a compelling case that the limited labor market success of low-skilled individuals is due as much to the lack of openings as to the lack of skills. The majority of entry-level jobs in the United States essentially require that a worker be on time, learn to do three-to-five simple tasks, and have a good attitude and basic motor skills. The challenge for low-skilled individuals is not that they are unable to do the work, but that there are too many people eligible for the same jobs.

This explains why most job training efforts have had limited success: they do not address the root problem. Even more than skills, workers on the margin need job openings. The most obvious way to create these is through government programs that provide work opportunities and income. There are four major difficulties with this approach. First, it is unsustainable because the individuals only have jobs as long as the government pays for them. Second, it is unlikely that these individuals would be efficiently employed. Third, such a program would most likely need to continually grow as there has been a 40-year trend of low-skilled work declining as a share of employment (Autor, Levy, and Murnane 2003). Furthermore, even if this were an efficient use of resources, it has proven to be politically infeasible.

Sadly, federal workforce development programs have not achieved their goal of decreasing poverty, nor have they made labor markets more efficient. In 1982, the occupations that employers described as important and difficult to fill with qualified candidates included "computer programmers, systems analysts, word processors, data processors, medical and laboratory technicians, machinists, and electricians" (Lafer 2002, p. 53). Today, only word and data processors can be removed from that list. This inability to address the needs of employers hurts regional and national economies. For example, Microsoft has opened offices in Canada in order to take advantage of that nation's skill-favoring immigration policies (Gohring 2007). When firms select work sites, the availability of a suitable workforce is usually a top consideration. Regions that are adept at training individuals for more skilled work are attractive to employers. This is illustrated by the subsidized, custom training programs provided by North Carolina's community college system, which have been credited for playing an important role in the strong growth of the state's Research Triangle region (Schmidt 1997).

WIA's tiered service system limits the ability of its programs to benefit employers because training is directed to the clients with the least skills. Data on the skills of those who receive training are not available. However, intensive training is reserved for people who are unable find work for an extended period of time, and it is reasonable to assume that training participants are less skilled than the people who find work through Workforce Investment Board (WIB) postings. A Government Accountability Office survey (2006) of firms that posted positions with one-stop centers operated through WIA found that two-thirds of the people hired from these postings were low skilled. Given the weak fundamental skills of people who are unable to secure even the most basic entry-level work, the hard-to-employ people that the workforce system focuses on are unlikely to succeed in midskilled careers. In order to address employers' needs, the workforce system would have to target training resources away from the least skilled and toward people with strong basic skills.

The U.S. workforce development system spends an overwhelming majority share of its resources on people who are not employed. However, it lacks mechanisms for helping people with jobs, or those who are able to find their own jobs, to advance in their fields or to change careers. This would not be a problem if our economy were made up of nothing but large employers; such entities can hire people for entry-level positions, learn about their aptitudes, and provide training for them to progress within the organization. However, 34.9 percent of employees at for-profit firms in the United States work at companies with fewer than 100 employees; another 14.1 percent work at firms with 100–499 employees (U.S. Bureau of the Census 2010). For these people, advancing often requires changing employers.

The system of one-stop centers operated through WIA does provide a variety of training, but most clients either are not given access to these resources or they choose not to use them. Of the 3.1 million people served under WIA throughout the United States from October 2007 to September 2010, only 382,626 (12.4 percent) received training services, and 15.9 percent of these were provided on-the-job or customized training.[3] This means that less than 2 percent of the adults and dislocated workers served by the WIA system during this time span received on-the-job or customized training, the forms that are most connected to the vision of refocusing the workforce development system on advancement.

The primary public mechanisms in place to help people advance are community colleges and career centers.[4] These are vital institutions, which deserve continued support and growth, but are insufficient in terms of capacity, affordability for students, and services offered. Unlike that provided by the WIA, individuals must pay for community college and career center training. As will be discussed in more detail, it is difficult for people who have the goal of becoming more skilled to get the information they need about employment opportunities and options for training. This uncertainty about how to move up and the clear upfront costs of training are part of the reason that there is an imbalance between job seekers and openings for midskilled occupations.

When someone advances to a higher-paying career, society as a whole benefits. The individual has more disposable income and consumes a portion of the incremental funds, causing economic growth. Such workers also pay more taxes. Importantly, one person advancing can start a chain of other people progressing, too. Suppose Jane has been working on the Geek Squad at Best Buy and becomes a computer programmer. Best Buy may promote a customer service worker into the Geek Squad and then hire a new customer service worker. Presumably, Jane's advancement has led to wage increases for one or two other workers and created an entry-level opening, which people who want to enter the labor market most need. These benefits are not just hypothetical; Persky, Felsenstein, and Carlson (2004) show that adding 100 midskilled jobs to a local economy creates 80 openings in lower-skilled positions.

POLICIES AND PROGRAMS TO PROMOTE ADVANCEMENT

Workforce development focused on advancement would play several roles lacking in our current system:

- identify occupations with the highest ratio of vacancies to eligible candidates;

- assess individuals interested in career change or advancement to determine their occupational aptitude;

- encourage people with high aptitude for an in-demand occupation and who earn less than they would in that field to pursue training to become qualified for the area;

- work with employers and educators to identify bottlenecks so that a larger portion of those pursuing in-demand occupations eventually become qualified.

There are a number of programs that could be introduced or expanded to facilitate advancement. To identify where public intervention would be effective, it is helpful to think about the stages of progression for an employed individual. Imagine Dave, a 20-year-old working at a "big box" retailer who wants to gain skills and increase his earnings. There are limited opportunities for him within the store because there are few supervisory positions, and much of the ordering and logistics is automated. Dave will find it easier to secure a promotion elsewhere. This means that his employer, even though it is large, has little incentive to invest in his advancement.

Dave's first step would be to identify a new career. Ideally, he would base this decision on the number of openings, wage and employment trends, and knowledge of his own aptitudes. But where would he get such information about different fields? For people who are working, one-stop employment centers provide self-service assistance—essentially showing them how to use computer resources to look up information on jobs and training opportunities. He might go to the admissions office of a community college or a proprietary school (a for-profit technical or trade school), though many people only take that step after they have identified a career. Most likely, he will talk to friends and family and accumulate anecdotal evidence about what careers are secure, pay well, and suit him. Depending on whom he talks to, he may or may not make a good choice. This is the first opportunity for improvement: provide easy access to more and better information on advancement opportunities.

After Dave selects a career, he has to choose a route for training. Some avenues are self-evident, such as community colleges and proprietary schools. Other paths do not have such clear entry points and, particularly in the case of on-the-job training (OJT), can require finding a supportive firm. Suppose Dave decides to become a chef. The general consensus is that proprietary culinary schools are not worth their cost and it is better to learn through on-the-job experience (Hallock 2011). But how would Dave know this? How would he judge which restaurant jobs will provide valuable OJT? How would he know whether a community college or a proprietary school has a program that is respected and valued by employers? Again, there is a critical lack of information available to guide people on their paths to better jobs.

Another factor in advancing is finding a program that accommodates Dave's work schedule and has slots available. Community colleges and proprietary schools have made great strides in accommodating working students' schedules, but community college programs that lead to careers in high-demand fields, such as nursing and radiography, often have long waiting lists. These programs could be expanded. While it is generally easy to borrow money for college, Dave may require assistance with child care or transportation. Help may also be needed to avoid predatory school loans, especially for students at proprietary schools.

If all goes smoothly and Dave does manage to get the training he needs to advance, he then has to search for work. If he chose a career well, this should be the easy part because he would be moving into a field where there are more openings than people. If not, he may need further assistance in identifying job opportunities. This is an area where help is usually readily available, either through local one-stop centers or the placement offices of individuals' alma maters.

This hypothetical case demonstrates four clear areas in which government policies and programs could facilitate advancement for Dave and others like him: first, improving information and available counseling to help people choose careers that are in demand and for which they have an aptitude; second, producing necessary information about community colleges, career centers, and proprietary schools; third, making it easier to get training through cost savings, convenient scheduling, and support services; and finally, matching individuals to the best available job through placement assistance.

Career Counseling

The first program that could facilitate advancement is one that devotes resources to making career counseling more broadly available. Workers need to know where they can turn to get guidance about how and where to advance. This could be achieved by refocusing WIA spending in order to make substantive career counseling available to everyone who is interested. Any such expansion of services needs to be paired with a comprehensive marketing campaign so that people are regularly reminded of the opportunity. The WIA route is attractive because it could be paid for by redirecting funds from existing WIA programs, rather than by finding new money to allocate to workforce development. Of course, more could be accomplished with additional resources, particularly since public spending on job training has been declining as a share of gross domestic product since the 1980s (Holzer 2009). The challenge would be overcoming public perception of the WIA-funded one-stop centers as places that help the unemployed.

Teenagers might feel more comfortable using the career services available at their local high schools. Even if they only serve their current students, counselors in high schools can make a large impact on students' career decisions. However, counselors are spread thin and have limited time available to give career advice. In 2006 there was one counselor for every 285 high school students in the United States (Barton 2006), and the number of students per counselors has most likely risen because of budget cuts during the recession (Flaherty 2013). Where counselors do remain, they primarily advise students how to find the right college, not the right career. This leaves students who would be well suited for skilled technical jobs without advice on that option. The lucky ones find their way to community colleges, where they may get better career direction. Many others will enter the workforce with no guidance about preparing for a career.

Information about Training Programs

One of the reasons that career counselors are so crucial is that there is little public information that can guide individuals toward job openings and training programs. Unlike four-year institutions, community colleges are not featured and compared in guides to finding the "best" program. Good career counselors become experts on local employers and training options. Therefore, the second option would be to give the public access to information about different career training options.

At a minimum, there are five pieces of information that need to be available to help individuals choose a career path and training program: 1) the proportion of people completing the program who are employed in a related field a year later, 2) the median monthly earnings of people a year after their completion of the program, 3) the average weekly hours the completers worked a year after finishing, 4) the percentage of people who start the program who also finish, and 5) the number of completers. This information should be gathered on a two- or three-year rolling basis so that it is up to date and also robust to idiosyncratic fluctuations. Such material would tell individuals how likely it is that the program would lead to a job, what they can expect to earn, and the probability of finishing the curriculum.[5] The data would come from annual surveys of students who have completed programs, which are currently used at some community colleges. These statistics would have to be collected for all the major types of training providers: proprietary schools, career centers, community colleges, and Internet-only schools.

Supporting the Training Process

The third way to facilitate advancement would be to provide support services while individuals are in training. Many such services have been put into place in the last couple of decades, but it would be worthwhile to expand them further. Policies that make training more affordable for individuals, such as repealing the automatic reduction of Pell Grants for students attending low-tuition schools and expanding the number of seats in community colleges, could also help people advance (Kazis et al. 2007). Working adults would especially benefit if subsidized student loans were extended to part-time students. Offering a complete set of courses when working people find it convenient has become more important with the increased need for lifelong learning and growth in single-parent and dual-earner families. People who go to school at night have difficulty finding child care, so expanding these programs is also important.

Community college is one of the best mechanisms we have in place for facilitating advancement. These institutions are usually lower in cost, and their students have higher earnings and employment rates five years after entering school than observationally similar proprietary school students (Deming, Goldin, and Katz 2012). Many are highly responsive to the requirements of local employers, which helps them prepare students for occupations with available openings. Community colleges welcome students who take one or two classes of their choosing, enabling people to get just the training they need, so continuing to improve and expand these institutions is essential. Three areas stand out as opportunities for development: 1) enlarging programs with waiting lists and strong placement records, 2) assessing students to ensure that those enrolling in high-demand programs are likely to succeed, and 3) steering students to programs that have high placement rates.

Even with limited information available, many people are able to find training that leads to jobs. As a result, many of the community college programs with the best placement records have waiting lists. This is especially true in health careers. For example, nursing and radiological technology programs often have one-to-two-year waiting lists.[6] If these programs could expand capacity, it would help individuals advance and assist hospitals in coping with the shortage of nurses and radiology techs. Of course, this is a difficult task, and two major factors that limit the growth of programs have proven hard to address: the lack of instructors (Yordy 2006) and the scarcity of opportunities for clinical training. Both stem in part from the choices of local employers: people qualified to be instructors can earn more practicing than teaching, and most clinical training happens at local hospitals. Partnerships between educational institutions and employers, such as Cincinnati's Healthcare Career Collaborative, are the most likely way to address these problems.

Until programs with waiting lists and strong placement records grow, we can facilitate advancement by doing a better job of allocating the limited spots available. Particularly in health career programs, a substantial minority of students drop out of training programs. Some community colleges now allocate seats in health sciences programs with wait lists based on students' academic aptitude (Moltz 2010). This should become standard practice for community colleges across the country.

Providing information and counseling to help people choose occupations and training programs is crucial to reorienting our workforce development system toward advancement. Improving student advising at community colleges is a relatively easy way to do this. In the last 10 years, tremendous gains have been made in creating longitudinally linked wage record files from the unemployment insurance system. Some states and community colleges are using these data to produce rich information about the employment and wages of students who have earned credentials. Many community colleges survey recent graduates as another way to learn about the career outcomes of their students. However, this knowledge is often not conveyed to students. Advising tends to focus on student desires, which may or may not include an awareness of the job prospects associated with different training paths. If advisers consciously direct students to programs that lead to employment, both students and the local economy will benefit.

Of course, advisers can only steer the students with whom they meet. According to the 2013 Community College Survey of Student Engagement, 50.8 percent of community college students never or rarely use career counseling; 20.2 percent responded "Don't know/ not applicable" (Center for Community College Student Engagement 2013). Career counseling is needed by more than the scant 29 percent of community college students that sometimes or frequently use it.

Placement Assistance

The last strategy that can help promote advancement is placement assistance. Not everyone knows the importance of finding a job that also offers a career. Placement support needs to help people find employers and also determine whether the employer will assist them in advancing further. Continuing to provide job readiness training, which has proven to be a cost effective way to help people retain their jobs (Holzer 2009), is also worthwhile.

PROGRAMS THAT HAVE SHOWN PROMISE

The Cleveland/Cuyahoga County Workforce Investment Board

Some exciting new workforce development programs have been implemented that also demonstrate how to facilitate advancement. The

Cleveland/Cuyahoga County Workforce Investment Board (CCCWIB) completely reinvented itself in 2010 because of a combination of budget cuts and disappointment with the share of participants who were unable to find work after completing training. Under the direction of Larry Benders, the agency shifted roles from that of a traditional WIB, which views itself as an organization that provides training for hard-to-employ individuals, to one more like an employment placement agency. Essentially, because of the 2007–2009 recession, the number of people with job skills coming into the CCCWIB's employment centers dramatically increased. This meant that the challenge was finding openings for them, not making them employable.

To find positions, the CCCWIB combines cold-calling employers with a sales force similar to that of a for-profit employment agency. The CCCWIB matches the openings to a database of people looking for employment. Qualified individuals receive calls informing them of an opportunity and its application procedure. Positions for which the number of qualified prospective workers is insufficient are targeted for job training. Individuals with an interest and aptitude for the opening are hired by the employer, who receives a grant to defray the cost of training the clients. This hews to the idea of advancement in that it focuses job training resources on cases in which qualified workers are hard to find and on those individuals who show strong potential for success.

The CCCWIB's new demand-facing approach has only been in place since July 2010 and has not been rigorously evaluated. However, the available evidence suggests that the strategy is producing better outcomes. Compared to the rest of Ohio in the program years since the new approach was implemented (2010 and 2011), the CCCWIB saw more improvement in the outcomes of exiters than did the rest of the state. The results are reported in Table 5.1. In 2011, the entered employment rates (the percent of exiters who were unemployed at the beginning of their program who were employed one quarter after exiting from the program) for both adult and displaced worker exiters were above the comparable rates in 2007, while for the rest of the state these two indicators were well below their 2007 levels. Similar patterns hold for the average earnings of adult exiters, but for displaced worker exiters the CCCWIB and the rest of the state had similar changes in earnings. The CCCWIB also had larger increases in the number of adults and displaced workers served during 2010 and 2011 than did the rest of the state.

Table 5.1 Exiter Outcomes for Cleveland/Cuyahoga County Workforce Investment Board (CCCWIB) and the Rest of Ohio, 2007–2011

Program year	Exiter's entered employment rate (%)				Average earnings (2012$)			
	Adults		Displaced workers		Adults		Displaced workers	
	CCCWIB	Rest of Ohio	CCCWIB	Rest of Ohio	CCCWIB	Rest of Ohio	CCCWIB	Rest of Ohio
2007	80.1	78.2	84.7	87.5	14,702	16,264	18,479	18,629
2008	75.5	75.3	82.6	85.1	19,118	16,085	20,005	18,833
2009	53.1	65.6	62.3	68.6	14,755	15,472	17,405	18,038
2010	79.8	66.4	79.5	73.1	14,889	14,965	18,885	19,519
2011	91.2	72.9	91.1	79.1	18,244	15,585	19,564	19,487

SOURCE: Author's calculations from data included in State of Ohio Workforce Investment Act Annual Reports for program years 2007–2011(Ohio Department of Jobs and Family Services 2013); Consumer Price Index for All Urban Consumers (U.S. Bureau of Labor Statistics 2013a).

At the same time that the outcomes of CCCWIB's exiters improved more than those for the remainder of the state, the Cleveland area was experiencing slower employment growth than the rest of Ohio. Table 5.2 gives the percentage change in employment during each program year for the Cleveland Core Based Statistical Area (CBSA)—which has the county served by the CCCWIB as its core—and for the rest of Ohio.[7] In each program year from 2007 to 2009, the Cleveland CBSA lost a larger share of its employment than did the rest of Ohio. In 2010 and 2011, the Cleveland CBSA had less growth than did the rest of the state. This is especially true in program year 2011, when employment grew by 0.51 percent in the CBSA and 2.31 percent in the rest of the state. The fact that the Cleveland area was growing less than the rest of the state during the implementation of the demand-facing approach makes the larger improvement in the outcomes of the CCCWIB's exiters all the more impressive.

The experience of the CCCWIB also gives hope that the public job training system can be radically transformed without additional funding. Due to the formulas for allocating WIA dollars, the CCCWIB saw its budget cut in half from 2007 to 2011. This means that the WIB served more clients and improved their outcomes at the same time it was cutting staff and services. Other WIBs may also find it possible to achieve better results without increasing budgets by focusing on finding open positions, matching workers to those jobs, and training people when there are not enough qualified applicants.

While the CCCWIB's new approach has only been in effect since July 2010, this innovative program has performed exceptionally well in a difficult time. More people are being placed into jobs (Perkins 2011), and those individuals are earning more than in the past. Anecdotally, employers are finding it valuable to partner with the WIB. People are receiving training that actually leads to jobs, and firms are getting help preparing people for hard-to-fill positions. This is a leading example of how the workforce system could promote advancement and make labor markets more efficient.

Other Workforce Development Initiatives

A pilot program that has shown promise is the Frontline Decision Support System (FDSS), which was a partnership between the W.E.

Table 5.2 Percentage Change in Employment in Cleveland Core Based Statistical Area (CBSA) and the Rest of Ohio, 2007–2011

Program year	Cleveland CBSA	Rest of Ohio
2007	−1.31	−1.12
2008	−6.43	−6.13
2009	−0.64	−0.22
2010	0.57	0.97
2011	0.51	2.31

NOTE: WIA program years run from July of the indicated calendar year through June of the following year. The employment percentage changes are calculated from June of the indicated calendar year to June of the following calendar year.
SOURCE: Seasonally adjusted Current Employment Statistics June 2007 to June 2012 (U.S. Bureau of Labor Statistics 2013b).

Upjohn Institute for Employment Research and the Georgia Department of Labor.[8] The Upjohn Institute has developed a methodology that takes advantage of aggregate labor market and administrative data from the unemployment insurance system and the Georgia Career Centers. For individuals served, the FDSS determines job prospects using advancement-oriented criteria: the chance of finding work in the client's most recent industry, the likely pay in the client's next position, and the occupations related to, growth prospects of, and available job openings in the client's most recent occupation.

The job counselors at Georgia Career Centers have been able to use this information to help clients target their job searches or pursue training that will help them secure a job. The FDSS also assisted with this task by giving counselors data on which class of service was most effective for prior clients who were similar to the current client. This helped counselors guide individuals to the type of training that has the best prospects for success. The two pilot implementations of this program have received positive feedback from both staff and clients (Eberts and O'Leary 2009), but the state of Georgia has cancelled the program.

The FDSS has promoted advancement in three ways. First, it has helped individuals to develop realistic expectations about their job prospects, which prevents them from declining positions that pay less than what they want but more than they should expect. Second, it has given individuals a sense of the prospects for their occupation, which helps people in fading fields choose to train for another career. Finally, it has provided guidance on which services are most likely to lead to employment. Giving counselors more relevant information should increase the number of job seekers who pursue training that helps them advance.

In the arena of workforce development, programs that focus on specific sectors and on developing career pathways are seen as the most promising route forward (Holzer 2009). Sectoral initiatives with a successful track record, such as the Wisconsin Regional Training Partnership and Jewish Vocational Service of Greater Boston, combine close relationships with employers and, relative to most WIA-funded activities, long and intensive training that addresses basic skills (8th grade–level math, reading, and critical thinking), field-specific skills, and job readiness (Maguire et al. 2010). Participants also have substantially larger earnings increases than do those in the typical WIA program. The average earnings gain was $4,000 per year for participants in the most successful sectoral program (Maguire et al. 2010), versus only $1,200 per year for WIA participants (Holzer 2009).

Sectoral workforce programs share many of the features that an advancement-focused workforce system would need. First, they screen applicants and work only with those who are anticipated to succeed in training, which typically requires 6th-grade reading skills. This means that they are better targeting their services to people who are likely to advance than the WIA system does. Public/Private Ventures evaluated three of these programs and found that 7.0 percent of their participants did not have a high school degree or general equivalency diploma (GED), compared to almost 16.7 percent of people who received intensive services through WIA in program year 2005 (Maguire et al. 2010; Social Policy Research Associates 2010). This difference is statistically significant at the 0.1 percent level. Second, sectoral programs foster close relationships with employers, helping to focus training on occupations with available openings. Finally, these programs stress developing technical competencies related to specific occupations, rather than basic skills or job readiness. This emphasis on hard skills training is essential to advancement.

In fact, the success of these sectoral programs may make the best case for shifting to an advancement-focused workforce system. They all have a mission to serve disadvantaged workers, a pool of individuals that typically find it more difficult to succeed in training. It is likely that similar efforts would produce even more impressive results if they placed less emphasis on socioeconomic status and more emphasis on aptitude. This is not to say that programs that serve disadvantaged workers and job seekers are unimportant. We should maintain and grow efforts like these while simultaneously introducing similar programs to promote advancement that serve a broader cross section of the workforce.

These notable workforce development programs all have a greater focus on advancement than is typical. Each of them has shown promise, although only sectoral training has been experimentally evaluated. Collectively, they suggest that reorienting our workforce development system toward advancement can be successful, both in theory and in practice.

CONCLUSIONS

Workforce development policy has two fundamental goals: to assist individuals who are struggling in the labor market, and to help employers find workers with the skills they need. The track record on helping individuals is mixed; the one on helping employers is even weaker. We could do better at both goals if we reoriented our workforce development system toward helping people advance into open positions. This would require redirecting resources away from individuals who are not working toward those who are and who have good potential for promotion. Given the small benefits disadvantaged workers typically get from government-sponsored training, it is important to not overstate the value of the existing programs for this group of individuals.

Promoting advancement is especially important in the Rust Belt for several reasons. Targeting resources to help people upskill into open positions would speed the process of adapting to further losses of manufacturing employment. Increasing the supply of workers eligible for midskilled jobs that manufacturers report having difficulty hiring, such as machinists and industrial equipment mechanics, may reduce employment losses by encouraging manufacturers to stay in the region. Finally, the incremental improvements in skills associated with advancements can add up and reduce the gap in skills between the Rust Belt and the nation as a whole.

It may be possible to reorient our workforce development system toward advancement without additional funding. This new approach would probably provide more intensive services, but it would also serve fewer people. This is because people would be trained for open positions; the best estimates are that there are usually 10 times as many people (employed and unemployed) looking for new jobs as there are available jobs (Lafer 2002). Both individuals and employers would be better assisted by a program that moves fewer people into open positions than by one that provides many people training that does not lead to jobs. In fact, the CCCWIB was able to greatly improve its placement results by becoming "demand facing" despite simultaneously suffering large budget cuts.

It is reasonable to hope that this strategy would also assist the disadvantaged people who are currently the focus of the U.S. workforce development system. Research and common sense suggest that the primary obstacle faced by these individuals is the chasm between the large number of people searching for low-skilled work and the smaller quantity of available positions. Helping people advance can lessen the gap by moving people from this market to more-skilled labor markets. Furthermore, it is likely that having more people progress to skilled employment will stimulate the economy because of increases in both productivity and earnings. As the experience of the 1990s showed us, sustained economic growth is the most reliable way to assist disadvantaged workers on a large scale.

Notes

1. These are averages of the occupation group-level Help Wanted OnLine data (Conference Board 2013) from the first month data are available to the beginning of the most recent recession.
2. Based on Table 5.2 in Persky, Felsenstein, and Carlson (2004) and adjusting wages for inflation from 1992 to 2012.
3. These figures are the author's calculations from the Annual WIASRD Data Books for program 2007–2009 (Social Policy Research Associates 2010).
4. A career center is a Perkins Act vocational educational venue that serves high school students and adults. The centers provide classroom and cooperative training, usually for a smaller set of occupations than would a community college.
5. Completion can be hard to define because sometimes students get enough training

to be hired for a skilled technical job prior to finishing a program. Whether or not these people should be counted as completers is a difficult question. The premise here remains relevant: students need to know if the program leads to employment and the pay and hours associated with that work.

6. While there are not good aggregate data on the length of community college wait-lists, there are reports from the popular media, such as Korry (2010). Data are available on the number of eligible students turned away from entry-level baccalaureate nursing programs. In the 2010–2011 academic year, 101,060 students were accepted to these programs while 58,327 eligible students were turned away (American Association of Colleges of Nursing 2012). This implies that admissions would increase by more than half if there were sufficient capacity.

7. WIA program years run from July of the indicated calendar year through June of the following year. The employment percentage changes are calculated from June of the indicated calendar year to June of the following calendar year.

8. This description of FDSS summarizes Eberts and O'Leary (2002).

References

American Association of Colleges of Nursing. 2012. "New AACN Data Show an Enrollment Surge in Baccalaureate and Graduate Programs Amid Calls for More Highly Educated Nurses." Press Release, March 22. Washington, DC: American Association of Colleges of Nursing. http://www.aacn.nche.edu/news/articles/2012/enrollment-data (accessed August 1, 2013).

Aspen Institute. 2003. *Grow Faster Together or Grow Slowly Apart: How Will America Work in the 21st Century?* Boulder, CO: Domestic Strategy Group.

Autor, David H., Frank Levy, and Richard J. Murnane. 2003. "The Skill Content of Recent Technological Change: An Empirical Exploration." *Quarterly Journal of Economics* 118(4): 1279–1333.

Barton, Paul E. 2006. "One-Third of a Nation: Rising Dropout Rates and Declining Opportunities." Educational Testing Services Policy Information Report. Princeton, NJ: Educational Testing Services. http://www.ets.org/Media/Education_Topics/pdf/onethird.pdf (accessed August 5, 2013).

Borjas, George J., Stephen G. Bronars, and Stephen J. Trejo. 1992. "Self-Selection and Internal Migration in the United States." *Journal of Urban Economics* 32(2): 159–185.

Bound, John, J. Groen, G. Kezdi, and Sarah E. Turner. 2004. "Trade in University Training: Cross-State Variation in the Production and Stock of College-Educated Labor." *Journal of Econometrics* 121(1-2): 143–173.

Center for Community College Student Engagement. 2013. "2013 Community College Survey of Student Engagement." Austin, TX: Center for Community College Student Engagement. http://www.ccsse.org/survey/reports/

2013/standard_reports/CCSSE_2013_coh_freqs_support_std.pdf (accessed July 31, 2013).

Conference Board. 2013. Help Wanted OnLine. New York: The Conference Board (accessed through Haver Analytics on March 6, 2013).

Deming, David J., Claudia Goldin, Lawrence F. Katz. 2012. "The For-Profit Postsecondary School Sector: Nimble Critters or Agile Predators?" *Journal of Economic Perspectives* 26(1): 139–164.

Eberts, Randall W., and Christopher J. O'Leary. 2002. "A Frontline Decision Support System for Georgia Career Centers." W.E. Upjohn Institute Working Paper No. 02-84. Kalamazoo, MI: W.E. Upjohn Institute for Employment Research.

———. 2009. "Tools to Transform the Workforce Development System." *Employment Research* 16(3): 6.

Feyrer, James, Bruce Sacerdote, Ariel Dora Stern. 2007. "Did the Rust Belt Become Shiny? A Study of Cities and Counties That Lost Steel and Auto Jobs in the 1980s." *Brookings-Wharton Papers on Urban Affairs*: 41–102.

Flaherty, Colleen. 2013. "School Counselors Vulnerable to Across-the-Board Cuts." *Education Votes*, April 1. http://educationvotes.nea.org/2013/04/01/school-counselors-vulnerable-to-across-the-board-cuts/ (accessed August 5, 2013).

Glaeser, Edward L., and Joseph Gyourko. 2005. "Urban Decline and Durable Housing." *Journal of Political Economy* 113(2): 345–375.

Gohring, Nancy. 2007. "Microsoft Vancouver Responds to Immigration Woes." *InfoWorld.com*, July 5. http://www.infoworld.com/t/business/microsoft-vancouver-responds-immigration-woes-068 (accessed April 11, 2013).

Government Accountability Office. 2006. *Employers Found One-Stop Centers Useful in Hiring Low-Skilled Workers; Performance Information Could Help Gauge Employer Involvement*. GAO Report GAO-07-167. Washington, DC: GAO.

Groen, Jeffrey A. 2011. "Building Knowledge Stocks Locally: Consequences of Geographic Mobility for the Effectiveness of State Higher Education Policies." *Economic Development Quarterly* 25(4): 316–329.

Hallock, Betty. 2011. "Some Up-and-Coming Chefs are Skipping Culinary School." *LATimes.com*, July 28. http://www.latimes.com/features/food/la-fo-cooking-school-or-not-20110728,0,4625622,full.story (accessed April 11, 2013).

Holzer, Harry J. 2009. "Workforce Development as an Antipoverty Strategy: What Do We Know? What Should We Know?" *Focus* 26(2): 62–68.

Holzer, Harry J., and Robert I. Lerman. 2009. "The Future of Middle-Skill Jobs." Brookings Center on Children and Families Brief No. 41. Washington, DC: Brookings Institution.

Kazis, Richard, Abigail Callahan, Chris Davidson, Annie McLoed, Brian Bos-
worth, Vickie Choitz, and John Hoops. 2007. "Adult Learners in Higher
Education: Barriers to Success and Strategies to Improve Results." Employment and Training Administration Occasional Paper 2007-03. Washington,
DC: U.S. Department of Labor.

Korry, Elaine. 2010. "Nursing Backlog Hits California Community Colleges." *NPR.org*, April 5. http://www.npr.org/templates/story/story.php
?storyId=125594201 (accessed August 1, 2013).

Lafer, Gordon. 2002. *The Job Training Charade*. Ithaca, NY: Cornell University Press.

Maguire, Sheila, Joshua Freely, Carol Clymer, Maureen Conway, and Deena
Schwartz. 2010. "Tuning in to Local Labor Markets: Findings from the
Sectoral Employment Impact Study." Philadelphia: Public/Private Ventures. http://www2.oaklandnet.com/oakca/groups/ceda/documents/report/
dowd021455.pdf (accessed April 11, 2013).

Manning, Alan. 2003. *Monopsony in Motion: Imperfect Competition in Labor
Markets*. Princeton, NJ: Princeton University Press.

Moltz, David. 2010. "Vying for Limited Seats." *Inside Higher Ed*, July 21.
http://www.insidehighered.com/news/2010/07/21/nursing   (accessed
August 1, 2013).

Moretti, Enrico. 2012. *The New Geography of Jobs*. Boston: Houghton Mifflin
Harcourt.

Ohio Department of Jobs and Family Services. 2013. "Workforce in Investment Act Program Year Annual Report." Columbus, OH: Ohio Department
of Jobs and Family Services.

Perkins, Olivera. 2011. "Employment Connection Finds Success Running
like a Private Placement Firm." *cleveland.com*, January 22. http://www
.cleveland.com/business/index.ssf/2011/01/employment_connection_
finds_su.html (accessed April 11, 2013).

Persky, Joseph, Daniel Felsenstein, and Virginia Carlson. 2004. *Does "Trickle
Down" Work? Economic Development Strategies and Job Chains in Local
Labor Markets*. Kalamazoo, MI: W.E. Upjohn Institute for Employment
Research.

Schmidt, Peter. 1997. "States Turn to Community Colleges to Fuel Economic
Growth." *Chronicle of Higher Education*, June 6, A29.

Shapiro, Jesse M. 2006. "Smart Cities: Quality of Life, Productivity, and the
Growth Effects of Human Capital." *Review of Economic Statistics* 88(2):
324–335.

Social Policy Research Associates. 2010. *Program Year WIASRD Data Book*.
Prepared for the Office of Performance and Technology, Employment and

Training Administration, U.S. Department of Labor. Oakland, CA: Social Policy Research Associates.

U.S. Bureau of Labor Statistics. 2013a. Consumer Price Index for All Urban Consumers: All Items. Washington, DC: U.S. Bureau of Labor Statistics (accessed through Haver Analytics on March 15, 2013).

————. 2013b. Current Employment Survey: Seasonally Adjusted. Washington, DC: U.S. Bureau of Labor Statistics (accessed through Haver Analytics on March 12, 2013).

U.S. Census Bureau. 2010. 2010 Statistics of U.S. Businesses. Washington, DC: U.S. Bureau of the Census. http://www.census.gov/econ/susb (accessed August 7, 2013).

Yordy, Karl D. 2006. *The Nursing Faculty Shortage: A Crisis for Health Care.* Princeton, NJ: Robert Wood Johnson Foundation.

6

Distinctly Cleveland

How the Arts are Helping
to Revitalize Rust Belt Cities

Gregory M. Sadlek
Joan Chase
Cleveland State University

Faced with the decline of the traditional manufacturing-based economic engine, a handful of fading Rust Belt cities turned to the arts as a means for revitalizing their local economies. Among them is Cleveland, a city known for its rich cultural heritage. While the arts may not replace the number of high-wage factory jobs lost in manufacturing, it does offer different types of benefits related to quality-of-life that help redefine a community's concept of prosperity.

Downtown Grand Rapids, Michigan, was once in decline. Hurt by international competition, its manufacturing plants were closing, and, at the same time, residents began moving out of the city to the suburbs. In the mid-1990s the situation started to change, and the turning point seemed to be the opening of the Van Andel Arena in the middle of downtown (Thompson 2006). Civic leaders, however, realized that revitalization was not simply a matter of constructing large public buildings; they needed a grand strategy to draw people back into the core of the city.

In 2005, under the leadership of Urban Marketing Collaborative, a new "Arts and Entertainment Strategy: Downtown Grand Rapids" report was created (Urban Marketing Collaborative 2005). The vision captured in this document called for Grand Rapids to capitalize on "its growing reputation as a destination arts and entertainment area" (p. 1). It would have three distinct arts "attitude districts," interconnected but distinct, that would draw audiences and enable them to be immersed in a vibrant city core containing a broad cross section of arts. The values reflected in this large arts district were to be "diversity, eclecticism, urbanity, sophistication, high culture," and it would become "a living laboratory to experiment, explore, learn and share" (p. 2).

Although the document called for better marketing and promotion efforts, no mention was made of what would become one of the most important revitalization tools of Grand Rapids: the annual fall ArtPrize contest. Created in 2009 by Rick DeVos, grandson of Amway founder Rich DeVos, this contest annually transforms downtown Grand Rapids into a living museum of art. But the distinguishing feature is that the substantial prizes, until recently, were awarded not by professional art critics, but by the visiting public.[1] In 2011, the festival drew approximately 322,000 visitors, who experienced the works of 1,580 artists in 162 separate venues (Linn 2012).

The payoff to the city is the financial boost given by the visitors to the community. A study by Anderson Economic Group (2011) of East Lansing, Michigan, estimates that the 2011 ArtPrize competition added $15.4 million to the local economy. In addition, the *Detroit Free Press* reports that the competition has been so successful that it is now being copied in such cities as Akron, New York, and Los Angeles (Stryker 2012). Clearly, the arts strategy envisioned in the 2005 strategic plan has succeeded in a significant way, and it presents a model of urban revitalization for other midwestern Rust Belt cities.

Milwaukee is also steeped in a manufacturing heritage but is now counting on the arts to develop a new economic future. The Cultural Alliance of Greater Milwaukee spearheaded the creation of a regional arts economic development strategy, entitled Creativity Works! The approach focuses on design, performing arts, visual arts, media and film, and culture and heritage organizations (Creative Alliance Milwaukee, n.d.). The Milwaukee region possesses a strong concentration of creative workers and hopes to leverage this advantage through four arts-based initiatives. The steps include growing the creative industries, expanding the local creative talent base, developing sustainable infrastructure for creative industries, and fostering leadership systems to integrate these industries (Creative Alliance Milwaukee 2011a).

A recent redevelopment effort that followed the strategy developed in Creativity Works! occurred when Milwaukee launched an innovative program to animate a faltering retail space. The Shops at Grand Avenue in downtown Milwaukee were "dedicated to presenting quality creatives and small business owners a place in which to teach, work, perform, and exhibit their work" (Creative Alliance Milwaukee 2011b). This program filled the underutilized retail spaces with local artists, artisans, and performers.

While the final outcome of the Shops at Grand Avenue is not yet known, Milwaukee advocates are committed to the Creativity Works! strategy. Indeed, a recent study indicates that in 2010, nonprofit arts organizations had a $300 million impact on the Milwaukee economy, representing a 20 percent increase over the 2005 figure (Creative Alliance Milwaukee 2012).

PERSPECTIVES ON THE ARTS AND URBAN REDEVELOPMENT

The turn to the arts for urban economic redevelopment follows upon the publication of several influential studies. The contribution of arts and creative industries has been recognized at least since the release of Richard Florida's *Rise of the Creative Class* (2002), and it has been developed further by Ann Markusen, Greg Schrock, and Martina Cameron (2004) in their work on "the artistic dividend." Florida links twenty-first-century economic vitality to concentrations of people who earn their living through creativity and innovation, including artists, artisans, performers and writers, of both popular and high art, as well as to a regional cultural ecosystem that innovative people find attractive. Markusen and her colleagues show that the work of artists is connected in interesting and important ways to the growth of urban economies, although there is "no clear relationship between artistic strength and either overall regional employment size or recent growth rates" (p. 19).

Cleveland is yet another manufacturing-oriented city in the Midwest that has suffered from changes in the global economy. As if to prove Markusen's point, although the area has traditionally had strong arts institutions, it has suffered significant losses of jobs and population. Like Grand Rapids and Milwaukee, however, the city is now looking hard at building upon the arts to help its economic recovery.

Indeed, there are already intriguing signs of improvement, including the refurbished Euclid corridor, a transformed Gordon Square, the Global Center for Health Innovation (a part of the new Cleveland Convention Center), the Horseshoe Casino, the continued growth and development of Playhouse Square, and the renewal of Cleveland State University's campus (Farkas 2013).

In addition, despite population losses citywide, the two districts that actually gained population in the 2010 census were downtown and University Circle, suggesting that hip young members of the creative class are finding urban life in Cleveland appealing (Smith and Exner 2011). Since 2000, for example, the downtown neighborhood has experienced a 73 percent surge in population (U.S. Census Bureau 2011). These residents are well educated: 49 percent have at least a bachelor's degree, compared to only 25 percent of the population in the Cleveland metropolitan statistical area (MSA). Downtown inhabitants are also youthful: 71 percent of the population is 44 years of age or younger (U.S. Census Bureau 2011).

Finally, while the economic recovery has stalled in much of the nation, Northeast Ohio has been buoyed by manufacturing growth (Helper, Krueger, and Wial 2012). As confirmation of this forward movement, it is interesting to note that Portland, Oregon, a city widely regarded as one of the top magnets for the creative class, has recently sent a delegation to study Cleveland's economic progress. "Cleveland is an innovative city," wrote the delegation's organizers, and it excels "in the areas most critical to urban success: talent, connections, innovation, and distinctiveness" (Miller 2012).

In discussing Cleveland's distinctive arts scene, we will also use the term "cultural ecosystem" because we want to suggest a broad definition of "arts" that includes both high and low forms, a wide range of related nonprofit organizations, commercial art, and both formal and informal activities. Bulik et al. (2003) argue that to be a vibrant and distinctive community, a city must have a large range of arts activity, "from large arts organizations to street festivals, world-class artists to amateurs" (p. 8). We believe that Cleveland has such a strong mix.

How can Cleveland leverage its traditional strengths in the arts to further this economic recovery? There are many theories of how cities prosper, 18 of which are ably summarized and categorized in Joseph Cortright's *City Success: Theories of Urban Prosperity* (2008). Cortright argues that while cities share many common problems, "each city will need to fashion its own distinct solution" (p. 4). Among the most relevant approaches to Cleveland's revitalization, we believe, are those he entitles the "attraction city," the "amenity city," and the "distinctive city," respectively. The "attraction city" theory suggests that cities succeed by developing "iconic attractions" that appeal to visitors and establish a city's unique brand (p. 50). The "amenity city" theory suggests that cities grow and thrive by providing social amenities, not only good schools, safety, and parks, but also various kinds of appealing entertainment (p. 53). The "distinctive city" theory holds that cities flourish by creating a special identity and related attitudes that clearly differentiate the city from others (p. 59). We believe that building upon Cleveland's traditionally strong arts scene will help the community achieve all three goals, becoming a distinctive city with nationally known attractions and plentiful amenities.

The significance of a city's distinctiveness is underscored by Cortright in a 2002 article in which he analyzes the unique nature of the Portland, Oregon, region; he concludes that, like Portland, each city has its "own unique set of opportunities, shaped by its residents' tastes and previous development" (p. 13). Moreover, the cities that will best thrive are those that do not try to copy the successes of others but build upon the facets of their own histories and the special tastes and skills of their current populations. Although many midwestern industrial cities, like Grand Rapids and Milwaukee, are now turning to the arts for revitalization, we believe that Cleveland has a distinctive arts profile that will serve it well as it rebuilds in the new global economy.

CLEVELAND'S STRATEGIC PLAN

The examples of Grand Rapids and Milwaukee underscore the importance of having a strategic plan, and, indeed, Cleveland has one. In 1997 the Community Partnership for Arts and Culture (CPAC) was created by the Cleveland and George Gund Foundations (CPAC 2011). The partnership was immediately commissioned to write a strategic plan for the arts in Cleveland. That plan was completed in 2000, and since then, CPAC has sought to facilitate its implementation.

Under the leadership of its president, Thomas Schorgl, CPAC promotes a closer connection between a lively arts scene and a vigorous community (T. Schorgl and M. Van Voorhis, personal communication, August 26, 2011). CPAC advocates for public policy that will sustain the local arts and culture community, provides assistance to individual artists and arts organizations, and conducts research related to the arts sector.

As examples of the proactive nature of CPAC's activities, we can cite its two conferences entitled "From Rust Belt to Artist Belt." The first was held in 2008 and focused on the opportunities created by the arts for the traditional manufacturing centers of the upper Midwest. The second was held in 2010, and its focus was artist-based community development. The report of the first conference emphasizes the mutually beneficial relationship between artists and the communities in which they reside. Rust Belt cities can offer artists affordable housing and workplaces as well as a context rich with already existing high-quality arts institutions. Artists can provide renewed population for inner cities; sweat equity (as they restore dilapidated houses and studios with their own hands and thus increase property values); and, finally, a positive impact on the economies of the cities they adopt (CPAC 2008). The second conference resulted in a program to encourage artists to settle in the Collinwood arts district on Cleveland's East Side. The initiative is a partnership between CPAC and New York–based Leveraging Investments in Creativity (Ott 2011).

For 14 years, then, CPAC has been promoting community growth by helping to build and unify the local arts culture. Are its efforts paying off by luring more of the creative class to Cleveland? Thomas Schorgl believes they are. He points to two recent articles that suggest that young artists in the culturally rich city of New York are moving to Cleveland. In Crain's *New York Business*, Souccar (2010) describes the severe difficulties experienced by artists who try to live in New York; she then notes the increasing interest of New Yorkers in a housing development for artists in Cleveland's Collinwood area. Collinwood is working to continue this trend with the funding provided by CPAC and Leveraging Investments in Creativity.

This phenomenon is explored in more detail by Alter (2009) in a *Wall Street Journal* article. Alter discovers artists working to revamp houses in Cleveland's Detroit-Shoreway neighborhood and in Collinwood. What's more, Cleveland has adopted artist-driven renovation as a strategy to counteract recent depopulation, investing $500,000 in 50 citizen-led pilot projects to reclaim vacant property. Alter focuses on the journey of two New York artists, Michael Di Liberto and Sunia Boneham, to a Collinwood project planned by Northeast Shores Development Corporation. Di Liberto, Boneham, and others are being lured to Cleveland by its rich arts offerings coupled with a low cost of living.

Collinwood's commercial district, the centerpiece of a once rundown neighborhood, is being renovated by a collective of 12 artists, named Arts Collinwood. The group bought a 5,000-square foot building in 2004 and has transformed it into an art gallery, a café, and nine art studios. This initial investment opened the door to "a flood of musicians, painters, and sculptors" (Alter 2009). The new residents, in turn, opened three new art galleries, a recording studio, and a stained glass studio. All of these serve as tangible evidence of urban revitalization. This trend needs to be better documented through further research, but the two articles in New York publications suggest that Cleveland is becoming a magnet for young artists.

THE CITY'S ARTS PROFILE

Major Cultural Institutions

If Cleveland must develop its distinctive cultural ecosystem in order to prosper, what is its characteristic arts profile? Here one must begin with the older, established arts institutions. Eric Wobser, executive director of Ohio City Incorporated, identifies "the big five" cultural institutions of the community as the Cleveland Orchestra, the Cleveland Museum of Art, Playhouse Square, the Rock and Roll Hall of Fame, and the West Side Market (E. Wobser, personal communication, July 25, 2011). No one who has listened to the Cleveland Orchestra play in the majesty of Severance Hall or who has spent hours either exploring the Rock and Roll Hall of Fame or navigating the various booths in the West Side Market could disagree. The Cleveland Museum of Art, which opened in 1916, houses 43,000 works of art and is especially noted for its Asian and Egyptian collections. It closed in 2005 to begin a major renovation and expansion to 592,500 square feet, a project designed by New York architect Rafael Viñoly. The work is expected to cost $350 million, an amount that dwarfs anything else comparable in Ohio (Litt 2008). In 2008, the museum began reopening in stages. When completed, 30 percent more gallery space, including new east and west wings and a large central court, will have been added.

While a dwindling population base has turned Cleveland into one of the smaller major-league cities, it is remarkable that the community has such high-quality and long-established cultural landmarks (T. Schorgl and M. Van Voorhis, personal communication, August 26, 2011). The "big five" institutions play a key role in making Cleveland an "attraction city," and they certainly draw tourists. For instance, more than 90 percent of visitors to the Rock and Roll Hall of Fame come from outside the Cleveland region (Rock and Roll Hall of Fame 2011). The strengths of these institutions are sources of civic pride for a town that has endured many difficult setbacks. Karen Gahl-Mills, the director of the region's recently founded public arts-granting organization, Cuyahoga Arts and Culture, comments that "growing up in Cleveland, one just assumes that great cities have great cultural institutions" (K. Gahl-Mills, personal communication, July 7, 2011). Her experiences in different parts of the country, however, suggest that this is not always true of other American cities of comparable size. It is clear that these major organizations can play a role in attracting the young professionals Cleveland needs in order to increase its size and dynamism, but they are not sufficient.

Additional Cultural Assets

Indeed, Cleveland has significant riches beyond the big five. The city, for example, is the birthplace of "rock and roll," and the presence of the Rock and Roll Hall of Fame indicates the importance of that musical genre to the community. The popular music scene in Cleveland is alive and well, with exciting performance venues, such as the Grog Shop, the Beachland Ballroom, and the Happy Dog, regularly featuring a large selection of musical choices to a local audience that Sean Waterson, co-owner of the Happy Dog, finds to be very sophisticated in its musical tastes (S. Waterson, personal communication, July 26, 2011).

In addition, Cleveland has a large number of nonprofit arts organizations that sponsor a wide variety of arts experiences. Cuyahoga Arts and Culture, for example, funds 150 different arts organizations, and more than half of these have budgets of under $1 million (K. Gahl-Mills, personal communication, July 7, 2011). Thomas Schorgl commented that Cleveland is indeed a kind of laboratory for small-scale arts development.

Another distinctive element to Cleveland's cultural ecosystem is that it is not concentrated in one area. Of the big five, only the Rock and Roll Hall of Fame and Playhouse Square are located in downtown Cleveland. The Cleveland Orchestra and the Cleveland Museum of Art are five miles to the east in University Circle. As a part of the City Beautiful campaign in the early twentieth century, Cleveland's leaders chose to develop University Circle to house the community's new arts establishments, as well as some of its major educational institutions. University Circle was chosen because of its pastoral setting, which presented a sharp contrast to the industrialized sector to the west. According to Charles Michener, former senior editor of *The New Yorker* and *Seattle*, this decision created in effect two centers, which has made it harder to unite the city (C. Michener, personal communication, June 20, 2011).

> In addition to downtown and University Circle, other small pockets of arts activity are scattered throughout the city. Three such centers on Cleveland's near West Side are the Gordon Square district, which is home to Cleveland Public Theatre and the Capitol Theater; the Tremont area, which is now bustling with visitors to new upscale restaurants; and the Ohio City area, which is concentrated around the West Side Market and is now dense with new bars and restaurants, including Great Lakes Brewery. There are others; there is no single arts and culture center to Cleveland, and this poses a problem when one raises the question of where Cleveland's development dollars should be spent. Some observers see this dispersal as a major disadvantage, complaining that Cleveland's cultural ecosystem lacks coherence and connectivity. Others, like Evan Lieberman, Professor of Film at Cleveland State University and guitarist with the rock group Poland Invasion, find this to be an attractive aspect of the city [E. Lieberman, personal communication, July 14, 2011]. A native of Atlanta, Georgia, Lieberman has become one of Cleveland's most enthusiastic

supporters. Lieberman finds the arts ubiquitous in Cleveland, part of the terrain and cultural landscape, and as a musician and film-maker, he could not be happier.

Other Unique Features

Cleveland is also a place of binary divisions. The famed East Side-West Side split is perhaps the most entrenched, as it goes back to the very earliest days of the city and the legendary battle between Cleveland and Ohio City over competing bridges in 1836 (Miller and Wheeler 1997). Beyond the obvious topographical distinctions, the two sides find themselves divided along lines of class, race, and ethnic cultures. But this is also true for the cultural ecosystem. Raymond Bobgan, Director of Cleveland Public Theatre, for example, finds a significant difference in arts funding opportunities between the two areas. He finds the established institutions on the East Side to be "massively capitalized," while the newer arts organizations on the West Side struggle (R. Bobgan, personal communication, August 4, 2011).

Michener sees this difference as an opposition between the old East-Side elites and Cleveland's working classes. Society members of the East Side were descendants of Cleveland's early industrial tycoons, who viewed the city as the last outpost of the great Northeast and looked toward New York for their ideas of good art and culture. On the West Side are the descendants of the men and women who labored in the tycoons' factories and plants, often of various ethnicities recently emigrated from Europe. It is probably an oversimplification to see the East Side-West Side divide as reflecting only Michener's binaries, but those elements certainly have played a role in creating this situation.

What does seem to be true is that the arts scene in the University Circle area is largely more established and has a more formal atmosphere. Other parts of the Cleveland cultural ecosystem are more contemporary and edgy. The Museum of Contemporary Art Cleveland (MOCA) in its new and strikingly contemporary building (designed by Farshid Moussavi and located in University Circle) is, perhaps, the exception that proves the rule (Museum of Contemporary Art Cleveland, n.d.). Cleveland Public Theatre (CPT), located on the West Side, is also dedicated to the work of contemporary artists, specifically those from Northeast Ohio.

The story of the founding of CPT is perhaps one of the best examples of arts helping to revitalize a neighborhood. In 1982, James Levin founded a New York–style experimental theater in Cleveland, and he was encouraged to look to the East Side, particularly to University Circle, as a place to begin (J. Levin, personal communication, July 14, 2011). In those days, it was difficult for people to imagine a major cultural organization being located outside of University Circle. Levin rejected that notion and wanted his theater to have a part in city rejuvenation. He settled on the Gordon Square District, which in those days was a run-down, crime-infested neighborhood. His venue was to be an old vaudeville theater, which was then a used-furniture store. He launched the project, made progress, and, in 2005, handed over the leadership of CPT to Raymond Bobgan.

According to Bobgan, no other market in the United States has a theatre exactly like CPT. Across the street is the refurbished Capitol Theater, which is the sole arts cinema on Cleveland's West Side. Building on momentum, a $3 million dollar streetscape project visually unified the neighborhood (Gordon Square Arts District 2012). Today, the square is home to a variety of attractive businesses, and CPT's major fund-raising event, *Pandemonium*, in Gordon Square each fall, is a night of raucous carnival and a feast of contemporary arts of all sorts. In sum, Gordon Square has become the kind of hip and authentic neighborhood that draws young professionals back to the city, and its transformation began with an investment in the arts.

Two other aspects of Cleveland's arts scene differentiate it from larger, better-known destinations. First, as noted earlier, the town's affordability is a major attractive feature for the creative class. Second, unlike New York and Los Angeles, Cleveland is not a leading center for the arts and entertainment industries, although work by Ivan Schwarz and the Cleveland Film Commission, especially on the promotion of the Ohio film tax incentive, has recently been paying dividends (E. Lieberman, personal communication, July 14, 2011). In 2011 alone, seven major movies were shot in Cleveland, and notable producers on the West Coast are starting to look to the city as a venue for filming. Lieberman notes that Cleveland is rich in different kinds of topography and architecture, making it ideal for just about any kind of film. The same attributes that attract individual artists to Cleveland also appeal to commercial studios. Cleveland is an affordable place to make motion pictures, and the city works diligently to ensure that it is easy for film companies to obtain the required permits.

> The fact that Cleveland is not an industry center is especially important to Evan Lieberman, who has lived and worked in Los Angeles. In Los Angeles, he argues, the industry and the bottom line dictate what artists write. In Cleveland, because artists are not tied directly to the commercial entertainment industry, they can be more authentic. Indeed, "authenticity" is a common theme when talking about the Cleveland cultural ecosystem and the neighborhoods in which it resides [e.g., T. Schorgl and M. Van Voorhis, personal communication, August 26, 2011]. In Cleveland, artists don't have to take a stand either for or against commercialism, and they are less likely to obtain huge contracts. Instead, they are more inclined to simply want to translate their life experiences into art. Indeed, Lieberman insists that the value that the arts contribute to the quality of life goes well beyond the economic. Arts, he argues, give us new ways of viewing the world, and they help us to lose ourselves in the artistic moment. They either surround our worlds in beauty or help us explore life's misery and problems, and in the end, they help us to imagine new possibilities. In a culturally rich city like Cleveland, especially one that is not tied directly to the commercial entertainment industry, these noneconomic aspects of the arts also directly improve the everyday lives of the region's citizens. (J. Michener, personal communication)

Cleveland, then, has a base in the arts that can be used to attract members of the creative class, but what needs to happen to make that base stronger? When asked what could be done to improve Cleveland's arts scene, Michener remarked that "the cultural institutions need to do a better job of knitting the city together." Indeed, the need to increase connectivity—bridging Cleveland's geographical and social divisions, creating new partnerships among arts organizations, and bringing people together with art—was high on the list of most of the experts we interviewed. In Cleveland, art is everywhere, but it needs to be drawn together more coherently and efficiently. Schorgl, for example, spoke of the need to grow cross-sectional partnerships between various segments of the city's economy. In addition, the established institutions need to attract wider (and younger) audiences, and the smaller, more popular arts institutions need to further the sense of community in their own neighborhoods.

The good news for Cleveland is that the arts community under-stands these imperatives. The more established organizations, for example, have developed aggressive outreach and educational pro-grams. With a lead endowment of $20 million from the Maltz Fam-ily Foundation, the Cleveland Orchestra has created an initiative, the Center for Future Audiences, to draw a new generation of patrons to its concerts (Cleveland Orchestra, n.d.). The goal is to create the youngest symphony audience worldwide by 2018 (Suttel 2011, p. 12). During the summers, the orchestra performs at Blossom Music Center, located in Cuyahoga Valley National Park, just south of Cleveland. This venue is much more family friendly than Severance Hall, and it has an expan-sive grass campus on which people can picnic and listen to the orches-tra play. The Orchestra's Director of Communications, Ana Papakhian, revealed that, as of the summer of 2011, anyone under 18 years old has been able to attend these summer concerts for free, a key strategy for building a new and younger audience (A. Papakhian, personal commu-nication, August 18, 2011). The hope is that an even more dynamic and youthful arts scene will be the catalyst not only to retain young artists and professionals in Cleveland but also to draw additional members of the creative class to make Cleveland their home.

INITIATIVES FOR THE FUTURE OF THE ARTS

The arts leaders we interviewed were optimistic about Cleveland's future: there is a sense that the Cleveland cultural ecosystem is part of a larger movement toward a more vibrant city. As noted, although Cleveland's population again dropped in the 2010 census, key areas of the city, downtown and University Circle, defied that trend. Indeed, downtown is alive with new additions like the Global Center for Health Innovation and the Horseshoe Casino on Public Square, and these point the way to greater density and traffic in the downtown area. Euclid Ave-nue has been fully renovated with a sleek new rapid transit system, the Health Line, running down the center, linking downtown with Univer-sity Circle. In the concluding pages, we highlight four important initia-tives, both large and small, that are creating a more dynamic arts scene for Cleveland and, thus, hope for Cleveland's further development.

Classical Music Moves West

Sean Waterson moved back to Cleveland several years ago with the intent to have a direct positive impact on his community. The result was Happy Dog, a music venue that serves specialty hot dogs to accompany upbeat music. Waterson's goal is to help build a community on the near West Side, and he wants Happy Dog to be the Gordon Square District's "living room." Happy Dog features live music five nights a week, and 85 percent of its repertoire is rock. But what makes this venue so special is that it also offers classical music and polka on a regular basis. "If New Orleans is jazz, Cleveland is rock and classical," says Waterson, and his programming reflects that belief.

Waterson started offering classical music at the Happy Dog after meeting Cleveland Orchestra flutist Joshua Smith. Together they invented "Orchestral Manoeuvres at the Dog," a regular series of classical concerts. The first concert was a sellout, with lines of interested customers running out the front door and down the block. Waterson thought that the risk inherent in playing in a less-than-perfect environment actually created a palpable energy in the bar. In his blog, Smith (2010) agrees that the evening was a big success, but he points out that playing classical music in bars is not a new idea. Nevertheless, the concept seems to have caught on particularly well at the Happy Dog, and the promise is that this classical music programming will continue. If a major problem in Cleveland arts is interconnectivity, Waterson has found a way to link West Side residents with the classical music scene, which heretofore has been largely an East Side, Severance Hall phenomenon.

> Sean Waterson was not satisfied, however, with his success in "Orchestral Manoeuvres at the Dog." He wanted to build more bridges between West Side audiences and the heritage arts institutions on the East Side. Thus was born "Gordon Square Goes to the Orchestra" and "Gordon Square Goes to the Art Museum." Both of these efforts were organized through Facebook. The idea was to gather an audience from the Gordon Square area, hire a bus, and transport the participants to East Side art institutions. After the visits, the group dined at Happy Dog. Both trips were sold out in 24 hours. (Smith 2010)

Public Support for the Arts

A second reason for hope is the availability of significant public arts funding in Cuyahoga County, which includes Cleveland and its suburbs. Michener describes past funding of the Cleveland arts community as basically top-down, the result of a sense of noblesse oblige on the part of the East Side elite toward the entire community, but this, he says, is changing. Cleveland has a long history of active grant-making organizations, such as the Cleveland Foundation and the George Gund Foundation, but what is new and absolutely essential for the community is the advent of a public arts financing mechanism.

In 2006, the citizens of Cuyahoga County passed a 10-year cigarette tax to be used to fund the arts. As a result of this ballot initiative, Cuyahoga Arts and Culture (CAC) was born, with a mandate to spend approximately $20 million each year to promote the arts in the county. The scale is massive. Schorgl commented that, if Cuyahoga County were a state, it would have the third-largest public state budget for the arts in the country, just behind New York and Minnesota. This large infusion of funds has been transformative.

As noted earlier, CAC assists about 150 arts organizations. In addition, although CAC is not permitted to finance individual artists directly, the organization does play a role in cultivating local artists through the agencies it supports. Cleveland's Creative Workforce Fellowship, for example, which is funded by CAC, gives out $20,000 fellowships to individual artists on an annual basis. Gahl-Mills argues that, if you want to find the best indicator of the city's distinct arts and culture scene, you need to look at what is happening in the neighborhoods; there Cleveland offers a rich variety of experiences, many at least partially financed by public tax dollars.

Arts and Education Partnerships

The growth of creative partnerships among arts and educational institutions provides a third positive force. These collaborations will be important components in the bid to make the city's arts scene even more vibrant. Downtown Cleveland has a concentrated theater center located just blocks east of Public Square, with massive venues from the heyday of classic movies in the early twentieth century. Forty years ago, this neighborhood was run-down, and all the theaters except the Hanna were closed. Because of the pioneering efforts of people like Raymond Shephardson and Joseph Geary, the Cleveland community rallied to save this area and created Playhouse Square, making it the world's largest theater-restoration project.

Today, with all the theaters going through at least one round of significant renovations, Playhouse Square is the second-largest live theater district in the country, right behind Lincoln Center in New York. Nine separate performance spaces, including the State, the Ohio, and the Palace Theaters, are currently in operation. Playhouse Square draws 1 million visitors per year, and it is estimated that it has a $43 million impact on the city economy (Playhouse Square 2011).

One of these spaces, the Allen Theater, a classical old movie house in Italian Renaissance style, was underutilized, being occupied only about 90 days per year (Collins 2011). At the same time, two other community players were facing operational challenges. The art and drama programs at Cleveland State University (CSU), located just east of Playhouse Square, were operating in antiquated, substandard buildings, and university leaders wanted to build a new Fine and Performing Arts Center to house both disciplines. The cost of such a new building, however, was prohibitive. The state's capital budget would not sustain such expenditures, and only two major community donors came forward to offer support for the plan. The university was caught in a difficult situation. Sixty blocks to the east of Cleveland State was the Cleveland Play House, the oldest and perhaps most prestigious regional theater in the country. Located near the world-famous Cleveland Clinic, the Cleveland Play House found itself with an extensive physical plant to maintain and diminishing audiences. Michael Bloom, former Artistic Director of the Cleveland Play House, commented that the organization was facing a very uncertain future.

Faced with the Great Recession of 2008–2009, the leaders of these three organizations came to realize that a partnership could be a cost-effective way to solve their problems. The vision was to move both the Cleveland Play House and CSU's drama and dance programs into a remodeled Allen Theater. Through cooperation, both organizations could move into affordable new space right in the middle of a thriving arts district in downtown Cleveland, building upon the critical mass of live theater that was already available there.

This visionary project is now complete, but many obstacles had to be overcome to make it happen. First, money needed to be raised to remodel the Allen Theater into a contemporary venue with multiple performance areas. As it was, the Allen had a relatively new and well equipped stage house, whose existence would save the project about $10 million in construction costs. However, the theater itself was much too large for the kind of intimate experience envisioned by CSU and the Cleveland Play House. Its 2,500-seat theater had to be cut back to about 500. In addition, two theater venues needed to be created in the parking lot adjacent to the Allen. These would be a new lab theater and a 250-seat highly adjustable Second Stage, a novel performance space that would not have been possible if each of the partners had tried to accomplish this separately.

A team of seasoned fundraisers from all three partners, called "The Power of Three," was assembled, with the goal of raising $32 million. But a second building was needed to house offices, classrooms, and rehearsal spaces for both CSU and the Cleveland Play House. Located around the corner from the Allen is the Middough Building, a five-story edifice, in which two floors were completely vacant. The "Power of Three" team then created yet another partnership, with Middough Inc., one of Cleveland's most distinguished architectural and engineering firms. As a result of this arrangement, all of the partners, excluding Playhouse Square but including CSU's art department, now fill Middough's five large floors, and a new CSU Fine Arts campus has been created. The campus includes not only the Allen Theater and the Middough Building, but also a structure on the corner of 13th Street and Euclid, which gives CSU's art gallery, now called the Galleries at CSU, storefront space in Playhouse Square. All in all, several powerful partnerships will boost Playhouse Square's artistic profile, and make this region a national model for creating synergies between education and entertainment. Playhouse Square is certainly one more element that will transform Cleveland into a major attraction city.

Arts Festivals

A fourth encouraging factor that is helping to create a more dynamic arts scene is the growth of distinctive arts festivals in Cleveland. These events are important because they draw large numbers of people together from different parts of the city. Two programs that are especially noteworthy are the Cleveland International Film Festival and the Ingenuity Festival.

In 1977, Jonathan Forman inaugurated the Cleveland International Film Festival, screening eight films from seven countries at the Cedar Lee Theater (Cleveland International Film Festival 2013). Over the years, the festival, supported by the Cleveland and George Gund Foundations, as well as CAC, grew significantly, and in 1991, it moved to Tower City, located downtown in Cleveland's iconic Terminal Tower. By 2011, the festival was screening approximately 150 feature films, grouped thematically, from 60 different countries. It had a budget of over $1.5 million and about 1,000 members (Magaw 2011). Filmmakers from around the world were drawn to Cleveland, and there was also a markedly engaged audience of about 78,000 fans, a 122 percent increase in attendance over the past eight years (Blackaby 2011; Magaw 2011).

Meanwhile, the Ingenuityfest was created in 2005 by James Levin and Thomas Mulready as a celebration of creativity at the nexus of arts and technology (Brown 2010). Over the years, it has continuously moved: from the Warehouse District to Playhouse Square to the lower deck of the Detroit-Superior Bridge, and, finally, to Piers 30 and 32 of the Port of Cleveland. At its current location, it literally brings together Cleveland's East and West Sides. In 2011 it drew about 40,000 people to the center for three days of festivities (Ewinger 2011). Some exhibitions are pure art; others focus squarely on technology; and still others, like Jared Bendis's surround-sound audio game, "Treasure of the Wumpus," combine both in interesting ways (Rosenberg 2011).

In some respects, there is no more appropriate way to celebrate the existence and achievements of what Florida (2002) has called the creative class, and this festival continues to draw ever-larger crowds paying homage to creativity, in whatever form it takes. Like the ArtPrize contest in Grand Rapids, both Ingenuityfest and the Film Festival are well on their way to becoming iconic attractions, drawing more and more people into the heart of the city.

THE ARTS AS A PATH TO REVITALIZATION

A dean of the Levin College of Urban Affairs at CSU once remarked that Cleveland's size put it in a sweet spot—large enough to enjoy major league sports and many other big-city amenities, but small enough not to suffer from a variety of urban problems, especially the curse of gridlock and giant traffic jams. Whether or not this is true generally—Cleveland still has plenty of big city challenges—it does seem to be the case with respect to the arts. On one hand, Cleveland has world-class arts organizations that are the envy of many other cities its size or even bigger. On the other, Cleveland is small enough for one man or one woman, like James Levin, to make a significant difference by building upon the arts to promote city development.

As in Grand Rapids and Milwaukee, the arts are playing a crucial role in community revitalization, but Cleveland's path to greater prosperity is building upon its own distinctive amenities, iconic attractions, and arts profile. Nevertheless, several critical aspects of this momentum are transferable. As we have seen, the multiple Cleveland strategies for urban development through the arts include

- having a thoughtful and detailed strategic plan,
- strengthening the city's major artistic infrastructure and cultivating new initiatives,
- making purposeful efforts not only to tie together widely dispersed artistic venues but also to capture younger audiences for the fine arts,
- creating significant arts and education partnerships,
- supporting art through significant public funding,
- providing artists and arts organizations an affordable and welcoming place to work, and
- creating multiple festivals to highlight the arts and draw audiences from the suburbs and beyond into the city.

It may well be that the broad scope and unique profile of these combined efforts is the most distinctive aspect of Cleveland's arts development strategy.

Rocco Landesman, Chairman of the National Endowment for the Arts, has offered independent confirmation of the importance of the arts to Cleveland's redevelopment efforts. Appointed by President Obama in 2009, Landesman has made the linkage between artistic activity and economic development a centerpiece of his strategy to build the Endowment (Litt 2011). After visiting Cleveland and touring its arts attractions, he concluded that local arts organizations were indeed helping to revitalize the city. "We're talking about it; you're doing it," he said. Overall, Landesman believes that Cleveland is "an arts city," and that other cities would do well to follow its lead.

Notes

1. As of 2012 there is also a juried prize.

References

Alter, Alexandra. 2009. "Artists vs. Blight." *Wall Street Journal*, April 17. http://online.wsj.com/article/SB123992318352327147.html (accessed April 16, 2013).

Anderson Economic Group. 2011. "The Economic Impact of ArtPrize 2011." East Lansing, MI: Anderson Economic Group. http://www.andersoneconomicgroup.com/Portals/0/upload/EcnImpct_ArtPrize2011.pdf (accessed August 8, 2013).

Blackaby, Linda. 2011. *They Make it Look Easy: CIFF's Lights! Camera! Action! Steps! and More*. San Francisco: National Alliance for Media Art and Culture. http://www.namac.org/node/25759 (accessed April 16, 2013).

Brown, Tony. 2010. "Ingenuityfest 2010, So In-the-Moment, Is History—and Has a Bright Future." *cleveland.com*, September 27. http://www.cleveland.com/onstage/index.ssf/2010/09/ingenuityfest_2010_is_history.html (accessed April 16, 2013).

Bulik, Bill, Carol Coletta, Colin Jackson, Andrew Taylor, and Steven Wolff. 2003. *Cultural Development in Creative Communities*. Washington, DC: Americans for the Arts.

Cleveland International Film Festival. 2013. About: History. Cleveland, OH: CIFF. http://www.clevelandfilm.org/about/history (accessed April 16, 2013).

Cleveland Orchestra. n.d. Center for Future Audiences. Cleveland, OH: Cleveland Orchestra. http://www.clevelandorchestra.com/support/future-audiences .aspx (accessed July 31, 2013)

Collins, Joanna. 2011. "The Renaissance of Cleveland's Allen Theatre: How Theatre Renovation Brought Together Three Institutions." *cleveland.com*, September 18. http://www.cleveland.com/arts/index.ssf/2011/09/the_ renaissance_of_clevelands.html (accessed April 16, 2013).

Community Partnership for Arts and Culture. 2008. "From Rust Belt to Artist Belt: Challenges and Opportunities in Rust Belt Cities: Executive Summary." Cleveland, OH: Community Partnership for Arts and Culture. http://www.cultureforward.org/Reference-Desk/Research-Library/ Neighborhoods/From-Rust-Belt-to-Artist-Belt (accessed April 16, 2013).

———. 2011. Organization, Programs and Services Summary. Cleveland, OH: Community Partnership for Arts and Culture.

Cortright, Joseph. 2008. *City Success: Theories of Urban Prosperity*. Chicago: CEO's for Cities.

———. 2002. "The Economic Importance of Being Different: Regional Variations in Tastes, Increasing Returns, and Dynamics of Development." *Economic Development Quarterly* 16(1): 3–16.

Creative Alliance Milwaukee. n.d. About. Milwaukee, WI: Creative Alliance Milwaukee. http://creativealliancemke.org/about/ (accessed April 16, 2013).

———. 2011a. "Creative Industries: A New Economic Growth Opportunity for the Milwaukee 7 Region." Milwaukee, WI: Cultural Alliance of Greater Milwaukee and the Greater Milwaukee Committee. http://creativealliancemke .org/wp-content/uploads/2011/11/Executive_Summary.pdf (accessed April 16, 2013).

———. 2011b. "Creativity Works Here Program Launches." Milwaukee, WI: Creative Alliance Milwaukee. http://creativealliancemke.org/2011/06/ creativity-works-here-Program-launch/ (accessed April 16, 2013).

———. 2012. "Study Shows Milwaukee-Area Arts had $300 Million Impact." Milwaukee, WI: Creative Alliance Milwaukee. http://creativealliancemke .org/2012/06/study-shows-milwaukee-area-arts-had-300-million-impact/ (accessed April 16, 2013).

Ewinger, James. 2011. "Ingenuityfest Brimming with Bright Ideas." *cleveland.com*, September 18. http://blog.cleveland.com/metro/2011/09/ ingenuityfest_brimming_with_br.html (accessed April 16, 2013).

Farkas, Karen. 2013. "Medical Mart in Cleveland Now Named Global Center for Health Innovation." *cleveland.com*, March 6. http: www.cleveland.com/ cuyahoga-county/Index.ssf/2013/02/medical_mart_in_cleveland_now.html (accessed July 31, 2013)

Florida, Richard L. 2002. *The Rise of the Creative Class: And How It's Trans-*

forming Work, Leisure, Community, and Everyday Life. New York: Basic Books.

Helper, Susan, Timothy Krueger, and Howard Wial. 2012. "Locating American Manufacturing: Trends in the Geography of Production." Advanced Industries Series Report No. 2. Washington, DC: Brookings Institution. http://www.brookings.edu/research/reports/2012/05/09-locating-american-manufacturing-wial (accessed April 16, 2013).

Gordon Square Arts District. 2012. About Us. Cleveland, OH. Gordon Square Arts District. http://gordonsquare.org/about.html (accessed April 16, 2013).

Linn, Virginia. 2012. "An Art Extravaganza Engulfs Grand Rapids." *Pittsburgh Post-Gazette*, May 14. http://www.post-gazette.com/stories/life/travel/an-art-extravaganza-engulfs-grand-rapids-635715/ (accessed April 16, 2013).

Litt, S. 2008. "Cleveland Museum of Art Renovations Beginning to See the Light." *cleveland.com*, March 29. http://www.cleveland.com/entertainment/index.ssf/2008/03/cleveland_museum_of_art_renova.html (accessed July 31, 2013)

———. 2011. "National Endowment for the Arts Chairman Rocco Landesman Salutes Arts-Based Community Development in Cleveland." *cleveland.com*, September 21. http://www.cleveland.com/arts/index.ssf/2011/09/national_endowment_for_the_art.html (accessed April 16, 2013).

Magaw, Timothy. 2011. "On the Comeback Trail: Cleveland's International Film Festival." *Crain's Cleveland Business*, June 27. http://www.crainscleveland.com/article/20110627/FREE/306279964/0/SEARCH (accessed April 16, 2013).

Markusen, Ann, Greg Schrock, and Martina Cameron. 2004. "The Artistic Dividend Revisited." Minneapolis, MN: Humphrey Institute on Public Affairs, University of Minnesota. http:www.hhh.umn.edu/img/assets/6158/artistic_dividend_revisited.pd (accessed August 9, 2013).

Miller, Carol Poh, and Robert Wheeler. 1997. *Cleveland: A Concise History, 1796–1996*, 2nd ed. Bloomington, IN: Indiana University Press.

Miller, Jay. 2012. "Portland Leaders to Visit Cleveland, Study Region's Progress." *Crain's Cleveland Business*, April 23. http://www.crainscleveland.com/article/20120423/SUB1/304239976/1053/toc&Profile=1053 (accessed April 16, 2013).

Museum of Contemporary Art Cleveland. n.d. About the Building. Cleveland, OH: MOCA. http:mocacleveland.org/about/building (accessed July 31, 2013).

Ott, Thomas. 2011. "Waterloo Road to Court Artists with Money to Buy, Fix Homes." *cleveland.com*, July 24. http://blog.cleveland.com/metro/2011/07/waterloo_artists_can_get_money.html (accessed April 16, 2013).

Playhouse Square. 2011. A Message from Art Falco, CEO and Presi-

dent, PlayhouseSquare. Cleveland, OH: Playhouse Square. http://www
.playhousesquare.org/default.asp?playhousesquare=48&urlkeyword
=History (accessed April 16, 2013).

Rock and Roll Hall of Fame. 2011. Economic Impact. Cleveland, OH:
Rock and Roll Hall of Fame. http://rockhall.com/visit-the-museum/learn/
economic-impact/ (accessed April 16, 2013).

Rosenberg, Donald. 2011. "Cleveland's Ingenuityfest Kicks Off Friday with
an Intriguing Blend of Art, Technology." *cleveland.com*, September 15.
http://www.cleveland.com/musicdance/index.ssf/2011/09/clevelands_
ingenuityfest_an_in.html (accessed April 16, 2013).

Smith, Joshua. 2010. "Beethoven for Beer: Orchestral Maneuvers at the Dog."
Soloflute, October 22. http://soloflute.blogspot.com/2010/10/beethoven-
for-beer-orchestral.html (accessed April 16, 2013).

Smith, Robert L., and Rich Exner. 2011. "396,815: Cleveland's Population
Drops 17%." *Cleveland Plain Dealer*, March 10: A1.

Souccar, Miriam Kreinin. 2010. "Artists Fleeing the City. High Cost of Living,
Fewer Part-Time Jobs Drive Them out of New York." *Crain's New York
Business*, November 14. http://www.crainsnewyork.com/article/20101114/
FREE/311149985 (accessed April 16, 2013).

Stryker, Mark. 2012. "Artists Will Vie for $560,000 at 4th Annual ArtPrize in
Grand Rapids." *Detroit Free Press*, September 16.

Suttell, Scott. 2011. "Five NE Ohio Anchors Give to Orchestra." *Crain's
Cleveland Business*, July 11, p. 12.

Thompson, Doug. 2006. "The Revitalization of Grand Rapids." *Sustainable
Land Development Today*, November 19. http://www.sldtonline.com/
index2.php?option=com_content&do_pdf=1&id=132 (accessed April 16,
2103).

Urban Marketing Collaborative. 2005. "Arts and Entertainment Strategy: Downtown Grand Rapids." Toronto, ON: J.C. Williams Group.
http://grcity.us/design-and-development-services/Planning-Department/
Documents/1558_DDA_A%20and%20E%20Strategy%20-%20
Downtown%20Grand%20Rapids.pdf (accessed April 16, 2013).

U.S. Census Bureau. 2011. American FactFinder: 2010 Census Data. Washington, DC: U.S. Census Bureau. http://factfinder2.census.gov (accessed April
16, 2013).

7

How Energy Policy Enabled the Decline of Midwestern Cities, and How It Can Contribute to Their Rehabilitation

Andrew R. Thomas
Cleveland State University

Globalization can't be seen as the sole factor that led to the decline in cities in the upper Midwest. Another contributing factor is homegrown: domestic energy policy. For instance, subsidies for rural electricity, funded by midwestern cities, made it possible for manufacturing to move to the Sunbelt. Similarly, subsidies for an interstate highway system established a permanent preference for trucking over the Great Lakes shipping ports and railroad centers. However, there are a number of energy policies that, if adopted, could foster rather than impede economic growth in declining Rust Belt cities.

In 1986 Michael Kinsley wrote an essay in *The New Republic* that helped popularize the word *schadenfreude* in America. *Schadenfreude* is a German word meaning "glee at the misery of others," a word Kinsley noted that only the Germans, with their grim humor, could invent. Kinsley speculated that, after more than a decade of watching vast amounts of wealth being transferred from the Northeast to the Texas Gulf Coast, the Northeast would enjoy watching the collapse of the oil and gas industry, and with it, the Texas economy. Indeed, in the late 1980s prices for natural gas dropped from over $4 per thousand cubic feet (mcf) to below $1.50 per mcf, and prices for oil fell from nearly $40 per barrel (bbl) to below $15 per bbl (1980 dollars). As a result, the oil and gas industry began a major contraction in the late 1980s that continued through the 1990s. But the Texas economy, while damaged, did not collapse. Nor did the Rust Belt economies of the Midwest and the Northeast fully recover when oil and gas prices remained low throughout the 1990s.

For those of us who grew up in the Midwest, the 1970s were a difficult time. The cost of fuel at the pump had skyrocketed overnight. Families waited in long lines to buy gasoline. Ford station wagons were abandoned for Volkswagen Beetles. The expense of heating the family home with natural gas was even more painful, as prices rose from around $0.20 per mcf to over $3 per mcf in a decade. With the rapid increase in energy costs came rampant inflation. Life in the Midwest was forever changed, with the perception that Texas cowboys had hijacked our way of life—and in the process pocketed billions of our hard-earned dollars. So it is small wonder that residents of the Midwest and Northeast experienced *schadenfreude* when increased production and decreased consumption inevitably led to an oversupply of oil and natural gas and a price collapse in the 1990s.

To be sure, the advent of the Rust Belt economies of the Midwest had many causes. We have heard much about them: bloated unions, high taxes, globalization, and underperforming education are the most cited. However, there can be little doubt that the energy crisis of the 1970s was a principal catalyst for the decline of the cities in and around the Great Lakes region. It decimated the American automobile industry, as Japanese and European automakers stole market share with their smaller, more energy-efficient models. The effects cascaded throughout the Midwest but were particularly hard felt in the Great Lakes region, where automobile and steel manufacturing formed a large part of the economy.

The American Midwest was suffering from what economist Gail Tverberg subsequently described as the "high-priced fuel syndrome" (Tverberg 2012). In short, consumers are required to pay more for a necessity, and as a result they cut back on discretionary goods and services. If oil and gas prices go up, so do food prices, which are dependent on oil for transportation and natural gas for fertilizers. Commuting costs, electricity prices, and business expenses increase. The result is layoffs, cutbacks, and more pressure on discretionary goods and services. Property values and tax revenues decline, and the follow-on effects are magnified. Figure 7.1 shows how acute the problem with oil prices was for the Midwest in the late 1970s.

Figure 7.1 Historic Oil Prices, 1900–2011 (2011$)

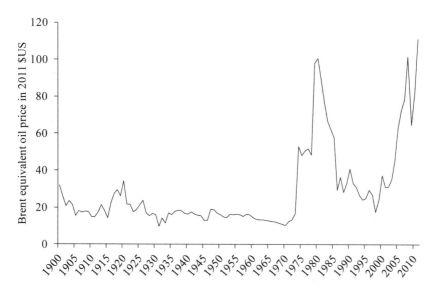

NOTE: "Brent equivalency" is the accepted international benchmark for crude oil pricing.
SOURCE: Tverberg (2012).

The result of the "high-priced fuel syndrome" in the late 1970s was an exodus out of the Midwest and the Northeast, especially of young people. A comparison of a timeline of inflation-adjusted oil prices with demographic change in the Northeast, Midwest, and the South demonstrates this: after decades of double-digit population growth, growth in the Northeast and the Midwest plummeted after the oil shock of the 1970s. In the South, on the other hand, population growth continued unabated, as shown in Table 7.1.

Yet when oil and gas prices crashed in the 1990s, the Northeast and the Midwest failed to regain their pre-energy-crisis population growth levels—clearly there were other forces at work. Some of these were energy related and are discussed later in this chapter. Others were not, although arguably the initial oil shock set in motion some of the pathologies that prevented a reversal of the trend. As of 2012, however, as shown in Figure 7.1, oil prices were again at near historic highs (trading at around $100 per bbl in 2011 dollars). The midwestern and northeastern economies are once more under the threat of the "high price fuel

Table 7.1 A Comparison of Oil Prices with Population Change in the Northeast, Midwest, and South, 1930–2010

	Price of oil per barrel (2011$)	% change in population		
		Northeast	Midwest	South
1930	19.00	16	14	14
1940	18.00	5	5	10
1950	17.00	10	11	13
1960	18.00	13	16	16
1970	17.00	10	10	14
1980	45.00	0	4	20
1990	38.00	3	2	14
2000	28.00	5	8	17
2010	90.00	4	4	14

NOTE: Oil prices are per barrel and based upon Brent Crude equivalencies.
SOURCE: Tverberg (2012); U.S. Census Bureau (2010).

syndrome," as they export more and more wealth to import expensive oil.

However, the advent of shale development promises some future relief. In 2010 oil imports accounted for over half of the American trade deficit (*Economist* 2010). For the Midwest, which reached "peak oil" (the inflection point at which oil consumption becomes permanently greater than concurrent reserve addition) long before the nation did, this deficit is even higher. While oil prices have not yet dropped, American oil imports have—principally as a result of the Bakken Shale in North Dakota. In Ohio, there is likewise potential for oil production from the Utica Shale. More importantly, domestic natural gas production has increased dramatically because of shale drilling, and natural gas prices are at historic lows. Indeed, for the first time ever, natural gas prices are completely decoupled from oil prices, creating a migration of truck fleets from gasoline-powered to natural-gas-powered engines. For the reasons discussed later, shale development provides considerable hope for an economic recovery in the American Midwest.

The volatility in oil and gas prices has hardly been the only energy problem facing midwestern cities since the 1970s—it has just been the most visible. This chapter will explore energy policies that have contributed to the decline of these cities and will consider strategies that might reverse some of the pathologies that have become so common-place in the Midwest.

Some policies have had an adverse impact on cities in general; other policies have had a deleterious effect specifically on the Midwest. Presumably all of these were unintended consequences: the policies were intended to produce desirable outcomes, but eventually had results that society did not necessarily want. Those energy policies that have affected cities in general will be considered first, and then those that have negatively affected cities specifically in the Midwest.

POLICIES THAT HAVE TENDED TO HARM CITIES IN GENERAL

Low-Cost Gasoline

There can be little doubt that the American migration to the suburbs has been enabled by cheap gasoline. There is also little question that federal and state policies have played a part in keeping gasoline inexpensive. The debate, rather, is about how much government support there really is. In other words, what is the actual cost of a gallon of gasoline at the pump, if you include all the externalities? Regardless of how one calculates this, it is clear that cheap gasoline has been a significant incentive for the exodus from the inner cities.

The public policy that can be most easily identified that has led to inexpensive gasoline in the United States is the relatively low excise tax on gasoline at the pump. Many people would agree that excise taxes on gasoline are necessary to generate funds for building and maintaining roads, and that those who drive the most ought to bear the highest burden of those costs. Many would probably also concur that we are currently undertaxed on gasoline at the pump; in 2010, for the first time since President Eisenhower signed the Federal-Aid Highway Act into law in 1956, the U.S. Highway Trust Fund was broke. Congress had to infuse $8 billion in general revenue funds into the Trust to keep it solvent. In 2011 Congress was forced to place another $19.5 billion into a fund that is supposed to be self-sustaining through gasoline taxes (Segedy, n.d.).

The issue that is most often debated now is not whether we should raise gasoline taxes, but rather when and by how much they should be increased. These taxes vary from state to state, but they average around $0.49 per gallon (American Petroleum Institute 2013).[1] In Europe, where migration from the central city has not devastated urban areas as severely as it has in the United States, gasoline taxes are as much as 10 times greater, and prices at the pump are typically double what they are in America (*New York Times* 2011). Figure 7.2 provides a comparison of gasoline prices internationally.

It is no coincidence that Europeans tend to live closer to their jobs than do Americans, or that Europe, as a result, tends not to suffer from as much residential abandonment of the inner city as does the United States. In short, the policy of making the cost of commuting by private vehicle inexpensive has also made it easier for Americans to flee urban problems rather than to solve them.

Of course, Americans today would choose to pay just about any price for gasoline if it means not having to live next to urban blight. But the difference in living conditions that has engendered the migration to the suburbs has been created gradually. When the migration first began, it was not a matter of escaping urban blight: it was about choosing to live in a marginally better environment. We might, for instance, expect a working-class family to stay in an inner-ring suburb, rather than to move further away from employers, if faced with the incremental increase in cost. With gasoline taxes at levels similar to those in the United Kingdom, moving 15 miles farther from the job might mean an extra $4,000 per year in commuting costs, rather than an extra $2,000 per year. For a working-class family, that would be a powerful incentive to stay put.

However, low gasoline taxes are only a part of the energy policies associated with inexpensive gasoline. A more difficult consideration is the so-called oil and gas subsidy, the tax incentives that President Obama called for an end to in his 2011 State of the Union address. Any government subsidy for oil inevitably makes it easier for commuters to move away from the downtown areas toward ever-longer commutes. Critics of U.S. energy policy have for years called for the termination of what they argue are massive subsidies to the oil and gas industry through federal tax policies. Unfortunately, energy policy is largely set in the United States through advocacy, and as a result it is hard even for

Figure 7.2 Global Gasoline Price Comparison, January 2011

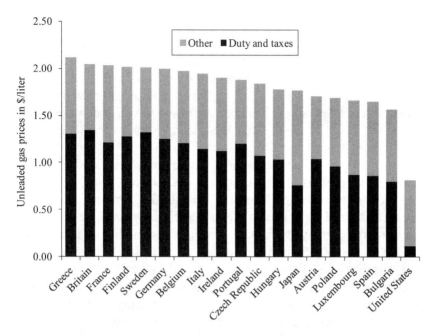

NOTE: "Other" refers to those costs associated with acquiring, delivering, storing and retailing gasoline at the pump.
SOURCE: Washington (2011).

experts, let alone the general public, to understand exactly what subsidies actually exist for oil and gas. Indeed, established energy interests frequently express outrage over subsidies granted to "clean energy," even as fossil fuel technologies enjoy over 10 times as much government support as do these newer approaches (Plummer 2010).

The American Petroleum Institute (API), not surprisingly, argues that there are no such subsidies. The ability to amortize investments, accelerate depletion allowances, and offset "intangible drilling costs" from tax obligations are, according to the API, standard accounting practices in the mining industry (American Petroleum Institute, n.d.). API points out that these accounting strategies are necessary to encourage the sort of massive investments required for such a high-risk business, and there is no reason to treat the oil and gas industry differently from other mining industries.

In the end, we can reasonably differ about what subsidies may or may not exist in the Internal Revenue code, how big those subsidies might be, and which of them are really necessary. But it probably does not matter, because we do know that one massive subsidy exists for imported oil that dwarfs all others: the United States spends billions of dollars every year policing the world's oceans, and it has done so for a long time. The total U.S. yearly military expenditure to patrol the world's petroleum supply has been estimated to range anywhere from $47.6 to $113.1 billion in 2003 U.S. dollars (International Center for Technology Assessment 2005).

It is this policy that makes the shipping of inexpensive oil from the Middle East possible. If this cost were passed along to the purchasers of gasoline at the pump, there is little doubt that the price of gasoline would be several times what it is today. Such an undertaking would also be a boon to domestic oil production, which would be competing with the actual cost of delivering foreign oil to the United States rather than the subsidized cost. However, we are unlikely to see this "external" cost realized at the pump. The notion that much of our defense budget is in fact a massive subsidy to Saudi Aramco is not easy to understand or accept. Nevertheless, the price of gasoline at the pump is artificially low as a result of this subsidy, and this reduction has enabled mass migration to the suburbs.

Inexpensive gasoline and the resultant increase in automobile commuting have created another troubling consequence for urban centers that has led to outmigration: a rise in pollution. Suspended particulate matter, in the form of soot, dust, smoke, and other pollutants, has been distributed into the air by traffic exhaust fumes. In the United States, measures have been taken to reduce the air pollution generated by automobiles, including the banning of lead-based gasoline. Indeed, compared to other major urban areas of the world, American inner cities today have good air quality, or at least not greatly worse than that of suburban areas. Unfortunately, many of these measures were taken after the exodus from the central city had already begun.

Public Policies Encouraging Rural Electrification

We often hear that the solution to our energy problems is another of America's great collaborative undertakings in ingenuity and initiative, usually discussed in terms of either the Manhattan or Apollo projects. It has been posed, for instance, that if we undertook a major Apollo-type effort to develop a hydrogen filling-station infrastructure, we could shift to a new transportation economy. This would be based on ultraefficient fuel cells, which rely on cleaner, locally produced natural gas as the feedstock, and which produce clean water as a byproduct.

In fact, however, in the last century the United States has undertaken two "Manhattan-type" energy policy initiatives that have had a significant impact on midwestern cities. The first was the development of the interstate highway system, now fundamental to the fabric of American society. This program subsidized a nationwide preference for automobiles and trucks over railroads and waterways and will be discussed later as among those energy policies that have been particularly problematic for the Great Lakes cities. The second great American energy policy undertaking was the program to bring electricity to rural areas. It is this latter policy that has, over time, done the most to encourage migration out of the cities (and, as will be discussed later, out of cities in the Midwest, specifically).

In the early 1930s rural electrification was stalled, leaving what was then a majority of Americans, literally, in the dark. The reason why rural markets had failed was manifest: the infrastructure to connect widely dispersed houses to the grid had proven too costly. The Great Depression further delayed investment in rural electrification. The growing gap between living standards in rural and urban areas, a lag in productivity growth in the agricultural sector, and the untapped potential rural demand for manufactured items such as household appliances and telephones led President Roosevelt to create the Rural Electrification Administration (REA) in 1935. The REA (now the Rural Utilities Service) has since been touted as one of the most profoundly successful public policy initiatives in U.S. history. Some $410 million dollars were set aside by Congress in 1936 for a 10-year program subsidizing loans to construct the rural electrical supply infrastructure. Federally funded public works programs such as the Tennessee Valley Authority and the Hoover Dam were set in motion, designed not only to create jobs, but also to generate and deliver cheap electricity. Rural electrical cooperatives were granted preference in purchasing the cheapest power available, such as that generated by the Tennessee Valley Authority.

The result was that, just two years after the creation of the REA, electricity was being delivered to 1.5 million farms in 45 states. By the mid-1950s, almost all U.S. farms had electricity service. The cultural, educational, and commercial disparity between rural and urban America shrank considerably as electrification spurred growth in demand for electrical appliances, plumbing, and information media such as radio and television (Malone 2001).

But as with all social engineering, an unintended consequence inevitably followed: subsidized power in the suburbs meant people could abandon the city. The initial movement outward from city centers began with the rapid expansion of the streetcar system, itself a product of rural electrification. The first suburbs that developed in the 1920s and 1930s were laid out along streetcar lines. With the electrification of rural America, streetcar lines extended further, creating the next ring of suburbs, and a migration outward has continued to this day (El Nasser 2011; Shumsky 1996).

The absorption of much of the costs of rural electrification by those who lived in urban areas made possible the exodus to the suburbs. It became feasible for much of America to move "to the country"—and to leave behind them the developing urban pathologies. Amazingly, although the problem of rural electrification has been resolved for some 50 years, subsidies for rural electrification continue. Today our federal government subsidizes rural electricity with billions of dollars of tax-payer money through an assortment of guaranteed loans, grants, and preferred treatment; the most controversial of these strategies is support for new coal-burning plants—while the rest of the country is trying to cut back carbon emissions (Slivinski 2009).[2]

An Artificially High Cost of Electricity in Urban Areas

The energy cost increases in the 1970s and 1980s were not restricted to oil and gas: electricity prices also rose significantly. For decades U.S. electricity generation, transmission, and distribution were all regulated, with utilities enjoying "cost plus" rate recovery for nearly all of their expenditures, regardless of their folly. The cost-plus strategy invited not only technology stagnation, but also bloated utility budgets, since there was no incentive to constrain costs. Inevitably, rates soared under this paradigm; average U.S. electricity rates rose 60 percent between 1969 and 1984, adjusted for inflation (Vaitheeswaran 2004). The biggest culprit for this problem lay with massive cost overruns associated with the building of large centralized nuclear generation plants (D'Ambrosio and O'Brien 2009).

Skyrocketing electricity prices were a major blow to urban areas throughout America because those economies, especially in the Midwest, relied heavily upon a healthy manufacturing base. Manufacturing, which even today consumes 30 percent of the nation's electricity (Ohio Manufacturers' Association 2010), was severely damaged by this, eventually leading to energy-intensive manufacturers championing electricity policy reform through deregulation. Ultimately this resulted in what one energy writer calls the "Quiet Revolution": governments around the world began liberalizing their energy markets for both natural gas and electricity (Vaitheeswaran 2004).

This regulatory reform, unfortunately, has not been uniformly enacted throughout the United States, and even when it has, it has been too late for many struggling urban areas that depended upon manufacturing jobs for their economic health. Even worse, many cities that reside in deregulated electricity markets are captive to transmission and peak capacity constraints, leading to excessive capacity (grid standby power) and other charges by utilities, passed through on wholesale power costs via regional transmission organizations. These capacity charges threaten the value proposition provided by deregulation.

Energy reform legislation

The reform was motivated in part by the energy shocks of the 1970s and the resulting legislation: the Natural Gas Policy Act (1978) and the Public Utilities Regulatory Policy Act (1978). Both laws were passed to deal with the energy crisis that had gripped the nation and catalyzed the onset of the Rust Belt in the Great Lakes region. The Natural Gas Policy Act froze "old" gas sold on the interstate market at unsustainable prices but rewarded companies that drilled for new natural gas production with market prices, thereby eventually alleviating the natural gas crisis. The Public Utilities Regulatory Policy Act, however, was less successful in resolving electricity problems. Its goal was to resolve electricity shortfalls by encouraging conservation and mandating that utilities purchase power from independent wholesale power producers. Nevertheless, the existing regulatory framework caused electricity prices to continue to rise even as new generation was brought on line.

Under the Public Utilities Regulatory Policy Act the individual states were to encourage new generation from small (below 80 mega-watts [MW]) facilities that used something other than fossil fuels, or used waste heat. Utilities were required to purchase power from these producers at "avoided cost," the cost the utility would have had to pay if it had built new, centralized electricity generation of a like amount. But avoided costs were not based on market prices; there was no wholesale market for electricity at the time. Instead, prices were based on "but for" forecasts, that is, the generation cost expected to be incurred had no such new generation been developed, and regulators soon found that electricity prices had no relation to market realities. Independent power producers had no incentive to innovate or to provide electricity at a lower cost (Lesser and Giacchino 2007).

By the 1990s a wholesale electricity market was beginning to develop (partly in response to the Energy Policy Act of 1992). Further, because of a sluggish economy, demand for electricity was stagnant, and surplus capacity developed. Yet power costs remained high because of the massive cost overruns and the cost-plus regulatory recovery schemes. Residential and commercial end users, with limited voice for advocacy at the time, could do little about this. Energy-intensive indus-trial users, on the other hand, had the wherewithal to influence energy policy in the United States and began to lobby for the right to bypass utilities and to take their loads to an open wholesale generation market. As a result, in 1994 deregulation was introduced to America through sweeping regulatory reform in California (Lesser and Giacchino 2007).[3] Deregulation thereafter spread throughout the nation and continues to develop to this day.

The impact of deregulation on electricity production and distribution

It has taken nearly 20 years for wholesale markets to develop for electricity, and the jury is still out on how well deregulation will work. Ohio, which first deregulated in 2001, suffered through a deep recession before wholesale electricity prices finally began to drop. Even then, states like Ohio that have restructured their energy markets continue to have electricity prices higher than those that did not (American Public Power Association 2012).

One reason why deregulation has failed in some urban areas is that the regional transmission organization (RTO) remains captured by constrained transmission. As a result, utilities are forced to maintain large and expensive amounts of standby (backup) power for peak periods of use. This results in an RTO capacity charge passed through with the wholesale price that can be on the same order of magnitude as the actual cost of electricity. Nowhere is this problem more evident than in the urban areas of northern Ohio, where a 2012 capacity auction held by the RTO resulted in an increase in capacity charges by 2015 that will approach or exceed in magnitude the wholesale price of power actually delivered. In theory, these high capacity charges should encourage utilities to build more local capacity. In fact they do not: utilities do not build new generation in an unregulated environment in response to short-term price signals, since there is no guarantee of a return on their investment. If anything, high capacity charges have the opposite effect—they encourage utilities to underinvest, thereby distorting the generation technology mix toward more expensive peaking units (Meunier 2010). The result is that utilities will pass through capacity charges—the cost of expensive standby generation—onto wholesale power costs that can be nearly as much as the cost of the power actually consumed.

But for Ohio and other midwestern states, the damage was already done before deregulation. Electricity-intensive manufacturing—e.g., steel, aluminum, glass, and chemical industries—has traditionally made up a large part of the urban workforce in Ohio. These industries struggled to remain competitive in the face of high electricity prices, and the loss of jobs severely damaged urban areas throughout the Midwest.

Yet even while generation has been deregulated, the transmission and distribution side continues to be devoid of competition. Electricity, natural gas, and telephone grids fall into what are traditionally considered to be "natural monopolies," instances where we cannot build and maintain multiple grids. The best we can do is to provide alternatives to the grid. Indeed, this was exactly what happened in the telephone industry: wireless networks provided the competition that drove down the cost of wired phone systems.

For electricity, however, utilities have no desire to see their principal asset—the grid—devalued. Not surprisingly, utilities have lobbied hard to protect this resource. For instance, one way of introducing competition for the grid is for end users to generate their own electricity on site. Utilities have perceived on-site generation, the most common form of distributed generation (DG), as a threat to the grid and have not welcomed it. Utilities have been very successful in advancing regulatory barriers to DG that continue intact to this day.

Generation alternatives

Nevertheless, the next "quiet revolution" will be the introduction of competition to the regulated side of electricity. The first place this is likely to happen will be in the shift from centralized to distributed electricity generation. It has long been thought that energy-intensive industries like steel, glass, and chemical manufacturing could be "ground zero" for rethinking how energy is generated and used in the United States. These industries consume large amounts of fossil fuels and electricity to melt scrap iron, iron ore, and sand, and to produce chemicals. Recycling the waste heat from these industries could itself generate some 5 percent of America's electricity needs. Likewise, in Gothenburg, Sweden, two refineries use waste heat to provide nearly half the 450,000 residents of that town with district heating. None of the 150 refineries in America recycles waste heat for use in residential heating (Vaitheeswaran 2004).

Utilities initially disfavored DG because they found value in economies of scale: large-scale coal plants in particular were more efficient and capable of producing less-expensive power than smaller plants. However, large-scale coal plants were not amenable to being located in crowded urban areas, rendering the waste heat produced from such plants difficult to use. Waste heat has a limited value unless buildings and homes are spaced closely together and are located near the source of the heat.

Once utilities became heavily invested in the grid, they had little interest in local generation. What's more, deregulation of the generation market cemented the utilities' distaste for DG. Utilities today nearly always favor investment in the grid, with its guaranteed return, to risky generation ventures. Indeed, the bigger the grid became, the more money utilities made. So when large-scale power users began to push for opportunities to self-generate, utilities pushed back with an assortment of obstacles, ranging from exit and standby fees to heavy-handed interconnection standards. DG was simply not cost effective except for very large industrial users.

The effects on cities were twofold. First, because cogeneration (also called "combined heat and power," or CHP) was not cost effective, few cities developed heating networks to use waste heat. And second, as large industrial users departed from the grid through the deregulation of power generation, captured urban residential and commercial users were left behind to pay a larger share of the cost overruns associated with nuclear and other expensive power. Rural residents, on the other hand, were able to avoid this capture through their cooperatives.

Successful lobbying by the clean energy industry and others, including smaller industrial users and new aggregated power purchasing cooperatives, has led to some regulatory reform. Most notably, net metering (where meters run backward when excess power from DG is placed into the grid) rules have enabled a recent increase in small-scale renewable DG. However CHP, the most cost-effective form of DG, continues to be ineligible for net metering in most jurisdictions, and standby fees continue to render most CHP projects uneconomical. Moreover, the changes that have been made have been mostly too little too late: the longtime preference for centralized power has made it difficult for cities now to develop waste heat networks similar to those that exist in Europe. A hostile regulatory environment and a lack of a heat transportation infrastructure have colluded to play a role in the decline of urban economies.

ENERGY POLICIES THAT HAVE TENDED TO SPECIFICALLY HARM MIDWESTERN CITIES

Cheap Air Conditioning

For all the angst over public policies that have led to the exodus from the Midwest to the South and Southwest, none would matter but for the advent of inexpensive air conditioning. Around the same time that the energy crisis gripped the Midwest, air conditioning had begun to be widely available, cheap, and commonplace throughout the United States. Until this transformation, the climates of the American South and Southwest were miserable to live in year-round.

It is difficult to overstate how cheap air-conditioning has changed U.S. society. It catalyzed the population boom in the South and Southwest (Cooper 1998), and it reformed the American political landscape (Pfiffner 2009).[4] We have become so dependent on air conditioning that some have likened it to a drug. Anyone who has stepped into an air-conditioned store on a hot summer day can attest to the sense of instant gratification climate control can provide. Fifty years ago a third of the U.S. population resided in the South and Southwest; now it is over half. The relocation of manufacturing, businesses, and jobs to the American South is a direct result of air conditioning and of the energy policies that made it cheap (Evans 2005).

The policy that has most enabled this transformation has been the Rural Electrification Act (REA), which provided the largely rural south with the favorable electricity rates that allowed it to grow (Diamond and Moezzi, n.d.). Without the REA, it would have taken generations longer for air conditioning to become affordable in the South, if ever. But it is hardly the only energy policy that enabled cheap air conditioning: the failure to account for external environmental costs associated with the emission of refrigerants has also served to artificially suppress the cost of air conditioning. In the 1980s, wealthier countries, such as the United States, moved away from using chlorofluorocarbons (CFCs) for air conditioning to save the atmosphere's ozone layer, but the replacement refrigerants are still highly potent greenhouse gases. North America, with 6 percent of the world's people, accounts for 40 percent of the world refrigerant market (Cox 2007). The South and the Southwest represent the vast majority of this usage—and our policies ignoring the actual cost of air conditioning have made it easier for businesses and manufacturing to move there.

In the Midwest, summers can be uncomfortably hot for short periods, but brief spans of heat are not debilitating to labor. Long periods of cold, on the other hand, can be inexpensively managed with proper clothing and heating systems. Manufacturing has historically thrived in cold climates and could not have been successfully implemented in a climate where intense heat dominated for half the year. Cities like Houston, Dallas, Atlanta, and New Orleans in the past were home to sleepy societies where work often shut down during the long summer. There was no interest by captains of industry to relocate manufacturing to the U.S. South or Southwest—or to Mexico or other subtropical countries, for that matter—due to the toll taken on both the workforce and machinery.

Cheap air conditioning changed all of that. With the emergence of mechanical cooling, working conditions in factories improved and entire manufacturing industries rose up in the South, facilitating the explosive economic development and population growth in the Sunbelt region. Air conditioning did more than make the workplace bearable; it also enabled the South to manufacture products sensitive to heat and humidity, such as textiles, color printing, pharmaceuticals, and food processing. In addition, the office environment improved, with air conditioning becoming an important factor in workplace efficiency (Steinmetz 2010). One study tested federal employees and found a 24 percent increase in output by typists when transferred from an environment without air conditioning to one with it (Cooper 1998).

Before air conditioning, the extreme heat in the South was not only uncomfortable and counterproductive, it was also a major health concern, as it facilitated the spread of disease. With the introduction of air conditioning, infant mortality was reduced and malaria eliminated (Arsenault 1984). The South became a more pleasant and attractive place to live as air conditioning and technological advances brought about improvements in public health.

Air conditioning was originally implemented in industrial and commercial settings but eventually proliferated in residential homes and automobiles, as the technology became not only cheaper, but also smaller and less dangerous with the development of nontoxic coolants. Several types of air conditioners were available on the market starting in the 1930s, but as they were both expensive and cumbersome, they remained a novelty for home use for the next 20 years. In 1951, an inexpensive, efficient window air conditioning unit was finally introduced and became popular. By 1965, central air conditioning had entered the market and could be found in 10 percent of homes in the United States (Carrier, n.d.). With technology steadily improving, most new homes were being built with central air conditioning, and window air conditioners were increasingly financially accessible (Great Achievements 2013). By 1975, air conditioning existed in 50 percent of American homes. By the 1980s, when depopulation of the Rust Belt in favor of the Sunbelt had begun in earnest, 90 percent of new homes in the South had adopted central air conditioning (Pipe Doctor Plumbing, Heating, and Air Conditioning, n.d.).

Paralleling this development was air conditioning in cars. Air conditioning in automobiles was first available as a factory-installed accessory in 1940 with the Packard line, but with the onset of World War II, growth in this sector was stunted along with the rest of the air-conditioning market. Even in the 1950s, the air-conditioned car was considered an extraordinary luxury and the ultimate status symbol, to the degree that some people in Texas drove around with their windows rolled up in the 100-degree heat just to give the impression that their car had air conditioning installed. By 1973, however, more than 80 percent of new cars in the South were being outfitted with air conditioning (Fergusson 2006).

Today we live in a very different world, where the hot climate is considered a reason to live permanently in the South rather than a reason to avoid it. This is more than a little bit due to the advent of inexpensive air conditioning. Most Americans prefer suffering through a short walk in intense heat from their air-conditioned house to their air-conditioned car to digging out of a snow drift and scraping ice off their car windows. Corporations are eager to blame their decisions to relocate manufacturing to the Sunbelt on unfavorable tax rates, unions, and other dollars and cents considerations. But one wonders how much executive distaste for midwestern winters controls decisions about relocations for manufacturing. So long as air conditioning is cheap and readily available, no amount of tax incentives or union concessions can compete with a lifestyle preference for mild winters.

Promotion of Trucking over Railroads and Waterways

The U.S. government undertook a major social initiative in the 1950s and 1960s designed to make interstate transportation by automobile easier and less expensive. This energy policy would have interesting and momentous consequences for the American Midwest. The program was promulgated during the Eisenhower Administration as the American Federal-Aid Highway Act. The initiative consisted of the development of a national trust for the purchase, through eminent domain, of large amounts of private land, and the subsequent building of an interstate highway system unlike anything ever seen. In short, the United States embarked upon a strategy to build a highway and bridge infrastructure that would transform the American landscape forever, making travel across the country easier, faster, and less expensive.

Change the landscape it did—and a great deal more: it forever altered American culture. Trucking benefited relative to railroads and waterways, helping it to become the transportation mode of choice for shipping a wide range of goods and materials throughout America. This contributed to the decline of the traditional midwestern transportation economy—railroads and waterways—and with it, to the decline of the Great Lakes port communities.

Developing a network of major interstate highways was certainly a laudable public policy: driving time and costs were reduced significantly, and travel efficiencies inured to the benefit of all, as the expenses of transporting goods dropped. Moreover, the indirect subsidy to the automobile industry was a short-term boost to the Great Lakes cities that manufactured trucks, automobiles, and parts. However, the long-term effect on these cities manifested itself later in another, less desirable manner: Great Lakes shipping ports and railroad terminals became largely obsolete. The advent of subsidized high-speed interstate highways, combined with subsidized cheap gasoline and diesel fuel, inevitably led trucking to become the preferred method of transportation of goods and materials across America. From Duluth to Buffalo, Great Lake cities watched their once-busy harbors turn into ghost ports. Railroad terminals across the Midwest also shut down, and with them disappeared the livelihoods of many Midwestern families who had worked on those trains for generations.

Although the majority of the people in America at that time were located in the Midwest or the Northeast, the new superhighways crisscrossed the country in equally spaced patterns without regard to population. The goal of the new interstate system was, after all, to make travel among the states easier—and this included crossing the underpopulated regions of the South and Southwest. The consequence, however, was to indirectly support migration to the rural South and Southwest. The new interstate highway system not only helped render obsolete the traditional transportation economy of the Midwest, it also subsidized the inevitable movement of workers to the South and Southwest by making it cheaper to transport goods and materials to and from those regions.

Failure to Embrace Change in Energy Policy

A third category of energy policy that generally has had a troubling result for midwestern cities stems from a behavioral disorder common to all leaders who set public policy: the failure to identify and understand social change, and to respond to that change in a timely way. The general reason for this shortcoming is that vested interests, especially in the trillion-dollar-a-year energy business, usually resist change mightily. Steps that may be good for society in general may not be good for a particular sector of the economy, and that segment may be particularly persuasive in helping government leaders to set public policy. In a society where policy is made by competing advocacy groups, alignment with the status quo has a significant advantage.

The best example of how this culture can be shortsighted relates to the political resistance to the adoption of Corporate Average Fuel Economy (CAFE) standards. These guidelines were originally established as a means of improving automobile efficiency in response to the 1973–1974 Arab oil embargo, which caused crude oil prices to triple and exposed the United States to vulnerabilities in relying on imported petroleum. In the period leading up to this first oil shock, new-car fleet fuel economy had dipped from 14.8 miles per gallon (mpg) in 1967 to 12.9 mpg in 1974. With the Energy Policy Conservation Act of 1975, CAFE standards required the passenger-car program to achieve new-car fleet fuel economy standards of 27.5 mpg by 1985.

Control over the passenger-car program remained in the hands of the Secretary of Transportation, and standards could be adjusted within a range of 26 to 27.5 mpg without requiring Energy Policy Conservation Act amendments and the subsequent approval of Congress. Under the same act, the National Highway Traffic Safety Administration (NHTSA) was given authority over the structure and alterations of the light-truck program (Yacobucchi and Bamberger 2007). CAFE standards set by the NHTSA were only held to the "maximum feasible fuel economy standards," broadly defined by Congress as having technological feasibility, economic practicability, and consideration for the effect of other standards on fuel economy and the need of the nation to conserve energy (Moulton, n.d.).

The predictable reaction from the automobile and petroleum industries was to resist any change as long as possible. This strategy worked. Since achieving the first target of improving fuel economy to 27.5 mpg in 1985, no improvement in standards has been made, and none is anticipated until 2017. Further, those energy efficiency standards that were adopted were easily circumvented. A sport utility vehicle (SUV) loophole was exploited that encouraged American families to buy trucks (including SUVS) instead of cars. Light trucks with a gross vehicle weight rating of 8,500 pounds are exempt from CAFE standards. For light trucks under this weight, fuel economy standards only increased by 2 mpg, from 20.2 to 22.2, during the 15 years between 1992 and 2007 (NHTSA 2013). Buoyed by the SUV market, truck sales in America exploded, eventually overtaking car sales by the late 1990s.

Unfortunately, this only served to put the U.S. automobile industry at a competitive disadvantage to its European and Japanese counterparts, who continued to build more efficient cars. As oil prices rose sharply in the mid-2000s, truck sales faltered (see Figure 7.3). By 2008, with the economy in free fall, car sales caught up with truck sales for the first time in over a decade, as sales for trucks dropped to half of their 1990 numbers. American car companies, notably the Detroit Three (GM, Ford, and Chrysler), were in no position to weather the storm, as profits had become heavily dependent on SUV and truck sales, and these firms required government support to stay afloat. Resistance to the CAFE standards, in response to a perceived threat to the viability of the American automobile industry, contributed to the near bankruptcy of this entire U.S. industry. Midwestern cities, especially Great Lakes cities, suffered grievously in the process.

The resistance to deregulation of electricity markets and to DG provides other examples where vested interests have conspired to thwart job creation in the Midwest, especially in traditional manufacturing industries such as steel, glass, and chemicals. The overall dependence of centralized generation upon the importation of fossil fuels has intensified the high cost of power for midwestern urban areas, insofar as this region has traditionally been an importer of coal, oil, and gas. DG, on the other hand, tends to rely on local fuels such as waste heat, solar, and wind, and as a result usually returns more money to the local economy.

Figure 7.3 U.S. Car and Truck Sales, 1950–2010

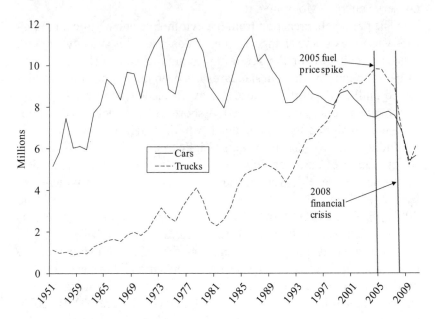

NOTE: "Trucks" includes Sport Utility Vehicles (SUVs).
SOURCE: Ward's Automotive Group (2012).

According to one expert, as much as 50 percent of every dollar spent on conventional centralized generation leaves the community. However, for renewable DG, about $1.40 is returned to the local community for every dollar spent (Sovacool and Watts 2009).

There will always be resistance to change by those who stand to lose from it. But when it comes to energy, policymakers are particularly vulnerable to short-sighted decisions. The stakes for energy generation choice are enormous. We can expect parties to aggressively advocate their own interests in the status quo. Unfortunately for midwestern cities, this intransigence has too frequently been harmful to local economies.

ENERGY POLICES THAT WILL HELP MIDWESTERN CITIES RECOVER

U.S. energy policy in the past 70 years has encouraged migration of jobs and residents out of the Midwest, and this needs to change. Yet we do not want to rebuild midwestern cities at the expense of rural areas, or at the expense of the South or Southwest. Certainly no one would advocate a return to poverty and misery for the South so that the Midwest could once again enjoy a more robust economy. Similarly, with so much of our commercial activity now moved to the suburbs, we cannot abandon those spaces. But we can at least try to redress some of the imbalances in our energy policies that have so decimated the cities in the Great Lakes region. New approaches that do not directly encourage migration out of the cities certainly would help. Some of the most important energy strategies that could be deployed are those that can help deliver clean, inexpensive energy to midwestern communities. Several of those policies are set forth in the following discussion.

Policies That Encourage DG

The shift to clean and high-efficiency energy systems is key to both sustainability and economic growth. This change will transform virtually every aspect of the economy, transportation systems, and construction, as well as the configuration of human settlements in the twenty-first century. Urban areas in particular are highly vulnerable to paradigm shifts in technology. Technological innovation is the "principal mechanism underlying the successive epochs of urban evolution." Throughout the history of American cities, changes in transportation and energy have been the root cause of fundamental transformation (Berry 1991). Forces are working together now that will transform the structure of urban society.[5] Cities throughout the United States need to understand these forces and prepare themselves for the changes that are coming.

One of those fundamental transformations will be the shift away from centralized generation toward a DG model. Developing a regulatory environment that is friendly to DG will help position communities for growth and sustainability. This will not only reduce the costs of energy in the inner city through such mechanisms as CHP, but will also create jobs locally. Moreover, since DG tends to be cleaner than centralized generation, it also tends to make for a more pleasant environment in which to live and work.

Advantages of DG for the Midwest

Midwestern cities are well placed to play a leading role in the development of DG. That is because the many locations where DG is likely to first become economical are those involving generation at industrial sites, and midwestern cities are among the nation's leaders in generation capability from industrial waste heat. According to the Environmental Protection Agency (EPA), Ohio, for instance, produces enough waste heat to "generate the equivalent power of 8 nuclear power plants" (Margonelli 2010). The Oak Ridge National Laboratory projects that waste-heat recovery systems can be available for around $1,500 per kilowatt (kW) installed (Margonelli 2010)—a price that should be attractive for electricity-intensive manufacturing. The potential to avoid future carbon taxes and to create jobs also makes this of considerable interest to midwestern cities.[6]

Three other factors will likely lead to the advancement of DG in the Midwest. The first is the April 2012 adoption of new federal EPA Clean Air Act pollution standards (the so-called Boiler MACT regulations [EPA 2013]) that will cause area-wide capital investment into new, cleaner steam-generation capacity.[7] Many midwestern industries have big, old coal boilers producing large volumes (over 100,000 pounds per hour) of steam. These boilers tend to work continuously, are inefficient, and require as fuel low-sulfur "compliance coal" (Casten 2012).[8] Industrial users that are considering an upgrade of their coal boilers in order to comply with the new rules may find this to be a convenient time to convert to more efficient heat-creating systems, such as CHP. With this approach, electricity made as a byproduct of generating heat can be converted for use on site, thereby dramatically improving systemic efficiency.

The second factor relates to grid congestion, especially in the Great Lakes areas. Northern Ohio, for example, has been grid constrained for a number of years. As a result, and in anticipation of retiring old coal-burning generation facilities, First Energy now plans to undertake a $1 billion transmission upgrade (Funk 2012). Indeed, the regional transmission organization (RTO) that Ohio utilities belong to, PJM, anticipates that there will be changes in the next several years to the generation fleet producing power for Ohio on an "unprecedented scale." PJM announced in May 2012 that it had purchased in an auction a "record amount of new generation" for 2015–2016. Northern Ohio suffered the highest prices in the PJM capacity market—$357 per MW, more than twice the PJM unconstrained price of $136 per MW (PJM 2012). All of these costs will be passed through to urban residents and businesses in the form of capacity charges on wholesale electricity bills. One expert projects that capacity costs alone in First Energy's Ohio region will increase by 700 percent by 2014 over today's charges, reaching $0.0317 per kilowatt-hour (kWh) by 2015 for a user with a 50 percent load factor (Brakey 2012). Such costs could be avoided if DG were strategically adopted in response to the constrained grid.

The third factor relates to another threat midwestern urban economies face: carbon regulation. Driven in part by EPA requirements to either clean up or shut down old coal plants and in part by a depressed natural gas market, much of coal electricity generation will be replaced by natural gas in the coming years. According to one recent study, even accounting for a marginal increase in life-cycle greenhouse gases generated through hydraulic fracturing, burning natural gas emits less than half the carbon that burning coal does (Hultman et al. 2011). This reduction in carbon emissions will likely become a critical element to the viability of midwestern economies, especially in urban areas that are so dependent on manufacturing, as increasing restrictions are placed on carbon emissions. CHP will in all likelihood become the most compelling solution to the problem of reducing greenhouse gas emissions: it not only uses natural gas (or biomass) as its principal fuel, it is also far more efficient than centralized generation.

CHP systems, however, do not as a rule enjoy the benefits of net metering. Utilities do not have to pay the full value of electricity when taking power back onto the grid. Instead, they pay what they consider to be the value of displaced power, calculated at the cost of generation at some distant centralized point. The actual electrons may be delivered to a manufacturer down the road 100 yards, but the utility is not required to compensate for the strategic location of the power generation.[9]

This policy, along with the general one of guaranteeing a "cost plus" recovery on expenditures on the still-regulated grid, has led to the traditional utility being incentivized to allocate as much of its costs as possible to building and operating the grid, and as little as possible to generateing electricity. Not surprisingly, we see as a result widely disparate estimates for the cost of power production from centralized generation. Utility accounting under this system, which may not include such things as the anticipated cost of decommissioning a power plant, typically sets a low generation cost for nuclear power. Yet the cost for nuclear energy generation, by most measurements, is very high (Vaitheeswaran 2004).[10]

Needed changes in policies

As noted by energy pundit Amory Lovins of the Rocky Mountain Institute, the old model of centralized generation with a ubiquitous grid was based upon the twentieth-century idea that generation was less reliable than the grid. But the twenty-first century reality turns this model on its head: today, generation, especially gas turbine, is more reliable than the grid. Accordingly, one of the fundamental reasons for centralized generation no longer exists. As Lovins (2001) notes, today "the cheapest, most reliable power" is that which is "produced at or near the customers" (p. xiii).

For DG to take hold in the Midwest, several policy changes will be required.

- Net metering and/or improved sales options for excess generation. Currently, in most jurisdictions excess generation cannot be "net metered" (i.e., the meter does not run backward), and must be sold back into the grid at the unbundled "generation rate" (i.e., the generation charge, without the transmission or distribution charge) for power. Under such circumstances, the return for generation is significantly diminished: there is no value attributed to the strategic location of the generation near a market. For smaller systems (below 138 kilovolts [kV]), however, utilities are often required to purchase the power only at the displaced generation price (i.e., the "avoided cost of generation.") In Ohio, the avoided cost has been set as low as $0.012 per kWh (Wissman 2012). Accordingly, smaller systems will likely not even recover the going rate for unbundled wholesale generation. Net-metering rules should be established for CHP, or at least regulations should allow for better sales options for excess power.

- Reduced standby rates. At the outset, it should be noted that the public policy case for the assessment of any standby fee is by no means clear. A strong argument can be made that both utilities and consumers benefit greatly from DG, and it is counterproductive to charge standby fees (Casten 2003). Any measures that reduce the need for repair or construction of distribution and transmission assets inures to the benefit of all users, not just the DG end users (Casten 2003; Miller 2012). Nevertheless, regulatory bodies are inclined to accept the utility arguments for the need for standby fees. The problem, then, is to determine what charges are reasonable under the circumstances—and what charges can be borne by distributed generators without rendering the project unviable. The EPA has determined that, unless the customer can avoid at least 90 percent of its otherwise applicable rate costs, CHP will not be viable (Weston et al. 2009). Unfortunately, this number is one that is not commonly met with existing standby charges in most jurisdictions. In a study by the Midwest Clean Energy Application Center, avoided-cost percentages from utilities in Iowa, for instance, ranged from a low of 74 to a high of 81 percent among Iowa investor-owned utilities (Miller 2012). Policies need to be established either doing away with or making manageable standby charges.

- Microgrid development. One way to capture the full potential of DG is through a distribution system architecture called a "microgrid." Unlike DG, a microgrid consists of more than a single point of generation. Like DG, however, a microgrid should have the ability to isolate itself (islanding) from the utility's distribution system during a grid disturbance. Islanding has the potential to give a higher level of reliability to end users than that provided by the macrogrid system as a whole.[11] The typical microgrid uses DG and cogeneration to provide both electricity and heat to multiple customers joined together on a local network. Microgrids also offer potential advantages in power quality and reliability over macrogrids, which tend to provide homogeneous power quality when customers may have heterogeneous requirements (Neville 2008). There is currently considerable uncertainty over how microgrids will be regulated, but under most jurisdictions, it appears that only utilities can operate microgrids. There will need to be clarity in the regulations over how microgrids may be operated and who may operate them before they can be deployed.

However, the policies necessary to enable DG are not just regulatory in nature. Urban universities, for instance, can play a critical leadership role in preparing cities for a transition to DG. To accomplish this, universities should change their approach toward technical education for the energy industry, and federal and state governments need to support this shift. Policies that promote DG will have little value if there is not a workforce that is capable of deploying the new technologies, and, importantly, of understanding the value proposition associated with DG. Without such a workforce, transactional costs threaten to slow the advancement of DG.

For centralized generation, professional services have traditionally comprised a small percentage of the total project cost. Accordingly, utilities have engaged the biggest and most expensive law firms, banks, architectural and engineering firms—and money has been no object. But in the world of DG, projects may cost $300,000 instead of $300 million. Yet many of the same legal, regulatory, financial, and engineering issues arise in small projects as in large projects; transactional costs do not go down in proportion to project size. Today's energy-systems professional needs to be nimble, trained in multiple disciplines, and capable of assessing value inexpensively.

State and federal resources should be brought to bear on urban four-year engineering and engineering technology programs throughout America, but especially in the Midwest, to create comprehensive, cross-disciplinary energy-systems training. Under current university models, applied technology is not a priority, and certainly the social sciences are not. Universities are rewarded with large research grants with generous overhead compensation for energy technology, especially through federally funded programs such as the National Science Foundation. But applied engineering programs and research on social impediments to the adoption of advanced energy do not generally get this same sort of support.

Midwestern urban areas have the most to lose if a transition to DG is not enabled. Ohio, for instance, is highly vulnerable to a carbon tax or a cap and trade system. Roughly 88 percent of Ohio's power generation comes from burning coal. In the meantime, Ohio, which is ranked seventh nationally in population, is ranked sixth in total energy consumption, fourth in industrial energy consumption, and fourth in greenhouse gas emissions (Consortium for Energy, Economics, and the Environment 2008). In short, Ohio's economy is dependent on traditional forms of energy generation that are patently unsustainable. Urban universities in Ohio and other midwestern states must take the lead in helping to rewrite regulatory law and in retraining their workforces for the inevitable paradigm shift from central to distributed power generation. State and federal resources need to enable this transition to be made without a massive disruption of midwestern economies.

Exploitation of Shale Formations

One of the most exciting and promising developments for the urban economies of both the Midwest and the Northeast has been improvements in drilling and completion techniques in the oil and gas industry. Specifically, horizontal drilling and new hydrofracturing technologies have enabled oil and gas companies to produce hydrocarbons from organically rich shale deposits that were laid down in sedimentary basins hundreds of millions of years ago. Previously, shale formations had been too impermeable to produce hydrocarbons in commercial quantities. Now, suddenly, vast commercially producible oil and gas reserves exist in areas of Ohio, Pennsylvania, West Virginia, North Dakota, and other places around the world. For the first time since the 1800s, the Midwest is poised to not only be self-sufficient, but even to export oil and gas.

This will of course be a badly needed shot in the arm for the flagging economies of the Midwest. Related job creation in financial and legal centers such as Pittsburgh, Cleveland, Columbus, Akron, Canton, and Youngstown has already begun. More will be coming as drilling picks up. In addition, shale development tends to be more service-industry intensive than traditional oil and gas exploration because of the relatively high cost of drilling and completing wells, and the high rate of production decline (requiring more drilling). In other words, there will be more wells and more completions, yet fewer failures, driving a robust new oil and gas service industry. Even though much of the early wealth to be generated from this industry will be for rural landowners, inevitably the urban areas of the Midwest will benefit greatly, not only from the reduced hydrocarbon prices, but also from professional service companies locating in cities to be close to a skilled workforce and to transportation hubs.

Pennsylvania has been the forerunner in economic development as a result of shale drilling. According to one study by Penn State University, the Marcellus Shale development has led directly to 44,000 jobs in 2009 in that state, creating around $3.9 billion in economic value added to Pennsylvania, with $8 billion more in 2010 and $10 billion more in 2011 (Considine, Watson, and Blumsack 2010). Likewise, in Ohio, economists have estimated that by 2014, 64,000 jobs will be supported as a result of developing the Utica Shale, adding some $4.9 billion to the state's gross domestic product (Thomas et al. 2012)

But setting aside these promising employment numbers resulting directly from oil and gas exploration, perhaps the best news for midwestern urban economies will be the long-term source of cheap natural gas. Shale gas has transformed the American energy landscape almost overnight: between 2006 and 2011, natural gas prices dropped from over $10 per mcf to under $4 per mcf (U.S. Energy Information Agency 2012a). Shale gas, which comprised less than 2 percent of the gas produced in the United States in 2000, now comprises 37 percent—and is rising (Yergin 2012). In the meantime, U.S. greenhouse gas emissions in 2012 were the lowest since 1992, due in principal part to the rapid replacement of coal with natural gas as a source of electricity (U.S. Energy Information Agency 2012b).[12]

States such as Ohio will no longer be experiencing huge trade deficits due to the purchase of oil from the Middle East. This newfound source of oil and gas promises a stable, 20–30-year supply of inexpensive hydrocarbons to heat homes, to generate electricity, and to fuel transportation. The Energy Information Agency projects natural gas prices of between $4 and $8 per mcf through 2035 as a result of the "shale gale" (U.S. Energy Information Agency 2012a). Further, petrochemical companies, which also rely on long-term, inexpensive and stable supplies of natural gas for feedstock, can justify the financial commitment to locate or expand manufacturing in the Midwest.

State and federal policies should encourage shale development. Regulation of the industry must be tight, sure, and comprehensive; any spills or contamination from wastewater generated by drilling will set back development enormously. State regulatory agencies and state geo-logical surveys must be completely independent from the oil and gas industry under their purview and be fully funded. This can be done through severance and other taxes generated by oil and gas production and also through long-overdue taxes on imported oil, especially from those locations where U.S. military presence is required to safely transport oil to American ports. This latter policy, more than any, has the potential to provide ample resources to enable the safe production of U.S. oil and gas supplies from unconventional sources while restoring wealth to American cities.

Importantly, midwestern cities should not use the newfound hydrocarbon wealth to go back to business as usual. While the oil and gas reserves located in shale beds in the Midwest and the Northeast provide a more climate-friendly alternative to burning coal, they are still an exhaustible resource that emits large amounts of carbon into the atmosphere. These reserves should be considered as a bridge to an economy based on hydrogen, electric transportation, and renewable energy generation—an economy where oil and gas are used primarily in the petrochemical sector rather than the energy sector. Policymakers in the Midwest have an opportunity to do something that their counterparts in Texas, Louisiana, and even the federal government have failed to do with their respective oil and gas largesse: plan for the inevitable transition to alternative energy supplies without a massive disruption of the economy.

Policies That Reflect the Actual Costs of Transportation and Power Delivery

For some 80 years our energy policies have placed the burden of growth in rural locales on the urban areas. That policy must be reversed. Now it is time for the rural areas, or at least the suburbs, to support growth in the inner city. The same sort of program that led to the development of rural electrification should now be put into place in our inner cities: subsidized loans and grants for DG and access to cheap, federally supported electricity. Municipal utilities in particular would benefit from having priority for the cheapest electricity available, from which savings could be used to attract business, industry, and residents back to the city.

Monetizing some of the external costs of power generation and gasoline consumption would also help cities, especially in the Midwest. For instance, if the actual cost of air conditioning were passed on to consumers, manufacturing management might reach a different conclusion about the benefits of relocating operations from the Midwest to the South or Southwest. Similarly, if the total cost of transportation were passed on to commuters, residents might reach a different conclusion about the benefits of moving ever farther from the city.

Just as we have seen decades of policy subsidizing rural electrification over urban electrification, we have also seen decades of policy subsidizing rural transportation over urban transportation. This is another policy that must be reversed. We cannot now abandon our reliance on interstate highways. However, we can fund programs that make life easier for residents of midwestern cities. This begins with better transportation systems.

Better, faster, and more comfortable public transportation would certainly be a major first step. It will require a significant and continuous subsidy to sustain such a program, because it will take decades to see the demographic response. In many of the Great Lakes cities, the hardest part about transportation is driving in snow. Public transportation could alleviate much of this problem.

Winter travel is problematic not just for commuting, however; it is also a problem for walking in the city. Many midwestern cities cannot afford to effectively plow and salt roads and sidewalks, and walking becomes an adventure. Funds should be directed to cities to enable them to respond quickly to winter storms. Sidewalks and crosswalks can be heated by underground steam systems to keep them free of ice. Better still, underground passageways can be built connecting downtown urban centers such as universities, museums, sports venues, commercial districts, arts districts, and office parks. Houston has such an underground tunnel system in its downtown, and it is used mostly in the hot, humid summer. A number of Canadian cities have downtown indoor walkways; Montreal's underground complex is so vast that it is known as the *ville intérieure*, the "indoor city." Midwestern cities could have a similar system in their downtown areas for winter activities. To be sure, these sorts of programs are not easily accomplished, especially in a bad economy. But the rural electrification program was established in a far worse economy. It will take the same sort of effort to rebuild midwestern cities to their former glory.

Regional Energy Planning

The Midwest today has an opportunity to reimagine sustainable industrialization. More than anything else, a return to a healthy manufacturing base would lead to a revitalization of urban areas. Manufacturing has long been the lifeblood of the midwestern urban economy, but it is also an energy-intensive business, especially for such industries that produce aluminum, steel, chemicals, and glass. Manufacturers account for roughly one-half of U.S. natural gas and 30 percent of its electricity consumption. Accordingly, a secure, reliable, and affordable source of electricity is a top priority for midwestern manufacturers. Those manufacturers for which electricity costs make up an especially significant portion of their product costs are most vulnerable to rapid rate increases (Ohio Manufacturers' Association 2010). The ongoing decline in manufacturing jobs throughout America has accelerated in recent years, reflecting not just high electricity costs, but also the return to $100 per bbl oil and the "high priced fuel syndrome." Ohio has lost some 117,000 manufacturing jobs in the the period of 2008–2012 alone—the second highest total in America (Thomas 2012).

With foresight and planning, the Midwest can develop energy policies to help reverse this trend. As outlined in this chapter, forces are coming together today that necessitate rethinking industrialization in the Midwest. Rising electricity capacity charges, EPA Boiler MACT laws, carbon emission reduction mandates, and the development of shale gas all demand that midwestern policymakers formulate strategies for enabling DG and a conversion of transportation fleets to natural gas or electricity.

Urban areas would benefit from collaboration between local governments and industries to develop regional energy-planning scenarios. This will be especially important in older, more densely populated areas of the Great Lakes and the Midwest, where DG holds so much promise. DG, especially CHP, will not be a "one size fits all" application; every situation requires an analysis specific to those circumstances. However, planning can help manufacturers identify strategies to use "off the shelf" technologies when possible.

In particular, for regions with a large variety of manufacturing and other electricity-intensive users, a coordinated CHP program can be useful to organizations trying to find a fit for their power and heat needs. Such a program might be set up to address three strategic areas:

1) commercial buildings and small industrial applications—deploying similar equipment and similar financial goals and capabilities;

2) institutional facilities—usually with larger power and heat requirements and with much longer-term financing abilities, which are more amenable to Energy Savings Company (ESCO) savings structures (arrangements whereby energy savings realized are used to fund efficiency upgrades); and

3) major industrial and district heating CHPs, where large-scale power is generated, visibility is high, and the returns to the districts and industries involved are potentially great.

The development of an energy master plan might begin with a Geographical Information System–based "energy map" that is prepared at a neighborhood, local authority, or subregional scale. It would include an assessment of existing building energy demands as a baseline, identify likely locations for new business development, and assess effects on energy demand. It might also include a "heat map," identifying anchor heat loads, such as large public buildings (King and Shaw 2010).

These energy maps could reveal CHP-generated district heating opportunities that local authorities or project managers might be willing to support. They may also inform growth options and serve as the starting point for energy planning for developers. A decentralized energy master plan could include technical, planning, financial, and legal support—all better enabling manufacturers to evaluate DG opportunities.

Local energy planning can provide a road map for manufacturing to identify strategies for developing on-site DG opportunities. For the reasons discussed earlier, transactional costs threaten small-scale generation. Manufacturers are generally unwilling to spend hundreds of thousands of dollars identifying potential DG projects. Regional energy planning reduces these costs for manufacturers by identifying not only potential projects, but also possible collaborators and sources of funding.

Traditionally, regional energy plans have been developed in the United States to address climate action plans and to decrease reliance on fossil fuels.[13] However, the type of energy-mapping strategies that were developed for London, England, will be required to enable manufacturing to identify opportunities to provide district heating through CHP projects. That approach included a 10-stage undertaking with, among other things, data gathering, project identification, financial modeling, and feasibility studies (King and Shaw 2010). This sort of information would significantly enhance manufacturing's appetite for undertaking DG.

Finally, any regional energy study should include an investigation into the transformation of transportation fleets to compressed or liquefied natural gas and to electric vehicles. Notwithstanding the advent of oil development from shale formations such as the Bakken in North Dakota and the Utica in Ohio, the United States will continue to be an oil-importing nation. By substituting natural gas or electricity for gasoline and diesel for our transportation fleets, we can reduce our nearly billion-dollar-per-day trade deficit (Bureau of Economic Analysis 2013), and in the process decrease greenhouse gas emissions. With natural gas trading for a fraction of the cost of oil for the foreseeable future, this transition would save money and repatriate dollars domestically.

Urban areas can facilitate this change by identifying infrastructure needs and by developing strategic locations for refueling and recharging stations. In areas where shale gas is abundant, additional planning may enable the development of refueling stations near gathering, transportation, compression, storage, and distribution infrastructure. Water use and discharge planning would further enhance shale development, as would road use and maintenance planning.

CONCLUSIONS

In American society, policy is set by advocacy. Unfortunately, under this system, those entities with a preference toward maintaining the status quo have a significant advantage in setting policy—even when that course of action is not in the general public interest. No field of enterprise suffers from this problem more than does the energy industry, in which the stakes are enormous, and change can be disruptive. Incumbent industries have propagated the notion that we cannot replace our current energy models with new ones. Even when unbiased information is set forth, the public struggles to understand it; an unsuspecting citizenry is unable to differentiate between a vested interest and an independent expert.

This problem helps to explain why programs such as subsidies for rural electrification continue to exist some 40 years after 99 percent of American farms have been connected to the grid. It also is a cautionary message to policymakers who may want to rectify the imbalance: energy policies that enable and encourage migration from the cities, especially from those in the Midwest, will be very difficult to change. Not only do these cities face the problem of overcoming vested interests, they are also dealing with reduced political might as a result of decades of population and wealth flight. It will require considerable political courage for policymakers to undertake the sort of long-term commitments to energy policy that will be needed for midwestern cities to return to the robust economies they once enjoyed. But this starts by recognizing the complicity that long-existing energy policies have had in creating the decline of urban economies in the first place.

Notes

The author gratefully acknowledges research and editing support for this chapter from Su Gao and Srikanth Sivashankaran.

1. The federal portion of this does not vary; it is around $0.18 per gallon. For a discussion of the history of the excise tax, see Pirog (2010).
2. As noted in Slivinski (2009), rural electricity is just one of a number of utility services subsidized by urban dwellers.
3. California was also the location for the first failures in deregulation. A combination of fixed retail prices and rising costs of generation, together with some market manipulation by Enron and others, nearly left several California utilities insolvent.
4. Pfiffner (2009) argues that the current partisan culture has its roots in the demographic change brought on by the advent of air conditioning.
5. Berry (1991) argues that massive change following technical innovation accelerates during times of "stagflation," such as we are arguably experiencing in America today. This acceleration in growth comes as a result of a combination of investors recognizing opportunity in depressed prices and public officials recognizing that help is needed to get the economy moving again. Both forces are at work today.
6. According to Policy Matters Ohio (2012), as many as 20,000 jobs could be created from cogeneration, and the release into the atmosphere of 13 metric tons of carbon dioxide would be avoided.

7. The Ohio Public Utilities Commission resolved in February 2012 to develop an educational forum to begin a pilot program to advance and share information about combined heat and power as a strategy for compliance with the new Boiler MACT rules. "Boiler MACT" refers to the set of adjustments to the Clean Air Act that the U.S. Environmental Protection Agency instituted December 20, 2012, specific to certain categories of boilers and solid waste incinerators. The adjustments made include emission limits for certain pollutants specifically targeted at categories of boilers and solid waste incinerators, changes to the subcategories of boilers in establishing standards, a revised implementation timeline, and adhering to established standards for the "highest emitting of the highest 0.4 percent of boilers" (EPA 2013).

8. Compliance coals run around $90 per ton, or $3.60 per mmbtu (million British Thermal Units, which measure energy content); 1 million btus are roughly equivalent to 1,000 cubic fee (mcf) of natural gas. If a boiler were 75 percent efficient, this means that the cost of delivered steam would be $4.80 per mmbtu.

9. Ohio's original net-metering law was enacted in 1999 as part of the state's electric-industry restructuring legislation. The Public Utilities Commission of OHIO (PUCO) later revised its net-metering rules in March 2007, prompted by the federal Energy Policy Act of 2005. Initially, PUCO required utilities to credit customers' net excess generation at the utility's full retail rate. However, in June 2002, the Ohio Supreme Court ruled that each utility must credit excess generation to the customer at the utility's unbundled generation rate. See http://energy.gov/savings/net-metering-29 (accessed October 24, 2013).

10. This policy of allocating costs when possible to the grid rather than to generation, in addition to ensuring the cost-plus return, makes certain that the utility generation is highly competitive in the wholesale market.

11. For purposes of this discussion, nongrid-connected microgrids are not considered, although these may have some application in more isolated areas.

12. Not all observers agree that shale gas has been a significant contributor to this trend. See Howarth (2011).

13. See, for example, Kane County (2011) and San Diego Association of Governments (1994).

References

American Petroleum Institute. n.d. Oil and Natural Gas Overview: API Key Tax Issues. Washington, DC: API. http://www.api.org/oil-and-natural-gas-overview/industry-economics/tax-issues/api-key-tax-issues (accessed April 17, 2013).

———. 2013. Oil and Natural Gas Overview: Motor Fuel Taxes. Washington, DC: API. http://www.api.org/oil-and-natural-gas-overview/industry-economics/fuel-taxes (accessed April 18, 2013).

American Public Power Association. 2012. Retail Electric Rates in Deregu-

lated and Regulated States: 2011 Update. Washington, DC: APPA. http://www
.publicpower.org/files/PDFs/RKW_Final_-_2011_update.pdf   (accessed
April 16, 2013.

Arsenault, Raymond. 1984. "The End of a Long Hot Summer: The Air Con-
ditioner and Southern Culture." *The Journal of Southern History* 50(4):
597–628.

Berry, Brian J.L. 1991. "Long Waves in American Urban Evolution." In *Our
Changing Cities*, John Fraser Hart, ed. Baltimore: Johns Hopkins University Press, pp. 31–50.

Brakey, Mike. 2012. "Skyrocketing FirstEnergy-Ohio Capacity Costs: Revo-
lutionary Pricing, Contracting, and Consumption of Electricity." Cleveland,
OH: Brakey Energy. Available by request at http://www.brakeyenergy.com.

Bureau of Economic Analysis. 2013. U.S. International Trade in Goods and
Services, May 2013. News Release. Washington, DC: U.S. Bureau of
Economic Analysis. http://www.bea.gov/newsreleases/international/trade/
tradnewsrelease.htm (accessed July 31, 2013).

Carrier. n.d. Carrier History. Farmington, CN: Carrier. http://www.carrier.com/
carrier/en/us/about/history (accessed April 17, 2013).

Casten, Sean. 2003. "Are Standby Rates Ever Justified? The Case Against
Electric Utility Standby Charges as a Response to On-Site Generation." *The
Electricity Journal* 16(4): 56–65.

———. 2012. "EPAs Boiler MACT Is an Economic Growth Opportunity." *Grist*,
June   15.   http://www.grist.org/article/epas-boiler-mact-is-an-economic
-growth-opportunity/ (accessed April 17, 2013).

Considine, Timothy J., Robert Watson, and Seth Blumsack. 2010. "The Economic Impacts of the Pennsylvania Marcellus Shale Natural Gas Play: An
Update." University Park, PA: Department of Energy and Mineral Engineering, Pennsylvania State University. http://www.marcelluscoalition.org/
wp-content/uploads/2010/05/PA-Marcellus-Updated-Economic-Impacts
-5.24.10.3.pdf (accessed April 17, 2013).

Consortium for Energy, Economics, and the Environment. 2008. "An Ohio
Perspective on Energy and Climate Change." Athens, OH: Voinovich
School of Leadership and Public Affairs, Ohio University.

Cooper, Gail. 1998. *Air-Conditioning America: Engineers and the Controlled
Environment 1900–1960*. Baltimore: Johns Hopkins University Press.

Cox, Stan. 2007. "Air-Conditioned Nation." *Synthesis/Regeneration* 42(Winter). http://www.greens.org/s-r/42/42-08.html (accessed April 17, 2013).

D'Ambrosio, Peter, and Kevin O'Brien. 2009. Nuclear Power Projects—
New Risks Require New Approaches. Chicago: American Bar Asso-
ciation.   http://www.winston.com/siteFiles/Publications/Nuclear_Power_
Projects_D%27Ambrosio_Article.pdf (accessed July 31, 2013).

Diamond, Rick, and Mithra Moezzi. n.d. "Changing Trends: A Brief History of the U.S. Household Consumption of Energy, Water, Food, Beverages, and Tobacco." Berkeley, CA: Lawrence Berkeley National Laboratory. http://www.epb.lbl.gov/homepages/Rick_Diamond/docs/lbn/55011-trends.pdf (accessed April 17, 2013).

Economist. 2010. "Oil and the Current Account." February 10. http://www.economist.com/blogs/freeexchange/2010/02/americas_trade_deficit (accessed April 16, 2013).

El Nasser, Haya. 2011. "Suburban Growth Focused on Inner and Outer Communities." *USA Today*, May 5. http://www.usatoday30.usatoday.com/news/nation/2011-04-26-suburbs-growth-census-demographics_n.htm (accessed April 16, 2013).

Energy Policy Conservation Act, Pub. L. No. 94-163, 89 Stat. 871 (1975).

Environmental Protection Agency. 2013. "Emission Standards for Boilers and Process Heaters and Commercial/Industrial Solid Waste Incinerators." Research Triangle Park, NC: EPA. http://www.epa.gov/airquality/combustion/actions.html (accessed April 17, 2013).

Evans, Stephen. 2005. "How Air-Conditioning Keeps Changing the U.S." *BBC News*, July 19. http://www.news.bbc.co.uk/2/hi/4697519.stm (accessed April 17, 2013).

Fergusson, James. 2006. "A Brief History of Air-Conditioning." *Prospect*, September 24. http://www.prospectmagazine.co.uk/magazine/abriefhistoryofairconditioning/ (accessed April 17, 2013).

Funk, John. 2012. "FirstEnergy Will Spend $1 Billion on High-Voltage Transmission Lines and Substations." *cleveland.com*, May 18. http://www.cleveland.com/business/index.ssf/2012/05/firstenergy_will_spend_1_billi.html (accessed April 17, 2013).

Great Achievements. 2013. Air Conditioning and Refrigeration Timeline. Washington, DC: National Academy of Engineering. http://www.greatachievements.org/?id=3854 (accessed April 17, 2013).

Howarth, Robert. 2011. "Greenhouse Gas Footprint of Shale Gas Obtained by High-Volume, Slick-Water Hydraulic Fracturing." Ithaca, NY: Howarth/Marino Lab at Cornell University. http://eeb.cornell.edu/howarth/Marcellus.html (accessed April 17, 2013).

Hultman, Nathan, Dylan Rebois, Michael Scholten, and Christopher Ramig. 2011. "The Greenhouse Impact of Conventional Gas for Electricity Generation." *Environmental Research Letters* 6(4): 1–9. http://www.iopscience.iop.org/1748-9326/6/4/044008/pdf/1748-9326_6_4_044008.pdf (accessed April 17, 2013).

International Center for Technology Assessment. 2005. Gasoline Cost Externalities: Security and Protection Services. Washington, DC: ICTA.

Kane County. 2011. "2040 Energy Plan." Geneva, IL: Kane County, Illinois. http://www.countyofkane.org/Documents/Office of Community Reinvestment/Energy Efficiency and Conservation Block Grants/Kane County 2040 energy Plan/KC2040EnergyPlan_final.pdf (accessed April 17, 2013).

King, Michael, and Rob Shaw. 2010. Community Energy: Planning, Development, and Delivery. London: Town and Country Planning Association. http://tcpa.org.uk/data/files/comm_energy_plandevdel.pdf (accessed April 17, 2013).

Lesser, Jonathan A., and Leonard R. Giacchino. 2007. Fundamentals of Energy Regulation. Vienna, VA: Public Utilities Reports.

Lovins, Amory. 2001. "Small Is Profitable: The Hidden Economic Benefits of Distributed Generation (and Other Distributed Resources)." Snowmass and Boulder, CO: Rocky Mountain Institute. http://www.rmi.org/Knowledge-Center/Library/U01-13_SmallIsProfitable (accessed April 17, 2013).

Malone, Laurence J. 2001. "Commonalities: The R.E.A. and High-Speed Rural Internet Access." Oneonta, NY: Hartwick College. http://www.arxiv.org/ftp/cs/papers/0109/0109064.pdf (accessed April 16, 2013).

Margonelli, Lisa. 2010. "The Case for Gray Power." The Nation, February 15. http://www.thenation.com/article/case-gray-power# (accessed April 17, 2013).

Meunier, Guy. 2010. "Capacity Choice, Technology Mix, and Market Power." Energy Economics 32(6): 1306–1315.

Miller, Graeme. 2012. "Iowa On-Site Generation Tariff Barrier Overview." Chicago: U.S. Department of Energy Midwest Clean Energy Application Center. http://www.iaenvironment.org/documents/energy/TariffBarrierOverview.pdf (accessed August 16, 2013).

Moulton, Sean. n.d. "Gas-Guzzler Loophole: SUVs and Light Trucks Drive Off with Billions." Washington, DC: Friends of the Earth. http://www.electrifyingtimes.com/gasguzzlerloophole.html (accessed April 17, 2013).

National Highway Traffic Safety Administration (NHTSA). 2013. "CAFE Fuel Economy." Washington, DC: NHTSA. http://www.nhtsa.gov/fuel-economy (accessed April 17, 2013).

Natural Gas Policy Act, Pub. L. No. 95-621, 92 Stat. 3350 (1978).

Neville, Angela. 2008. "Microgrids Promise Improved Power Quality and Reliability." Power, June 15. http://www.powermag.com/business/Microgrids-promise-improved-power-quality-and-reliability_134_p3.html (accessed April 17, 2013).

New York Times. 2011. "The Clear Case for the Gas Tax." New York Times, August 15. http://www.nytimes.com/2011/08/16/opinion/the-clear-case-for-the-gas-tax.html (accessed April 16, 2013).

Ohio Manufacturers' Association. 2010. "Retooling Ohio: A Bulletin for Leaders on Policy Issues Critical to Ohio Manufacturers." Columbus, OH: Ohio Manufacturers' Association.

Pfiffner, James P. 2009. "Partisan Polarization, Politics, and the Presidency: Structural Sources of Conflict." In *Rivals for Power: Presidential Congressional Relations*, James A. Thurber, ed. Lanham, MD: Roman and Littlefield, pp. 37–60.

Pipe Doctor Plumbing, Heating, and Air Conditioning. n.d. The History of Air Conditioning. HVAC Professionals. http://www.superhvac.com/learn/the-history-of-air-conditioning (accessed April 17, 2013).

Pirog, Robert. 2010. "The Role of Federal Gasoline Excise Taxes in Public Policy." Report prepared for members and committees of Congress, No. 7-5700. Washington, DC: Congressional Research Service. http://www.fpc.state.gov/documents/organization/130217.pdf (accessed April 16, 2013).

PJM. 2012. "PJM Capacity Auction Secures Record Amounts of New Generation Demand Response, Energy Efficiency." News release, May 18. Norristown, PA: PJM. http://www.pjm.com/~/media/about-pjm/newsroom/2012-releases/20120518-pjm-capacity-auction-secures-record-amounts-of-new-generation-demand-response-energy-efficiency.ashx (accessed April 17, 2013).

Plummer, Bradford. 2010. "Fossil-Fuel Subsidies Still Dominate." *The New Republic*, August 3. http://www.newrepublic.com/blog/the-vine/76750/fossil-fuel-subsidies-still-dominate (accessed April 18, 2013).

Policy Matters Ohio. 2012. "Capturing Energy Waste in Ohio: Using Combined Heat and Power to Upgrade Our Electric System." Cleveland and Columbus, OH: Policy Matters Ohio. http://www. policymattersohio.org/combined-heat-power-march2012 (accessed April 17, 2013).

Public Utilities Regulatory Act, Pub. L. No. 95-617, 92 Stat. 3117 (1978).

San Diego Association of Governments. 1994. San Diego Regional Energy Plan. San Diego: San Diego Association of Governments. http://energycenter.org/uploads/energy_plan.pdf (accessed April 17, 2013).

Segedy, Jason. n.d. "Moving Beyond 1956 . . . A New Vision for Transportation." Akron, OH: Akron Metropolitan Transportation Study. http://www.amatsplanning.org/2010/08/13/moving-beyond-1956-a-new-vision-for-transportation/ (accessed April 16, 2013).

Shumsky, Neil. 1996. *Urbanization and the Growth of Cities*. New York: Garland Publishing.

Slivinski, Steven. 2009. *Rural Subsidies*. Washington, DC: CATO Institute. http://www.downsizinggovernment.org/agriculture/rural-subsidies (accessed April 17, 2013).

Sovacool, Benjamin J., and Charmaine Watts. 2009. "Going Completely Renewable: Is It Possible? (Let Alone Desirable)?" *Electricity Journal* 22(4): 95–111.

Steinmetz, Katy. 2010. "Air-Conditioning." *Time*, July 12. http://www.time.com/time/nation/article/0,8599,2003081,00.html (accessed April 17, 2013).

Thomas, Andrew R., Iryna Lendel, Edward W. Hill, Douglas Southgate, and Robert Chase. 2012. "An Analysis of the Economic Potential for Shale Formations in Ohio." Cleveland, OH: Cleveland State University. http://www.urban.csuohio.edu/publications/center/center_for_economic_development/Ec_Impact_Ohio_Utica_Shale_2012.pdf (accessed April 17, 2013).

Thomas, G. Scott. 2012. "Long-Term Manufacturing Decline Affects All States." *The Business Journal: On Numbers*, July 11. http://www.bizjournals.com/bizjournals/on-numbers/scott-thomas/2012/07/longterm-manufacturing-decline-affects.html?page=1 (accessed April 17, 2013).

Tverberg, Gail. 2012. "High-Priced Fuel Syndrome." *Our Finite World*, September 26. http://ourfiniteworld.com/2012/09/26/high-priced-fuel-syndrome/ (accessed April 16, 2013).

U.S. Census Bureau. 2010. *Resident Population Data—Population Change*. Washington, DC: U.S. Census Bureau. http://www.census.gov/2010census/data/apportionment-pop-text.php (accessed October 29, 2013).

U.S. Energy Information Agency. 2012a. "Projected Natural Gas Prices Depend on Shale Gas Resource Economics." *Today in Energy*, August 27. Washington, DC: U.S. Department of Energy. http://www.eia.gov/todayinenergy/detail.cfm?id=7710 (accessed April 17, 2013).

———. 2012b. "U.S. Energy-Related CO2 Emissions in Early 2012 Lowest Since 1992." *Today in Energy*, August 1. Washington, DC: U.S. Department of Energy. http://www.eia.gov/todayinenergy/detail.cfm?id=7350 (accessed April 18, 2013).

Vaitheeswaran, Vijay V. 2004. *Power to the People: How the Coming Energy Revolution Will Transform an Industry, Change Our Lives, and Maybe Even Save the Planet*. New York: Farrar, Strauss, and Giroux.

Ward's Automotive Group. 2012. U.S. Car and Truck Sales. Southfield, MI: Ward's Automotive Group. http://www.wardsauto.com/keydata/historical/UsaSa01summary (accessed April 17, 2013).

Washington, R.A. 2011. "Energy Prices Tax Away Vulnerability." *The Economist*, February 23. http://www.economist.com/blogs/freeexchange/2011/02/energy_prices (accessed July 31, 2013).

Weston, Rick, Joel Bluestein, Bruce Hedman, and Rod Hite. 2009. "Standby Rates for Customer-Sited Resources: Issues, Considerations, and the Elements of Model Tariffs." Report prepared for the U.S. Environmental Protection Agency. Montpelier, VT: Regulatory Assistance Project, and Arlington, VA: ICF International. http://www.epa.gov/ehp/documents/standby_rates.pdf (accessed April 17, 2013).

Wissman, Kim. 2012. "CHP and PUCO." Columbus, OH: Public Utilities Commission of Ohio Workshop on CHP. http://www.puco.ohio.gov/puco/index.cfm/industry-information/industry-topics/combined-heat-and-power-in-ohio/ (accessed August 16, 2013).

Yacobucchi, Brent D., and Robert Bamberger. 2007. "Automobile and Light Truck Fuel Economy: The CAFE Standards." Prepared for members and committees of Congress. Washington, DC: Congressional Research Service. http://www.fpc.state.gov/documents/organization/82504.pdf   (accessed April 17, 2013).

Yergin, Daniel. 2012. "America's New Energy Reality." *New York Times*, June 9. http://www.nytimes.com/2012/06/10/opinion/sunday/the-new-politics-of-energy.html?pagewanted=all (accessed April 18, 2013).

8
Entrepreneurial Initiatives in Chinese Markets

Why They Are Important and What Firms Need to Know

Chieh-Chen Bowen
Cleveland State University

As China's role in the world economy grows, American firms and entrepreneurs—including those in Rust Belt cities—will need to find ways to gain entreé to its growing domestic marketplace. Understanding the culture, language, and economic mechanisms in place are crucial to gain access and establish a foothold.

Throughout the twentieth century, no single nation or block of nations had nearly as much economic power and influence as the United States. During much of that period, no region had as much industrial might as the Midwest. Now, however, as the early part of the twenty-first century unfolds, the age of total U.S. world supremacy is ending, so has the era of midwestern industrial superiority ended within the United States. China in particular is a vastly more prosperous and vibrant country than it was even 20 years ago. According to the World Bank, between 2007 and 2010 China's real GDP growth was at an average rate of 10.85 percent per year, as compared to 0.54 percent per year over the same period in the United States (World Bank 2012). China is now the second-largest economy in the world and is expected to become the largest around 2016 (Organisation for Economic Co-operation and Development 2013). China's growth and development are an inexorable and major aspect of the economic context within which any renewal in midwestern prosperity must occur.

At current growth rates, China's economy is doubling in real terms every seven or eight years. Between 2001 and 2010 average household income in China grew by more than 125 percent in inflation-adjusted terms (Rodriguez 2012). This was the fastest period of economic growth over a single decade of any nation in recorded history. China's ascendency is, moreover, not just seen in its growth rate but also in its immensely large population. As a consequence, we have started to witness a totally different structure in the world's economy, in which the United States and all of its cities and regions play a different and less influential role than in the past century.

While the economic context within which midwestern industrial cities must adapt and compete has changed, this is not necessarily a bad thing. It simply means that industry in these cities must take a few steps back and rebalance inside and out. They must become more efficient and successful at anticipating the jobs of the future, moving resources into new areas, redefining prosperity, and putting far more emphasis upon investments and exports to other countries, especially China.

Prosperity is created and renewed at the margin. It requires production and exchange of the goods and services people value. For midwestern industrial cities, this emerging economic context means, among other things, that the renewal of prosperity depends on how well local entrepreneurs and firms understand the economic, legal, social, and political environments in China. Such comprehension is necessary to successfully export and invest in new Chinese markets. In this author's view, export and investment are among the most important keys to renewed prosperity in midwestern industrial cities. The old saw rings true that one can buy in one's own language, but one must sell in the language of the buyer. Nowhere is this more important than when doing business with the Chinese.

This chapter aims to contribute to the renewal of prosperity in midwestern industrial cities by discussing and giving practical advice regarding the culture and traditions one must know about to successfully export to—and invest in—Chinese markets. The implications of understanding this environment are explained using the examples of the failure of Google when it was forced to pull its operation out of mainland China in 2010, and the success of Rupert Murdoch when the Chinese government granted him the first "landing rights" to sell foreign programs to cable system prime-time slots, then later, rights to provide media content to mobile users.

THE GROWING MARKET IN CHINA AND OPPORTUNITIES FOR U.S. AND MIDWEST INDUSTRY

There are many reasons for the surging U.S. interest in China, involving not only its pace of economic growth but also its sheer size of population, territory, and foreign reserves. China has quickly transformed from one of the largest suppliers of cheap labor and inexpensive goods to one of the largest consumer markets, where multinational corporations compete to grow their market shares (McGregor 2005). The People's Republic of China (PRC) has become one of the most popular host countries for global firms and the most appealing market for foreign investors since 2002, according to A. T. Kearney's Foreign Direct Investment Confidence Index (Laudicina 2010). China joined the World Trade Organization (WTO) in December 2011, as a condition of entering the WTO, China also agreed to open its markets to global producers without requiring technology transfer, a condition on which it used to insist. Thus, PRC's exports and imports of goods and services have been growing explosively. Even during 2011, when the world economy was mired in European economic crises and global slowdowns, PRC's total export value was $1,898.60 billion, a 20.3 percent increase from the previous year. The total value of imports was $1,743.46 billion, a 24.9 percent increase from the previous year (Ministry of Commerce of the People's Republic of China 2011). It is also worth noting that the PRC's imports are rising at a faster pace than its exports. This growth in imports signals enormous market needs that are not fulfilled by China's local producers, and its urge to reach outside its borders to purchase goods and services. The rapid growth rate of imports provides evidence of the PRC's interest in growing its consumer economy.

The fast-growing import and export sectors attract many U.S. companies to do business with China. According to U.S. Census data, China has become the second-largest trading partner with the United States; in 2012 the value of imports from China was $426 billion, and the value of exports to China was $110 billion (U.S. Census Bureau 2013). Trade stimulates growth in economic activities and creates jobs. Moreover, as the world economy globalizes, the effects of trade are increasing. In Ohio, 21.2 percent of jobs depended on trade in 2008, up from 10.5 percent in 1992. Also, exporting companies grew faster, paid higher salaries, and had broader consumer bases than did nonexporting companies. Furthermore, overseas competition tended to stimulate higher growth and development rates (Business Roundtable 2010).

China's burgeoning economy and expanding middle class have created a huge appetite for U.S. goods and services, including business technological solutions, construction materials, and consumer products. U.S. exports to China grew from $27.5 billion in 2003 to $108.6 billion in 2012, a 294 percent increase in a decade. During the same period of time, Ohio's exports to China grew from $823 million in 2003 to $3.656 billion in 2012, an impressive 344 percent increase in a decade. Ohio ranked eighth in exporting goods and services to China among all states in 2012. Other midwestern states also enjoyed a much faster growth rate in exports to China than that of the United States overall, as shown in Table 8.1. In many midwestern states, China ranks third among all foreign trading countries in export markets, trailing only the two large border countries of Canada and Mexico (U.S.-China Business Council 2013).

Knowing that the Chinese people are buying is only the first step. Figuring out what they are buying, exporting it, and selling it to them require deeper understanding of the cultural and social norms in China. Making products and services for the Chinese market necessitates knowledge of the entire business system, including the local social, cultural, legal, and political environment. All of these elements are interconnected, and changes in one are not isolated from changes in the others.

Numerous corporations have entered the Chinese market without substantial knowledge of the nation's business environment and practices, and have thus encountered many failures. The renewal of prosperity in midwestern industrial cities depends, in no small measure, on learning from these failures to improve the chance of success when doing business in China. Consequently, in the following sections, different key aspects of China's economic, political, legal, and social environment will be discussed.

Table 8.1 Exports to China from the United States and from Midwestern States, 2003 and 2012 (2003$)

	United States	Illinois	Indiana	Iowa	Michigan	Missouri	Ohio
2003 ($, millions)	27,500	1,167	454	566	439	463	823
2012 ($, millions)	108,600	6,092	2,601	3,151	3,703	2,227	3,656
% increase, 2003–2012	294	422	473	457	743	381	344
China's ranking in export market, 2012	3rd	3rd	3rd	2nd	3rd	2nd	3rd

NOTE: Percentages calculated from unrounded data.
SOURCE: U.S.-China Business Council (2013).

CHINA'S ECONOMIC ENVIRONMENT

China's economic reform was launched in 1978 by Deng Xiaoping when he pushed to open up and modernize the old and closed communist economy to improve the quality of life for the ordinary people. For the next three decades until 2010, the economic growth rate averaged 10.0 percent per year for real GDP growth (World Bank 2012). China has changed from a centrally planned and organized economy to a market-oriented one. Before the reform, the state directed and monitored a large share of the country's output and production goals, controlled prices, and allocated resources throughout most of the economy. China has also been transformed from an isolated economy with virtually no international trade and foreign investments to the top-ranked exporting country and the second-ranked importing country in global trade, as well as a very powerful player in foreign investment and exchange. Its high level of monetary reserves makes it a major force during worldwide economic crises (Central Intelligence Agency 2013).

The newest five-year economic and social development plan has continued China's commitment to open up the market, optimize foreign trade structure, and develop economic relations with mutual benefits and win-win results (Ministry of Commerce of the People's Republic of China 2012). To get close to this market, many companies have set up operations or joint ventures in China, which are practically impossible without first understanding how business functions in China.

The Chinese people have developed special principles for doing business using their own customs. Chinese business models are quite distinct from those in the United States. Research has shown that failing to recognize cultural differences in doing business is the most frequently cited reason for failures experienced by multinational corporations (Pan and Zhang 2004). Knowing the cultural norms and business practices in China is much more important for U. S. companies today, when they are trying to get a piece of the fast-growing Chinese market, than when they were mostly buying Chinese goods and services.

CHINA'S POLITICAL ENVIRONMENT

The political system in China plays an important role in controlling business activities. The Chinese Communist Party (CCP) took power in 1949 and has since had a strong hold on the central government. Not only does it control all political activities, it also controls all commercial ones, and runs the All China Federation of Trade Unions at the municipal, provincial, and national levels. Not recognizing and understanding the important part played by the CCP and by central and local government officials and authorities may stall business progress in China (Manners 2005).

Firms are expected to establish and maintain good relationships with governmental officials to ensure business transactions run smoothly. The combination of centralized political power and emphasis on the principle of the "rule of people" creates a potentially ripe environment for government officials to use public power for personal gain (Luo 2008). The principle of the rule of people is the opposite of the rule of law. The rule of people refers to "society operating on cultural norms rather than formal legal rules" (Chew 2005). Unpredictable and arbitrary human indiscretions are likely to enter into authoritative decisions which are made and executed by people at the top of the hierarchy. Therefore, whenever there is a shift in the power structure at the top, there will be major changes in how decisions are made. The uncertain nature of how things get done makes trade, foreign investment, and economic development more difficult than in societies that operate by the rule of law (Chew 2005).

The CCP has tight control over the central government and military and also has an iron fist over business activities, in a way that goes beyond regulation. It presides over large, wealthy, state-owned firms, and it exercises control over the selection of senior executives of all state-run firms, many of which are in the top tier of the Fortune Global 500 list. Multinational corporations are often confused and frustrated by the dual roles of regulator and competitor assumed by the same Chinese governmental agency. On one hand, foreign companies are mandated to disclose information to comply with Chinese regulations, but on the other hand, Chinese competitors can utilize this information to gain an advantage in the market. This conflict of interest is impossible to sort out when dual roles are assumed by the same individuals (McGregor 2010).

CHINA'S LEGAL ENVIRONMENT

The Chinese legal tradition developed from both Confucianism and Legalism, two influential, though adversarial, schools of thought. Confucianism assumes human nature is fundamentally good. Social order can be achieved by observing customs, morals, and norms rather than through governmental regulations and laws, which should be used minimally and only for the worst offenses against public well-being. Legalism assumes that moral order is inadequate in maintaining social order because innate human malevolence would constantly drive people into trouble. A well-ordered society can be established and maintained only through a set of formally and publically announced harsh rules. Heads of state had the duty to establish and enforce law with uniformity, certainty, celerity, and severity (Ren 1997). Unfortunately, the influence of Legalism has often been overlooked historically because of its association with despotism and cruelty during the Qin Dynasty, which lasted from 221 BCE to 206 BCE.

In the past, the legal system in China has not played an important role in keeping social order. However, the legal landscape in China has changed rapidly in recent years. More and more business legislation, law offices, and attorneys have emerged in China in the past couple of decades. This trend is due partially to an effort to present Western investors with an image of a stable and predictable business environment with legal protection and security (China Knowledge Press 2004), and partially to fulfill membership requirements of the WTO.

China has strengthened its legal framework and amended its intellectual property rights and related laws and regulations to comply with the WTO Agreement on Trade-Related Aspects of Intellectual Property Rights. There have been important updates and amendments regarding intellectual property rights: patent, trademark, and copyright laws. However, both patent and trademark laws adopt the "first to register" rule instead of the "first to invent" rule, even if the first filers are not the original inventors. In a situation where an estimated 20 percent of all consumer products in the Chinese market are counterfeit, companies are encouraged to file trademark applications with the Chinese Trademark Office and file patent applications with the Chinese State Intellectual Property Office to register their products even when they don't have plans to sell their product in China (U.S. Department of Commerce 2003).

However, having intellectual property rights does not provide necessary protection from commercial piracy. For example, China has more than 950 million mobile phone users. The demand for iPhones is so strong that the smuggling of real iPhones and sales of fakes are skyrocketing. Stores masquerading as real Apple outlets and selling smuggled genuine Apple products have sprouted up everywhere from Beijing in the northeast to Kunming in the southwest (Reuters 2011). The Kunming government eventually ordered two of the fake Apple stores to shut down for operating a business without a license, instead of based on concerns regarding any copyright violation, piracy, smuggling or intellectual property theft (*Today's Zaman* 2011).

In reality, no matter how modernized and Western-like the Chinese legal system may appear, and how similar the structure and process of business arbitration, dispute resolution, and mediation are, laws and business contracts alone will not, in the foreseeable future, bring in successful business deals for multinational corporations in China. The social outcome of implementing a codified law is often determined not by the form and language used in the statute or process that executes law, but by people's attitudes, expectations, and value systems regarding what ought to be restrained and what otherwise ought to be rewarded or compromised (Ren 1997). Legal rights and protections may mean very little in practical terms when legislation in China tends to be vaguely written and rarely enforced (Orts 2001). China's legal system is considered to be underdeveloped (Parekh 2005) and inefficient (Guvenli and Sanyal 2003), and has been criticized for its vague, ambiguous wording for decades (Lee 1999). To survive a weak, ambiguous, and inefficient legal system, the Chinese people tend to stay within a tightly connected group to seek reassurance, support, and protection as well as to adhere to the rule of people (*ren zhi*) principle.

Law in China bears the birthmark of its own history, culture, and tradition. This heritage is sometimes a force more powerful than the rule of law in foretelling the consequences of law and in dictating people's thinking about the role of law and legal authority (Ren 1997). Even if a company can convince the court and win a judgment, reluctance to enforce arbitration from provincial or district courts is a long-existing problem (*Economist* 2005; Kivela and Leung 2005). It is estimated that, at best, only 60 percent of court rulings are enforced, and that can drop to 10 percent when courts entrust officers in other jurisdictions to enforce rulings for them (*Economist* 2005).

In contrast, Americans tend to accept and, in a relatively large measure, to follow the principle of the rule of law (*fa zhi*) that legal rules are publicly known, consistently enforced, and fairly applied (Orts 2001). Law in the United States is designed to be applicable to everyone consistently. Laws and business contracts tend to be respected as well as enforced in the U.S. business environment. Accordingly, reliance on laws and business contracts guides business activities. The need for clear and explicit business terms and conditions stems from core cultural values. Individualistic Americans are likely to behave in a self-serving manner to maximize their personal gains from business opportunities. Such individualistically oriented social norms allow a wide range of acceptable behaviors for asserting persons' own particular rights (Doney, Cannon, and Mullen 1998). Under the assumption that everyone will maximize their own self-interests whenever they can, business transactions need to be regulated and sanctioned with explicit legal terms to clearly define the boundaries of individuals' rights and responsibilities and to provide equal protection for all parties involved. U.S. firms rely on legal protection and expect to follow contracts to the letter in case of any business disputes (Coulson 1984).

CHINA'S SOCIAL ENVIRONMENT

In Chinese culture, the concept of the self is conceived as an integral part of the collective. This interdependent view grants primacy to the relationship between the self and others. Traditionally, Chinese people do not have an independent individual identity. Their self-identity is heavily interdependent with their family, and this makes them more likely to act in accordance with the anticipated expectations of others (Chuang 1998).

The Chinese are known to be highly favorable toward insiders and extremely guarded toward outsiders. Friendships and trust are the foundations for doing business. Profits may not be the only consideration when making business deals. Extensive connections and trust building with local and central government officials seem to create profitable business opportunities at the right time (*Economist* 2004). Business deals are much more likely to be made with friends or people within the web of connections than with strangers solely based on mathematical reasoning and profit/loss analysis. Lam (2000) mentions that Americans use mathematical reasoning and utility analysis in business negotiation, but the Chinese use feelings, personal connections, and trust. Failing to address these different concerns in doing business may very well leave both sides empty-handed.

The collectivistic Chinese people tend to view themselves as tightly connected in a social web of relations, in which their own self-interests are suppressed and woven into the greater good of the group with which they identify. Overtly self-serving behavior is thus likely to be curbed by social sanctions. People who are perceived as acting solely in their own interests tend to be ostracized for acting selfishly. A narrow range of acceptable behavior is prescribed by one's social roles, and people act in unison to achieve order and harmony (Doney, Cannon, and Mullen 1998). Consequently, there is relatively little need for laws and business contracts to protect individual rights in Chinese societies. Instead, cultivating, sustaining, and maintaining long-term reciprocal relationships with individuals who are a part of a web of relations are guiding principles for business activities among the Chinese people. The Chinese show more subordination to in-group hierarchy than to outside authorities, which they often find ways to circumvent or ignore (Triandis, Brislin, and Hui 1988).

The rule of people principle depicts the basic Chinese social mechanism and can be described as a set of implicit and unspoken guidelines governing social interactions and relationships, and serving as a social control mechanism for survival in a legally, politically, and economically complex and uncertain environment. This set of rules allows social actors to behave in a more or less predictable way, which minimizes unnecessary conflicts and enhances social harmony (Cheng and Farh 2001). Davies et al. (2003) assert that, in Chinese business and social life, rule of people is of paramount importance. This principle is composed of the following three highly related elements: 1) *guanxi*, 2) *renqing*, and 3) *mianzi*. The boundaries among the three are blurred, as can be seen in the overlapping of each one's definition.

Guanxi

The Chinese characters for guanxi can be directly translated as connections and relationships. Guanxi is defined as "the process of using personal connections for political, social and economic benefit" (Fan 2002, p. 551). It determines one's place in the social structure and provides security, trust, and a prescribed role (Hammond and Glenn 2004). The art of guanxi is defined by Yang (1994, p. 109) as "involving the exchange of gifts, favors and banquets; the cultivation of personal relationships; networks of mutual dependence; and manufacturing of obligation and indebtedness." The Chinese are thus more likely to favor insiders with whom they have developed guanxi than outsiders with whom they have not.

Guthrie (1998) argues that guanxi is an inevitable characteristic of most societies, while the stickiness of guanxi practice in China, given modernization and globalization, is seen as arising from institutional underdevelopment. The practice of guanxi helps form self-sufficient circles of reciprocity and obligations to protect people from state control and reduce their dependency on the state for material resources and social sustenance during periods of political and economic uncertainty or hardship (Yang 1994). Guanxi is commonly used as a means of survival as well as obtaining prosperity in Chinese societies.

Renqing

The two Chinese characters for renqing can be directly translated as human and affection. Renqing is defined as "a normative standard for regulating social exchanges and a set of reciprocity rules to strive for desirable outcomes within a stable and structured web of social relations" (Hwang 1987, p. 946). It is typically based on ingratiation and contains affective components in addition to guanxi. To succeed in Chinese society, the receiver must understand and abide by the reciprocity rule and the necessary commitment to pay back in similar kind and extent.

Because of the expectation of future return, the Chinese may dole out renqing to others as a form of social investment, expecting to have more effective interactions with the receivers in the future. Renqing also implies a moral obligation to maintain the exchange relationship. Renqing could be either concrete or abstract, such as money, gifts, services, information, and/or affection (Hwang 1987). Renqing involves deliberated and calculated engineering of social interactions for future personal gains.

Mianzi

The third element is mianzi, whose Chinese characters can be directly translated as face. Mianzi is defined as "an individual's social position or prestige, gained by successfully performing one or more specific social roles that are well recognized by others" (Hwang 1987, p. 960). It involves constant consciousness of one's status in the web of social relations, the probability of being accepted by others, and the special power or privilege one enjoys for being recognized by others. In Chinese social relations, maintaining face is essential because it translates into power and influence. A loss of mianzi would likely result in a loss of prestige.

The common thread of these three elements is continuing and complex social interactions. Guanxi, renqing, and mianzi not only are unique and ubiquitous products of Chinese culture, they are also efficient means to maintain social order. The rule of people principle is philosophically in line with Confucius's teaching to maintain relationships, help those in need, and fully reciprocate favors. It forms the basis for collective pressure to maintain social harmony and thus sets the usually unspoken expectations of cooperation and lowers the transaction costs of doing business. Through implicit mutual agreement, this principle establishes a restrictive, even coercive, power upon every member of the web of social relations. These members enjoy privileges and at the same time incur obligations. The Chinese rely on this concept when conducting their daily activities.

The Rule of Law, the Rule of People, and Governmental Influence on Business Activities

The principles of the rule of law and the rule of people seem to operate at the opposite ends of the spectrum, and it is thus assumed that most people would use one as a substitute for the other. However, people function on different assumptions, traditions, customs, and values in different cultures. It is prudent to rely on empirical evidence instead of common sense when dealing with cross-cultural differences. Bowen et al. (2009) conducted such an empirical cross-cultural comparison between U.S. and Chinese societies on the rule of law, the rule of people, and governmental influence on business activities. The survey respondents were university students from the United States and China.

The results, presented in Table 8.2, show that there are no differences between how Americans and Chinese perceive the rule of law or the governmental influence on business activities. But significant differences exist in the perceptions of the impact of the rule of people. The Chinese perceive the rule of people to be more important than do Americans. A possible explanation for this is that the Chinese are known to be flexible and highly adaptable. They have learned to function in a global environment in which the rule of law principle needs to be respected and followed. In the attempt to modernize the Chinese business environment, the Chinese did not totally abandon the rule of people principle, either. As expected, the Chinese people's daily life is much more tied to the complex web of social interactions than is that of Americans.

Also interesting is that the rule of law and rule of people principles are found to be independent of each other, as illustrated by the correlation of these two principles, −0.04 among Chinese people and −0.08 among Americans. These nonsignificant correlations could be interpreted as the emphasis on trust, reciprocity, and long-term relationships to encourage cooperation may either substitute for or complement the equalizing and homogenizing power of laws and contracts. The empirical data indicate that the rule of law has not replaced the rule of people in modern Chinese societies. In practice, both principles are used as parallel systems to achieve business goals and objectives. The rule of people has worked smoothly in Chinese societies for millennia, and it is reasonable to expect such practice to persist into the future. It is

Table 8.2 Perceptions of the Influence of the Rule of Law, the Rule of People, and Government Influence on Business Activities, by U.S. and Chinese Respondents

Scale	U.S. mean (s.d.)	Chinese mean (s.d.)	t-value	Rule of people Chinese correlation (U.S. correlation)	Governmental influence Chinese correlation (U.S. correlation)
Rule of law	3.59	3.59	0.06	−0.04	−0.30***
	(0.49)	(0.48)		(−0.08)	(−0.42***)
Rule of people	3.53	3.67	−4.50***		0.44***
	(0.34)	(0.41)			(0.26***)
Governmental influence	3.30	3.32	−0.35		
	(0.57)	(0.63)			

NOTE: U.S. sample size = 233. Chinese sample size = 449. Perceptions were measured by a 5-point Likert scale with higher numbers representing more applicable the concept in the society. * = significant at the 0.10 level; ** = significant at the 0.05 level; *** = significant at the 0.01 level.

SOURCE: Primary data collected by the author.

valuable for any company that wants to conduct business in China to be familiar with this approach and to learn to practice the basic social mechanisms of guanxi, renqing, and mianzi.

The significant negative correlations in the perceptions of the rule of law and governmental influence among both Chinese and Americans support the belief that when laws are consistently applied to everyone involved, there is little room for governmental influence on business activities. However, the significant positive correlations in the perceptions of the rule of people and the governmental influence on business activities among both Chinese and Americans support the notion that the perception of the rule of people and the perception of governmental influence on business activities usually go hand-in-hand. This pattern is stronger among Chinese than among Americans. The combination of highly concentrated political power and the rule of people principle makes navigating Chinese markets particularly confusing for foreign companies. I will use two examples of big multinational corporations to illustrate this point.

Two Contrasting Experiences

There are plenty of examples of successful multinational corporations that sailed into China with unshakable confidence but were defeated either by their Chinese competitors, the Chinese government, or both. One such tale involves Google pulling its operations out of mainland China in 2010 (BBC News 2010). The other tale is

---

Box 8.1 Google and Star TV

Google. When Google.cn began operating in China in 2006, Google agreed to self-censor and to remove sensitive information before it reached Internet users. Google had to compromise the principle of freedom of speech in order to cash in on the fast-expanding Chinese market.

Four years later, in January 2010, Google's Web site stated that the company had decided to stop internal censoring of Internet search information so that it could provide unbiased and equal access to all of its users. Google waged a public battle against the Chinese government's media censorship (*Economist* 2010).

Box 8.1 (continued)

However, the Chinese government insisted that controlling media content was one of its centralized strategic policies along with national sovereignty, and it accused Google of violating a written agreement and politicizing an economic issue. Whenever the Chinese government responded to an event by citing controlling media content and national sovereignty at the same time, it clearly had no intention of backing down. At the end, even under pressure from U.S. Secretary of State Hillary Clinton, China refused to budge. "Foreign companies must abide by Chinese laws and regulations when they operate in China" (China .org.cn 2010). Two months after the standoff between Google and the Chinese government, Google stopped its operation in mainland China and moved it to Hong Kong.

The incident might have had a different outcome had Google executives taken the time and effort to enlist support from high-level Chinese government officials and to frame the win-win benefits resulting from free and open content on the Internet without exerting pressure from the U.S. Secretary of State to evoke the national sovereignty concern.

Star TV. The success of another media mogul, Rupert Murdoch, can serve as an exemplary model of doing business in China. His strong financial resources, patience, and adaptability to change proved to be the key to his success in China.

Murdoch's initial foray into China was disastrous. Shortly after he purchased the satellite broadcaster Star TV in Hong Kong for nearly US$1 billion in 1993, he made a speech in London that enraged the Chinese leadership. He said that modern communications technology had "proven an unambiguous threat to totalitarian regimes everywhere." However, the Chinese government promptly retaliated by outlawing private ownership of satellite dishes, which had proliferated on rooftops. Star TV thereby faced a threat to its viability (Kahn 2007). Although it took several years to repair the damaged relationship, Murdoch quickly changed his way of doing business in China. He masterfully selected partners with strong ties to the Chinese leadership and media regulatory agencies. He cultivated political ties to insulate his business ventures from regulatory interferences. Once he gained access to the web of complex social relationships, he abided by the principle of the rule of people and earned social prestige by building trust, reciprocating favors, fulfilling obligations, and enjoying privileges.

Box 8.1 (continued)

Murdoch cooperated closely with China's censors and state broadcasters. Star TV mindfully overhauled its programming to suit Chinese tastes. In 1994, it dropped BBC News, which had frequently angered Chinese officials with its reports on mainland China affairs (Kahn 2007). Murdoch adeptly provided highly desired access to Western news media to the Chinese government to present its own face to the world. He showed that Chinese media could become more sophisticated and dynamic without threatening the Communist Party's power. In exchange for permission to broadcast foreign programming in China, he also agreed to broadcast China-made English-language programming to the United States and Britain. Murdoch's helping hand in mentoring and modernizing the Chinese news media was recognized and rewarded by the government by granting him the first "landing rights" to sell foreign programs to cable system prime-time slots, and later, rights to provide media content to its mobile users (Kahn 2007; McGregor 2005).

---

how Rupert Murdoch expanded Star TV from Hong Kong to Mainland China (Kahn 2007).

LESSONS LEARNED

The stark contrasts between Google's and Murdoch's media ventures provide the following lessons for everyone who wants to initiate entrepreneurial effort in Chinese markets.

- It is a good idea to enlist help from people who understand the Chinese culture and have local connections. Neither the Google Translate nor a self-paced international culture software program would be adequate in preparing an American professional to do business in China. Hiring Chinese people educated in the United States seems to be a popular and wise option for corporate executives in starting this process. Not only do such individuals need to be fluent in both English and Chinese, they have to understand the business and be loyal to the company. Their connections in China might provide an access point into the complex web of social relationships.

- It is important to pay attention to government regulations and to understand that rules can change at any time and that they can either work for or against a company. Politics should be left out of business. Making negative comments about the CCP or the Chinese government in public should be avoided, especially regarding China's sensitive issues such as media censorship, human rights, the Tiananmen Square Incident, Fa Lun Gong, and oppression in Tibet.

- When conflicts arise, they should be dealt with quietly. It is much better to try to solve the conflicts behind closed doors by enlisting help from politically connected insiders privately than it is to enlist help from high-level U.S. officials. An all-out public fight with the Chinese government leaves no room for compromise. The Chinese government is not known to back down on central issues, such as media content censorship and national sovereignty.

- It is important to realize and to bear in mind that both the rule of law and the rule of people are applicable in Chinese culture. Americans who want to succeed in doing business in China should be prepared to invest and cultivate long-term social relationships. Becoming familiar with the rule of people principle and the complex web of social relationships is one of the best ways to enhance opportunities, smooth business processes, and lower transaction costs.

CONCLUSION

The fundamental business and economic principles for renewing prosperity in midwestern industrial cities are straightforward. The opportunities to generate income and wealth occur through individual business transactions, some of which start with new products and innovations, and some of which start with identifying demands, producing goods and services people value, and matching the demands with the supply of goods and services. These goods and services are then traded in exchanges in which both parties expect their well-being to improve. Wealth and prosperity within midwestern urban economies will be generated when production and exchange occur over and over again. The top exports to China from midwestern states were crop production, machinery, chemicals, transportation equipment, and second-hand scrap and recycled material, which are used in China for rebar steel and packaging (U.S.-China Business Council 2013). The ascendency of a vast and wealthy Chinese population brings tremendous possibilities for exports from the Midwest, but only if the basic Chinese social mechanism is understood and accepted as a crucial factor in the social and business environment.

Cultural differences can pose seemingly insurmountable obstacles for those wanting to get into Chinese markets. The basic Chinese social mechanism is a deeply ingrained part of daily life not likely to change any time soon. Westerners seeking to do business in China may find out the hard way that the American business model will not achieve their goals. While it takes relatively large up-front investments of time, effort, and other resources to search out potential business partners, negotiate trades, and close sales with Chinese firms, there is no other path to success in that social environment. The associated costs may be high, but the potential benefits in terms of generating wealth and prosperity are even greater.

References

BBC News. 2010. "Google Stops Censoring Search Results in China." *BBC News*, January 17. http://news.bbc.co.uk/2/hi/business/8581393.stm (accessed January 17, 2011).

Bowen, Chieh-Chen, Yuann-Jun Liaw, Aichia Chuang, and Yu-Cheng Su. 2009. "Cross-Cultural Comparisons of Reliance on Laws and Business Contracts versus Three Basic Social Mechanisms among U.S., China, and Taiwan." Paper presented at the Eastern Academy of Management's 46th Annual Meeting, held May 13–16 in Hartford, CT.

Business Roundtable. 2010. "Trade Creates Jobs for Ohio." http://

businessroundtable.org/uploads/studies-reports/downloads/Trade_Creates_ Jobs_for_Ohio.pdf (accessed April 23, 2013).

Central Intelligence Agency. 2013. *The World Factbook: China.* New York: Skyhorse Publishing. https://www.cia.gov/library/publications/the-world -factbook/geos/ch.html (accessed August 13, 2013).

Cheng, B. S., and Jing-Lih Farh. 2001. "Social Orientation in Chinese Societies: A Comparison of Employees from Taiwan and Chinese Mainland." *Chinese Journal of Psychology* 43: 207–221.

Chew, Pat K. 2005. "The Rule of Law: China's Skepticism and the Rule of People." *Ohio State Journal on Dispute Resolution* 20(1): 43–67.

China.org.cn. 2010. "Google 'Breaks Promise' for Censoring." China.org.cn, March 23. http://www.china.org.cn/wap/2010-03/23/content_19667604 .htm (accessed January 30, 2011).

China Knowledge Press. 2004. *China Business Guide.* Singapore: China Knowledge Press.

Chuang, Y.C. 1998. "The Cognitive Structure of Role Norms in Taiwan." *Asian Journal of Social Psychology* 1: 239–252.

Coulson, Robert. 1984. "From the President of the American Arbitration Association." *The Arbitration Journal* 39: 2.

Davies, Howard, Thomas K.P. Leung, Sherriff Ting-kwong Luk, and Y.H. Wong. 2003. "Guanxi and Business Practices in the People's Republic of China." In *Chinese Culture, Organizational Behavior, and International Business Management*, Ilan Alon, ed. Westport CT: Praeger, pp. 41–56.

Doney, Patricia M., Joseph P. Cannon, and Michael R. Mullen. 1998. "Understanding the Influence of National Culture on the Development of Trust." *Academy of Management Review* 23(3): 601–620.

Economist. 2004. "Face Value. The King of Guanxi: Vincent Lo's Career Shows What it Takes for an Outsider to Succeed in China." *Economist*, September 23. http://www.economist.com/businessfinance/displaystory .cfm?story_id=E1_PNTJJDN (accessed February 6, 2010).

———. 2005"China Courts. Winning Is Only Half the Battle: Congratulations, You've Won Your Case. Now Go Away." *Economist*, March 23. http://www .economist.com/node/3797564/print (accessed January 18, 2010).

———. 2010. "Flowers for a funeral: Censorship and hacker attacks provide the epitaph." *Economist*, Jan 14. http://www.economist.com/world/asia/ displaystory.cfm?story_id=15270952 (accessed Feb 6, 2010).

Fan, Ying. 2002. "Questioning Guanxi: Definition, Classification and Implications." *International Business Review* 11(5): 543–561.

Guthrie, Douglas. 1998. "The Declining Significance of Guanxi in China's Economic Transition." *China Quarterly* 154(June): 254–282.

Guvenli, Turgut, and Rajib Sanyal. 2003. "Perception and Management of

Legal Issues in China by U.S. Firms." *Journal of Socio-Economics* 32(2): 161–181.

Hammond, Scott C., and Lowell M. Glenn. 2004. "The Ancient Practice of Chinese Social Networking: Guanxi and Social Networking Theory." *Emergence* 6(1-2): 24–31. http://emergentpublications.com/ECO/eco_other/issue _6_1-2_6_ac.pdf (accessed April 23, 2013).

Hwang, Kwang-kuo. 1987. "Face and Favor: The Chinese Power Game." *American Journal of Sociology* 92(4): 944–974.

———. 1997. "Guanxi and Mientze: Conflict Resolution in Chinese Society. *Intercultural Communication Studies* 7(1): 17–42.

Kahn, Joseph. 2007. "Murdoch's Dealings in China: It's Business, and It's Personal." *New York Times*, June 26 . http://www.nytimes.com/2007/06/26/ world/asia/26murdoch.html?n=Top%2fReference%2fTimes%20 Topics%2fPeople%2fM%2fMurdoch%2c%20Rupert (accessed January 27, 2012).

Kivela, Jaksa, and Lin Fung-Lin Leung. 2005. "Doing Business in the People's Republic of China." *Cornell Hotel and Restaurant Administration Quarterly* 46(2): 125–152.

Lam, Maria Lai-Ling. 2000. *Working with Chinese Expatriates in Business Negotiations: Portraits, Issues, and Applications*. London: Quorum.

Laudicina, Paul. 2010. "Don't Give Up on Globalization." *Bloomberg Business Week*, March 5. http://www.businessweek.com/globalbiz/content/ mar2010/gb2010035_430768.htm (accessed August 15, 2013).

Lee, Jenny S. Y. 1999. "Organizational Learning in China." *Business Horizons* 42(1): 37–44.

Luo, Yadang. 2008. "The Changing Chinese Culture and Business Behavior: The Perspective of Intertwinement between Guanxi and Corruption." *International Business Review* 17(2): 188–193.

Manners, David. 2005. "Chip Forum Told How To Do Business in China: Get Yourself a Good Lawyer and Watch your IP." *Electronics Weekly* 2194: 22.

Ministry of Commerce of the People's Republic of China. 2011. Brief Statistics on China's Imports & Export in December 2011. http://english.mofcom.gov .cn/aarticle/statistic/BriefStatistics/201201/20120107927531.html (accessed April 9, 2012).

———. 2012. "MOFCOM Defined Major Tasks of Commercial Development during the 12th Five-Year Plan Period." News Release, January 9. http:// english.mofcom.gov.cn/aarticle/newsrelease/significantnews/201201/ 20120107919006.html (accessed January 11, 2012).

McGregor, James. 2005. *One Billion Customers: Lessons from the Front Lines of Doing Business in China*. New York: Free Press.

McGregor, Richard. 2010. *The Party: The Secret World of China's Communist Rulers*. New York: Penguin Group.

Organisation for Economic Co-operation and Development. 2013. Economic Survey of China 2013. Paris: OECD. http://www.keepeek.com/Digital-Asset-Management/oecd/economics/oecd-economic-surveys-china-2013_eco_surveys-chn-2013-en (accessed Aug 20, 2013).

Orts, Eric. W. 2001. "The Rule of Law in China." *Vanderbilt Journal of Transnational Law* 34(1): 43–115.

Pan, Fan, and Zigang Zhang. 2004. "Cross-Cultural Challenge When Doing Business in China." *Singapore Management Review* 26(1): 81–90.

Parekh, Rupal. 2005. "China Poses Unique Opportunities, Risks." *Business Insurance* 39(18): 19.

Ren, Xin. 1997. *Tradition of the Law and Law of the Tradition: Law, State, and Social Control in China*. Westport, CT: Greenwood Press.

Reuters. 2011. "Apple Struggles to Take Bigger Bite Out of China."http://www.reuters.com/article/2011/12/16/us-apple-china-idUSTRE7BF0DS20111216 (accessed Aug 20, 2013) .

Rodriguez, Peter. 2012. "China, India, and the United States: The Future of Economic Supremacy." Chantilly, VA: The Great Courses. http://www.thegreatcourses.com/tgc/courses/course_detail.aspx?cid=5892 (accessed April 23, 2013).

Triandis, Harry C., Richard Brislin, and C. Harry Hui. 1988. "Cross-Cultural Training across the Individualism–Collectivism Divide." *International Journal of Intercultural Relations* 12(3): 269–289.

Today's Zaman. 2011. "Chinese City Orders Two Fake Apple Shops to Close." *Today's Zaman*, July 25. http://www.todayszaman.com/newsDetail_getNewsById.action;jsessionid=2CFCD149CA5B5AA3563339E9582AF1B6?newsId=251575 (accessed February 6, 2012).

U.S. Census Bureau. 2013. Trade in Goods with China. Washington, DC: U. S. Census Bureau. http://www.census.gov/foreign-trade/balance/c5700.html (accessed July 30, 2013).

U.S.-China Business Council. 2013. "U. S. Exports to China by State 2003–12." Washington, DC: The U. S.-China Business Council. https://www.uschina.org/sites/default/files/2012%20State%20Exports%20Report%20Overview.pdf and https://www.uschina.org/reports/us-exports/national-2013 (accessed August 15, 2013).

U.S. Department of Commerce. 2003. "Protecting Your Intellectual Property Rights (IPR) in China: A Practical Guide for U. S. Companies." Washington, DC: U. S. Department of Commerce. http://www.mac.doc.gov/China/Docs/BusinessGuides/IntellectualPropertyRights.htm (accessed January 17, 2012).

World Bank. 2012. China—Key Economic Indicators. Washington, DC: World
Bank.   https://docs.google.com/spreadsheet/ccc?key=0AonYZs4MzlZbd
FNNUGVrVEJOWVlsVVB5Y0QyTURBNkE#gid=3 (accessed June 11,
2012).

Yang, Mayfair Mei-hui. 1994. *Gifts, Favors, and Banquets: The Art of Social
Relationships in China*. Ithaca, NY: Cornell University Press.

9
Barriers and Opportunities for Entrepreneurship in Older Industrial Regions

Ziona Austrian
Merissa C. Piazza
Cleveland State University

Manufacturing served as the main source of economic activity in many of the cities of the Midwest until its decline led to the creation of the term "Rust Belt." While entrepreneurship offers the promise of economic growth, Midwest regions need assistance to foster a sustainable entrepreneurial ecosystem and launch new businesses.

Postwar prosperity was built on the production of goods needed to satisfy pent-up demand from Americans, who wanted to improve their lives after World War II, and demand from Europe and Asia, where the populations were physically rebuilding their countries. This period of economic growth was concentrated in several leading industries—automobiles, steel, aluminum, tires, and chemicals—each with large dominant companies with significant market shares. The role of small businesses and entrepreneurship was diminished during the postwar decades; small companies were found to be less productive and innovative than larger corporations, and they offered lower wages. The industrial revolution of the early twentieth century, characterized as an entrepreneurial and individualistic era, had been replaced by an environment of large, structured, and hierarchical corporations. However, even with these developments, U.S. policy still tended to preserve small enterprises, and in 1953 Congress created the Small Business Administration. This policy was in stark contrast to Europe and the Soviet Union, which discouraged such ventures in order to focus on national industrial policies.

The recovery of Japan and Europe and the ensuing movement of labor to cheaper markets outside of the United States through globalization brought to an end the complete advantage the nation had enjoyed after World War II. Since the 1970s, the United States and its regions have been undergoing a dramatic transformation from manufacturing to knowledge- and information-based economies, shifting the focus from physical to human capital. By the 1980s, innovation and entrepreneurship emerged as the main components in the engine of economic growth, causing many scholars and policymakers to look to the factor of knowledge as a primary source of competitiveness. With this paradigm shift, national and regional decision makers needed to change public policy to ensure a more hospitable and nurturing environment for innovators and entrepreneurs.

This chapter links the assertion that entrepreneurship is associated with regional growth to the need for public policy that stimulates entrepreneurship in declining industrial areas. The discussion reviews some of the literature on the general role of innovation and entrepreneurship in economic growth, the barriers to entrepreneurship in older industrial regions, and the role that the nonprofit and public sectors play in accelerating entrepreneurship in these regions. Then examples are given of how private-sector-led organizations encourage the development of an entrepreneurial ecosystem and culture that could lead to economic growth in older industrial regions.

Entrepreneurship has been investigated as a potential means for economic growth throughout economic history. But with the recent framework of endogenous growth theory showing that technology advances lead to higher economic output, many people today are increasingly looking to entrepreneurs to facilitate these advances. In addition, some authors find that higher participation rates of entrepreneurial activity are strongly positively correlated with higher growth rates, even when establishment size and agglomeration effects are statistically controlled (Caree and Thurik 2010). Moreover, additional studies show that entrepreneurs are needed to bring new ideas to market because large existing firms do not have the capabilities to take advantage of the innovations that address market gaps (Audretsch, Bönte, and Keilbach 2008). With this concept in mind, it is important to ask what happens to regions that have been dependent on large firms throughout their recent economic history and that do not have the entrepreneurial culture to take advantage of innovations because individuals are risk averse.

These issues lead to the examination of the entrepreneurial makeup of lagging regions in the United States, specifically older industrial regions with a legacy of large and declining manufacturing firms. Much has been written about this topic in the literature for economic development practitioners, but little has been published in the academic literature. It is the hope that this chapter will begin to bridge the divide in order to provide adequate frameworks for practitioners implementing entrepreneurial policies, as well as to contribute to the academic literature on entrepreneurship and regional growth.

INNOVATION, ENTREPRENEURSHIP, AND ECONOMIC GROWTH

There is a vast amount of academic literature on entrepreneurship and its ability to revitalize regions (Acs and Armington 2004; Audretsch and Keilbach 2004; Baptista and Preto 2011; Caree and Thurik 2010; Dejardin 2011; Fritsch and Schroeter 2011; Mueller 2007). The economic fundamentals of entrepreneurship stem from the building blocks that economists have put forward over the last 200 years. In the beginning, neoclassical economic growth was the only model, and it was based on the idea that development occurs through an increase in productivity, by making more goods in a given amount of time. As economists began to investigate this relationship, they found a phenomenon that was spurring growth but could not be explained by neoclassical theory (Lerner 2009). It was not until 1956, when Abramovitz examined gross output in the U.S. economy from 1870 to 1950, that it became evident that 85 percent of the growth experienced during this period was due to innovation and increased productivity (Abramovitz 1956; Lerner 2009). According to Lerner (2009), Abramovitz showed, "there are ultimately only two ways of increasing the output of an economy: 1) increasing the number of inputs that go into the productive process (e.g., by having workers employed until the age of sixty-seven, instead of retiring at sixty two) or 2) developing new ways to get more output from the same inputs" (p. 44). In other words, Abramovitz's work indicated that it was the innovation and knowledge that transformed the economy, not traditional productivity increases.

Building on the work of Abramovitz, Solow (1956) found that economic growth is determined by the use of classical factors of production, especially capital and labor (Lerner 2009; Solow 1956). What Solow found was that "classical factors of production barely explained half the variance in national economic growth" (Stough, Desai, and Nijkamp 2011, p. 3).

Later in the 1980s, Romer (1988) and Lucas (1994) developed the endogenous growth theory, showing that innovation and technological progress have regional dimensions (Stough, Desai, and Nijkamp 2011), and may also be connected to entrepreneurship (Taylor 2008). Since knowledge and innovation are endogenous to the individual, entrepreneurship is a way in which there is a spillover of knowledge through commercialization (Thurik 2009). Stough, Desai, and Nijkamp (2011) state, "Only recently has the entrepreneur been envisioned as agent of regional economic growth" (p. 6). Through the entrepreneur as an individual actor, demonstration of innovation can take place and therefore build and spawn collective economic growth within regions. There has been a long tradition of examining the benefit of entrepreneurs as contributors to economic development, as in *The Theory of Economic Development* (Schumpeter 1934).

The Concept of Entrepreneurship

Even with this extensive entrepreneurial literature, there are multiple ways of defining who is an entrepreneur and what is entrepreneurship. In addition, there are confounding definitions of how to measure and define entrepreneurship. McQuaid (2011) discusses the perplexing definitions of entrepreneurship. He finds that entrepreneurs as individuals are absent in the theory, and that there are five perspectives on entrepreneurship: 1) entrepreneurship as new business creation, 2) entrepreneurship as the role of the owner/manager of a small or medium-sized company, 3) entrepreneurship as an economic function to allocate resources and capitalize on opportunities, 4) entrepreneurship as a personal behavior of an individual in the quest of a prospect, and 5) characteristics of entrepreneurs. This chapter is based on McQuaid's definition of entrepreneurship as new business creation, since a large amount of the literature focuses on business starts as entrepreneurship, and these provide a quantifiable metric.

The act of creating a new firm is risky for individuals because many times they leave behind the security and known career paths at existing companies. These factors make entrepreneurs unique. They do not only become engines of economic growth through their start-ups, but they facilitate knowledge growth by doing something that would not otherwise be accomplished (Audretsch, Bönte, and Keilbach 2008). Entrepreneurs are set apart from the common person by the act of taking risk in their ventures, and through this risk they enhance the economy by functioning to diffuse knowledge, innovation, and change (McQuaid 2011). "The reason for this positive assessment of entrepreneurial activity is the belief that entrepreneurship does not only create jobs and wealth for entrepreneurs but that there are substantial societal spill-over effects" (Rønning, Ljunggren, and Wiklund 2010, p. 195).

Spillover Effects

The risk taken by entrepreneurs benefits not only themselves, but also society through knowledge spillovers. It is important to begin to understand these spillovers, because they are the vehicle through which entrepreneurial processes can take root. According to Harris (2011), spillovers were first identified by Marshall, Arrow, and Romer (and are thus known as MAR spillovers), and they stem from efforts to minimize transaction costs attributable to firms that collocate near other firms of similar nature, in an agglomeration effect. Harris (2011) shows that these spillovers are greatly related to industrial specialization.

Many articles have built on the Knowledge Spillover Theory of Entrepreneurship (Audretsch 1995), which shows that individuals start a new firm because they are not able to translate their new idea into a product within their current firm, and therefore they start their own firm; and the spillover of knowledge from the old firm to the new firm takes place. In addition, knowledge spillovers created outside the firm allow the entrepreneur to capitalize on opportunities (Acs et al. 2009). This theory has evolved to show that spillovers of interfirm and intrafirm knowledge are important agents in the regional economy. Audretsch and Lehmann (2005) demonstrate that the presence of young high-tech firms in close proximity to a university advances the knowledge capacity in the region.

Moreover, there is a significant amount of literature that links the entry of firms in the economy to positive regional growth within the United States (Acs and Armington 2004; Mueller 2007) and in international cities (Audretsch and Keilbach 2004; Baptista and Preto 2011; Dejardin 2011). It is these new companies, and the entrepreneurs that run them, that take on the risk. Lerner (2009) points out that large firms do not provide incentives to innovate, while new entities may choose riskier projects than established firms. Mueller (2007) examines the impact of entrepreneurship on growth and finds that existing firms do not fully take advantage of new knowledge and that innovative start-ups are more effective effective at capturing this knowledge.

Examining start-up rates in the United States and internationally demonstrates that they contribute to a more vibrant regional economy. In a path-breaking article, Acs and Armington (2004) study business birth rates in 394 local market areas and find that "higher rates of entrepreneurial activity were strongly associated with faster growth of local economies" (p. 924). Their results provide strong evidence of the importance of regional entreprenuership in the United States. The solid positive association between entrepreneurship and economic growth points to the importance of looking at how entrepreneurship can help lagging regions, primarily in the Rust Belt, where manufacturing has been such a predominant industry sector. Moretti (2012) makes the argument that if the economic market were based solely around cost, then lagging regions would attract jobs because places like San Francisco would be hindered by their high costs. But he suggests that this is not the case, rather the opposite. It is a multitude of actors and agents within an ecosystem that helps commercialize knowledge into products (Fritsch 2011; Moretti 2012).

There have been a few academic articles written on entrepreneurship in the Great Lakes region. Using county-level data in Ohio, Acs, Plummer, and Sutter (2009) examine the role of new and incumbent firms in terms of translating "new knowledge (produced by research activities) into economic knowledge. This translation process has been referred to as the 'knowledge filter'" (p. 994). They find that new firms are more able to pass through the knowledge filter, turning ideas into products. Additionally, Faberman (2002) analyzes Rust Belt metropolitan statistical areas (MSAs), looking at employment and wages from 1992 to 2000. He finds that high-growth MSAs tend to be comprised of establishments that are larger and younger, while MSAs with low growth have establishments that are older and smaller. Faberman's results show a different entrepreneurial culture in the Rust Belt region.

BARRIERS TO ENTREPRENEURSHIP IN OLDER INDUSTRIAL REGIONS

As we have shown, the economic literature reveals strong connections among technological progress, innovation, and growing economic wealth. The linkages are especially impressive when innovations include both scientific discoveries and incremental changes in the way manufacturers and service providers work. However, the literature is inconclusive on whether innovations have primarily been created by large or small companies. Anecdotal evidence suggests that the size of highly innovative companies may differ by industry. In some cases, the enabling processes—such as in biotechnology and the Internet— were developed at universities with federal funding, but it is the entrepreneur and his or her small company that saw the potential for commercialization.

The Regional Impact of Entrepreneurship

A study conducted for the U.S. Small Business Administration (2005) finds that the most entrepreneurial regions in the nation experience greater growth in employment, wages, and productivity when compared with the least entrepreneurial regions. Moreover, that research noted that since innovation may be portable, by itself it is not sufficient for economic growth. Moreover entrepreneurship culture is place-based and can be influenced by local and regional policies. In other words, entrepreneurship enhances the regional economic impact of investments in innovations, and commercializing activities undertaken by local entrepreneurs are necessary to convert a region's innovation assets to long-term economic gain. This suggests that interventions aimed at increasing entrepreneurial activities, especially in regions where the birth rate of new start-ups is low, could contribute to increased economic growth.

The Regional Dashboard of Economic Indicators' framework, based on a study of 136 MSAs, suggests a positive relationship between entrepreneurship and growth in regional per-capita income, gross regional product, and productivity (Austrian, Yamoah, and Clouse 2009). This research compares the performance of Leading, Midwest, and northeast Ohio MSAs and monitors the economic performance of regions.[1] Austrian, Yamoah, and Clouse (2009) address the vitality of regions by including two entrepreneurship metrics (two of nine factors): 1) individual entrepreneurship, containing the percentage of self-employed among total employment and the share of business establishments with under 20 employees; and 2) business dynamics, encompassing the ratio of business openings and closings. The factor on individual entrepreneurship for the Midwest and northeast Ohio MSAs consistently ranks in the third and fourth quartiles from 2005 to 2007 (Austrian, Yamoah, and Clouse 2009). The business dynamics factor displays northeast Ohio MSAs solidly in the fourth quartile from 2005 to 2007, and the other Midwest MSAs scattered from the second quartile to the fourth. This study empirically illustrates that, in entrepreneurship metrics, localities in northeast Ohio and other Midwest regions lag behind the remainder of the cohort MSAs.

Regional Variations in Entrepreneurship

Globally, the entrepreneurial environment varies among countries, and within the United States, it varies significantly across regions (Caree and Thurik 2010). Why has the Midwest Rust Belt region been slow in the creation of start-ups? The Midwest was known for its innovation and entrepreneurship in the first half of the twentieth century. As a result, many firms were established in the Midwest, and some grew to become among the country's largest corporations, primarily in manufacturing industries. These companies were able to mass-produce record numbers of goods by taking advantage of economies of scale, with very high levels of efficiency. The dominance of large manufacturing companies in the Midwest provided lifelong job opportunities to both low-skilled and high-skilled employees. As a result, economic and social norms did not encourage individuals to see entrepreneurship as a career option. Therefore, over the past several decades many in the Midwest may have lost the spark, energy, and resources needed for innovation and entrepreneurship.

Several factors may have contributed to the relatively weak entrepreneurial environment in the Midwest during the second half of the twentieth century:

- the ability to get a job in large, established companies allowed individuals to have a comfortable standard of living;
- cultural and social norms did not favor postsecondary education since many manufacturing jobs available to high school graduates offered economic success;
- risk aversion discouraged potential entrepreneurs, employees, and the financial system from starting new companies (Booth 1986);
- culture in which one business failure was seen as an indication that an individual was not capable of starting a new firm, which prevented entrepreneurs from establishing additional companies;
- the lack of large numbers of start-ups and experienced entrepreneurs to encourage and assist future entrepreneurs;
- the difficulty of recruiting individuals, especially for leadership and professional positions, to work in start-ups when not many start-ups exist;
- the unwillingness of employees who work in large firms to leave their jobs for start-ups because of unfamiliarity with young companies and the higher risk of not being compensated;
- lack of a strong business support system for entrepreneurs, including banks, equity financing, and business services; and
- insufficient access to capital for start-ups in their different phases of development.

Access to capital is deemed by many to be one of the primary barriers to a successful start-up, and it merits more discussion. Generally, sources of financing for entrepreneurs include family and friends, owner equity, the Small Business Administration through its Small Business Innovation Research grant program, bank lending, angel investors, and venture capital. Traditionally, the wealth assembled and inherited in the

Midwest has been based on the success and profits of manufacturing companies. Many of the regions' affluent individuals have been less knowledgeable about the technologies being developed on the East and West Coasts, and thus, have been less inclined to become angel investors in these types of start-ups.

Angel investors are people who make investments from their own funds in private companies.[2] They not only provide an important source of early stage funding to start-ups, but they also provide value by having access to key stakeholders, offering strategic advice, providing operational assistance, and serving as confidants to entrepreneurs. Angels, individually or in groups, invest mainly in companies located in their region. Historically, Midwest regions had fewer angel investors than on the coasts, where angel groups grew organically as a result of a rich entrepreneurial ecosystem; in the Midwest, angel groups needed to be organized by either the public or the nonprofit sector. The relationship between angel investors and entrepreneurs is like "the chicken and the egg"; entrepreneurs need angel investors, but angel investors prefer to invest in companies that are located in a region with seasoned entrepreneurs, a relevant industrial base, strong universities, an entrepreneurship culture, and talent experienced with start-ups. Thus, in the Midwest region, the development of angel networks did not happen by market forces alone and required special policies or jump-starting.

Venture capital firms bring with them funds as well as knowledge and management expertise of how to grow start-up companies. However, being actively involved in the company's management or sitting on its board requires the venture capitalist to be in close proximity. As a result, an area has to achieve a critical mass in terms of deal volume before a venture capital firm will visit the region or locate a partner there. Even though some venture capital firms have opened offices in midwestern states and venture capital has started to flow to these regions, the industry has changed following the Great Recession. Venture capital is increasingly concentrated in a few industries and geographic regions, and it began funding companies in the latter phases on the continuum of seed money. In 2011, venture capital investments at the seed-funding stage in the United States declined about 48 percent over the prior year, and investments were concentrated in social media and software and less in biotechnology, genomics, and clean technology, particularly solar (Holstein 2012). Venture capital companies invest more in companies that do not require equipment or physical infrastructure so that the time to bring products to market is shorter. Consequently, with the early stage funding system in turmoil, the Midwest regions have suffered even more than the two coasts.

In addition, traditionally there has been imperfect information between banks and entrepreneurs when applying for credit, because entrepreneurs know the risk of their projects but banks do not (Stiglitz and Weiss 1981). This has been even more prevalent in the Midwest. The more such professionals become familiar with specific high-tech industries and early stage financing mechanisms, the better assistance and advice they can offer nascent entrepreneurs and financiers.

OLDER INDUSTRIAL REGIONS LAG BEHIND LEADING REGIONS IN ENTREPRENEURSHIP METRICS

Older industrial regions are believed to lag behind leading regions in terms of entrepreneurship because of their legacy and historical costs. An investigation of entrepreneurship and innovation metrics reinforces this argument empirically.

Thompson and Walstad (2012) have created the State Entrepreneurship Index, which includes information on income of entrepreneurs, business formation, innovation, and the increase in the number of entrepreneurs. This research is a continuation of previous analysis conducted on the state of Nebraska (Thompson and Walstad 2012; Tran, Thompson, and Walstad 2011). To create the index, the authors combined five components: 1) percent growth in employer establishments, 2) percent growth in employer establishments per person, 3) establishment births per person, 4) patents per thousand persons, and 5) average income per nonfarm proprietor (Thompson and Walstad 2012).

Table 9.1 shows the State Entrepreneurship Index for states considered to be innovative coastal states and industrial states for the years 2008, 2010, and 2011. The overall index value reveals that the raw scores between groups of states differ. In 2011, Washington had the lowest index value among the innovative coastal states (1.38), which

Table 9.1 State Entrepreneurship Index, 2008, 2010, and 2011

	2008		2010		2011	
	Rank	Index value	Rank	Index value	Rank	Index value
	Innovative coastal states					
California	4	1.81	6	1.77	3	2.39
Massachusetts	9	1.54	1	2.46	1	3.01
New Jersey	12	1.40	4	2.13	7	1.68
New York	1	2.04	3	2.24	4	2.23
Texas	34	0.82	11	1.61	8	1.61
Washington	3	1.88	2	2.38	13	1.38
	Industrial states					
Illinois	11	1.42	12	1.60	9	1.59
Indiana	39	0.73	45	0.59	40	0.75
Michigan	33	0.93	42	0.62	49	0.10
Minnesota	23	1.14	24	1.12	5	1.79
Ohio	27	1.06	40	0.68	22	1.09
Pennsylvania	28	1.06	15	1.39	11	1.54
Wisconsin	38	0.73	34	0.90	18	1.19

SOURCE: Rankings produced by Thompson and Walstad (2012); Tran, Thompson, and Walstad (2011).

was higher than four of the Industrial States. In the cases of Indiana, Minnesota, Ohio, Pennsylvania, and Wisconsin, their 2011 index values were the best performance they have marked.

There is no doubt that the economic crisis hit hard in the industrial states, as seen in the entrepreneurial index data between 2008 and 2010. The Great Recession caused some of them to slide backwards; Michigan is an example. Ranking 33 in 2008, Michigan had an Entrepreneurial Index score of 0.93, but by 2011, it showed an index of 0.10 with a ranking of 49. In contrast, between 2010 and 2011, all of the industrial states, except for Michigan, improved their rankings. As shown later in the chapter, some of these states have intermediaries tasked with building regional entrepreneurial ecosystems, and they may have contributed to the observed rise in rankings. More than ever, continued efforts to increase economic development capacity through entrepreneurial facilitation are needed.

Evaluating all metrics in Table 9.1 shows that the industrial states lag behind innovative costal states for entrepreneurship and innovation indices. Illinois in 2008 and 2011 and Minnesota and Pennsylvania in 2011 are exceptions to the lagging midwestern trend. One might infer that this shows the importance of dedicated policies to overcome the barriers resulting from the legacy costs of older industrial regions. One way to accomplish this is through tax policy and tax incentives, and another is through the development of intermediaries in these regions to help facilitate entrepreneurship. The following two sections of the chapter will examine tax policies in states and best practice approaches that foster and enhance entrepreneurship in older industrial regions.

TAX POLICIES AFFECTING ENTREPRENEURSHIP

In Chapter 11 of this book, David Elkins examines the overall role of taxation in entrepreneurial behavior. In regard to the Great Lakes region, Elkins concludes that policymakers must address the issue of high tax burdens and the low proportion of foreign born because these policy mechanisms spur entrepreneurship. In order to make the Great Lakes region more attractive to entrepreneurs, policymakers need to address the issue of high tax burdens (Elkins 2014). A study from the Goldwater Institute also shows that at a state level, a high percentage of taxes as a percentage of personal income lowers the rate of entrepreneurship (Slivinski 2012). This section presents a different aspect of taxation, as it looks specifically at state policies pertaining to investment tax credits targeted at enhancing investments in start-up companies.

States, like businesses, must remain competitive in luring investments so that entrepreneurs can obtain the early stage funding that is critical to facilitate business growth. Many states look to tax policy to help facilitate this investment since the environment for early stage lending has increasingly become risk averse.

Entrepreneurs looking for funding for their start-up companies face a different situation than existing small businesses; there is a heightened sense of risk on behalf of the investor, which in turns makes standard financing difficult for startups. As Keuschnigga and Nielsen (2002) state, "Financing early stage businesses involves special problems and is fundamentally different from financing mature and well established companies. Because of the lack of collateral and the absence of any past track record, and due to their informational advantages, pioneering entrepreneurs often face severe difficulties in convincing banks to finance projects with potentially high returns but high risks as well" (pp. 175–176).

Investment tax credits are a policy instrument used to foster investment and risk capital within a state. An examination of early stage investment tax credits by states shows that 22 states offer tax incentives to investors (Table 9.2).[3] Many states established these policies in recent years; five states initiated these tax credits in 2010, with three more in 2011. The earliest enactment was by Maine in 1988. Tax credit policies vary by state, but most are not for the full investment amount. Generally, states reimburse 25–50 percent of the investment, and this amount may be subject to a cap.

THE ROLE NONPROFIT INTERMEDIARIES PLAY IN ACCELERATING ENTREPRENEURSHIP

The shift from investment in physical capital to human and knowledge capital was not as seamless as the new growth theory implies. Despite investments in scientific research, many regions in the United States fell behind in economic growth, and not all of the newly created knowledge resulted in commercialized innovations. Many barriers prevent individuals from bringing their products to market. In order to overcome these hurdles, lagging regions need mechanisms and infrastructure to link ideas, knowledge, and creativity.

Four elements have contributed to the early lead in technology-based entrepreneurial activity on the East and West Coasts: 1) access to cutting-edge research, 2) access to early stage funding and venture capital, 3) a culture that encourages experimentation and risk taking versus looking down at failure, and 4) a national regulatory structure that enables firms to start up and enter new markets while making it possible for less-productive firms to exit (Council on Competitiveness 2007). Entrepreneurship is an activity that feeds on itself. In some parts

Table 9.2 Early Stage Investment Tax Credits, by State

	Name of tax credit	Credit (%)	Year established
Arizona	Arizona Angel Investor's Tax Credit	30–35	2007
Arkansas	Arkansas Equity Investment Tax Credit Incentive Program	33.3	2007
Connecticut	Connecticut Angel Investor Tax Credit	25	2012
Georgia	Georgia Angel Investor Tax Credit	35	2010
Illinois	The Angel Investment Tax Credit	25	2010
Indiana	Venture Capital Investment Tax Credit	20	2010
Iowa	Community-Based Seed Capital Funds	20	2011
Kansas	Angel Investor Tax Credit	50	2005
Louisiana	Angel Investor Tax Credit	35	2011
Maine	Maine Seed Capital Tax Credit Program	50–60	1988
Maryland	Biotechnology Investment Tax Credit	50	2005
Michigan	Michigan Small Business Investment Tax Credit	25	2003
Minnesota	Angel Tax Credit	25	2010
Nebraska	Nebraska Angel Investment Tax Credit Act	35–40	2011
New Mexico	Angel Investment Tax Credit	25	2007
North Carolina	Qualified Business Tax Credit Program	25	2002
North Dakota	Angel Fund Investment Credit	45	2003
Ohio	Technology Investment Tax Credit	25–30	1996
Rhode Island	Rhode Island Innovation Tax Credit	50	2006
Virginia	Virginia Qualified Equity and Subordinated Debt Investment Credit	50	2003
West Virginia	High Growth Business Investment Tax Credit	50	2004
Wisconsin	Wisconsin Angel Investor Tax Credit	25	2002

SOURCE: Individual state Web sites (accessed September 2012).

of the country, entrepreneurship developed organically, which may provide support to the view that capitalistic mechanisms offer the greatest promise of prosperity.

However, because of the economic history of other regions, such as those in the Midwest, and the barriers to entrepreneurship that have resulted from that legacy, these locations arguably need public tax dollars and philanthropic funding to "jump-start" the entrepreneurial ecosystem. Lerner (2002) highlights two arguments on why public investments in start-up companies are required: the certification hypothesis and the presence of R&D spillovers. Innovations and entrepreneurship create knowledge spillovers that are critical to regional economic growth and benefit the public at large. Start-ups bring new products and services to the market and often create industries that result in a social benefit beyond the returns to the individual firms. These social advantages, which many times happen down the road, justify public investments in innovation and entrepreneurship: the social benefits are not accounted for in the market price of the new company and are often greater than the private return of the individual firm. The development of a vibrant entrepreneurial ecosystem requires a long-term horizon.

In recent years, several states and regions have implemented initiatives designed to accelerate the first three of the four elements listed above. These approaches have an important role in cultivating a network to stimulate entrepreneurship that has not developed naturally. The objectives of these initiatives, which were established through nonprofit organizations, are to promote and support innovative start-up companies by providing pre–seed funding, developing networks of angel investors, and connecting new companies with follow-on funding through either private equity and/or venture capital firms. Many of these programs also provide technical assistance and support by helping entrepreneurs develop business plans, connect to mentors, and find the talent to manage and grow their company.

Table 9.3 highlights three nonprofit entrepreneurial-intermediary organizations that promise to help fill the gap the market left behind. They are JumpStart Inc., located in Cleveland, Ohio; Innovation Works in Pittsburgh, Pennsylvania; and Ann Arbor SPARK, in Ann Arbor, Michigan.

JumpStart Inc. is tasked with increasing the economic impact and sustainability of northeast Ohio's diverse entrepreneurial ecosystem (JumpStart 2012). JumpStart delivers vital, focused resources to entrepreneurs and accelerates the growth of early stage businesses and ideas into venture-ready companies with the hope of transforming northeast Ohio into a nationally recognized area of entrepreneurship and innovation.

JumpStart was modeled after Innovation Works. The mission of Innovation Works is to increase growth in the technology economy of southwestern Pennsylvania through direct investments and business expertise, and its goals are to help hundreds of entrepreneurs, researchers, and small manufacturers create new markets through ideas and innovations (Innovation Works 2012a). Innovation Works has a range of partners in government, business, investment, research, law, and academia.

Operating in another Rust Belt city, Ann Arbor SPARK is an inter-mediary in the greater Ann Arbor, Michigan, region aiming to advance innovation-based economic development. Ann Arbor SPARK has sev-eral goals: to be known as a "hot spot" for high-value, knowledge-intensive, and diverse talent; to build a unified region working together to achieve common economic objectives, without duplication of effort, utilizing the Open Source Economic Development concept; to be on a "short list" for site selectors and other influencers as a sought-after loca-tion; to be known as an innovation hub with access to funding and busi-ness creation/development support; to have national and international brand recognition; and to be recognized as one of the nation's best regions for innovation-based business retention and growth through a proactive business development effort (Ann Arbor SPARK 2012a).

CONCLUSION

As suggested, the transformation to knowledge-based economies has not occurred uniformly across the country. The academic litera-ture offers plenty of evidence that innovation and entrepreneurship are strongly correlated to economic growth. Moreover, regions with high levels of research and development, patents, start-ups, and venture cap-ital develop faster than other areas. The missing link for many regions is the component of entrepreneurship; it is the entrepreneur who brings fresh ideas forward, commercializes these innovations, and brings them to market.

Economic history and industry specialization differ among regions within the United States. In the 1970s, 1980s, and 1990s entrepre-neurship developed organically on the East and West Coasts, while it stagnated in the Midwest. During the initial development of high-tech industries on the two coasts—especially of semiconductor, informa-tion technology, and bioscience companies—Midwest regions were still focusing on large, hierarchical, traditional manufacturing indus-tries, and neither paying attention to the barriers to entrepreneurship nor

Table 9.3 Nonprofit Intermediaries: JumpStart, Innovation Works, and Ann Arbor SPARK

	JumpStart, Inc. Cleveland, Ohio	Innovation Works (IW) Pittsburgh, Pennsylvania	Ann Arbor SPARK Ann Arbor, Michigan
Mission and goals	Increase the economic impact and sustainability of northeast Ohio's entrepreneurial ecosystem.	Increase growth in the technology economy of southwestern Pennsylvania through direct investments and business expertise.	Advance innovation-based economic development in the greater Ann Arbor region.
Why established?	Established in 2003 by the region's civic, community, and philanthropic leaders to address the declining economy, employment losses, and lack of entrepreneurial growth.	Established in 2000 as part of the Benjamin Franklin Technology Partners to take Pittsburgh to where it was a century ago, when entrepreneurs came to start companies, find investors, and produce goods sold worldwide.	Created in 2005 by community leaders as a public-private partnership (business, government, and education to meet the needs of innovation-based companies at every stage of development.
Services provided: entrepreneurial, business, and funding assistance	• Providing one-on-one intensive assistance to entrepreneurs leading high-potential companies by experienced and successful entrepreneurs. • Establishing and achieving milestones of rapid growth. • Investing a minimum of $250,000 in companies with breakthrough and protectable technologies in high-opportunity markets. The portfolio companies are located across the region, but must have	• Investing directly (through IW Seed Fund) in early stage technology companies focused on high-opportunity markets. • Assisting entrepreneurs in developing a business plan, researching market opportunities, and attracting investment capital. • Launching (in 2007) a business accelerator specializing in rapid product development and commercialization—AlphaLab. Offering a 20-week program to	• Providing business accelerator services that enable companies to move quickly through the initial stages of business (idea, business formation, proof of concept, marketability, and commercialization). • Providing SPARK Business Accelerator to qualifying start-ups. Start-ups receive up to $50,000 of consulting and business development services.

less than $5 million in revenues.
- Operating inclusion-specific programs for minority, women, and inner-city-based entrepreneurs offering intensive hands-on assistance, access to capital, and connection to first clients.

launch start-ups in the software, entertainment technology, and Internet-related industries.
- Helping accelerate the development of alternative energy efficiency technologies in universities, national labs, and companies. Also provides investments and business assistance to start and grow energy-related companies.
- Providing manufacturing companies with up to $50,000 to develop new technologies.

- Operating the SPARK Regional Incubator Network, which includes two business incubators and one wet lab. Located in three different cities, the incubators offer physical space, business services, and business development guidance.
- Administering several state-funded programs for start-up companies in Washtenaw County. Grants are available to companies from $1,000 to $10,000. Microloans are available for product development, commercialization, and hiring. Equity investments of up to $250,000 are available through the Michigan Pre-Seed Capital Fund to fund product commercialization and growing the business.

Services provided: talent attraction

- Matching entrepreneurial job seekers with opportunities in start-up companies (advertising for opportunities, screening applicants, and introducing candidates to the start-ups).
- Training entrepreneurs on how to retain talent.

- Assisting entrepreneurs to find the right talent.
- Placing undergraduate engineering and MBA studnets as interns in early stage technology companies and manufacturers. More than half of the companies hired or planned to hire their interns.

- Connecting start-ups seeking managerial and technical talent with job seekers.
- SPARK created a job portal for high-value, knowledge-based positions, where job seekers and employers can post without charge.

Table 9.3 (continued)

	JumpStart, Inc. Cleveland, Ohio	Innovation Works (IW) Pittsburgh, Pennsylvania	Ann Arbor SPARK Ann Arbor, Michigan
	• Guiding entrepreneurs in the development and management of their boards		• SPARK issues a weekly Talent Search newsletter, featuring new postings and career events.
Services provided: other	Mentoring • Program established in 2012 was created in partnership with MIT's Venture Mentoring Service. • Mentors include founders and presidents of Fortune 500 companies, leaders of national high-tech companies, and venture capitalists. Marketing • Generating publicity and creating marketing materials for start-up companies. • Writing press releases and developing relations with media. IdeaCrossing • Developed and maintained by Jumpstart, the Web-based Idea Crossing connects and matches	University-related programs • Working with local universities to cultivate research ideas and help speed commercialization. Providing $25,000 grants for technology validation, market research, prototype development, and evaluation of intellectual property. • Accelerating commercialization of technologies developed by local universities and small businesses through the 16 agile innovation system. The program, funded by a federal grant, was developed in 2010 by IW and Carnegie Mellon University. The system includes workshops, mentors, funding, and space.	Entrepreneurial education and training • Organizing a 2-day Entrepreneur Boot Camp, offering advice about entrepreneurs' business model, management team, and market strategy. • Offering a full-day of training on how to start a business. • Providing one-on-one sessions with entrepreneurs. • Organizing monthly networking programs for entrepreneurs, investors, and others. • Offering a 9-session Business Law and Order Legal series. • Offering 10 monthly marketing sessions.

entrepreneurs, investors, mentors, and providers of business services.

Network Resources

• Connecting entrepreneurs to the Entrepreneurial Network, which includes incubators and accelerators, seed funds and pre–seed funds, venture capital and angel funds, educators, advisors, and other service providers.

Types of industries served

• Health care
• Cleantech (advanced materials and advanced energy)
• Information technology
• Electronics
• Business and consumer products

• Advanced electronics
• Consumer electronics
• Enterprise software
• Network infrastructure
• Information technology
• Internet
• Robotics
• Sensors
• Advanced energy
• Biotech and pharmaceuticals
• Health information
• Life sciences
• Materials
• Medical devices
• Medical diagnosis

• Information technology
• Cleantech (advanced materials and advanced energy)
• Life sciences

Table 9.3 (continued)

	JumpStart, Inc. Cleveland, Ohio	Innovation Works (IW) Pittsburgh, Pennsylvania	Ann Arbor SPARK Ann Arbor, Michigan
Impact	From inception in July 2004 through June 2012, JumpStart made 98 investments totaling over $26 million in 65 companies. These companies created and retained 1,305 direct jobs, held 144 patents with additional 344 patents pending, and raised $495 million in follow-up funding. The 2011 economic impacts of the companies assisted by JumpStart are: value of all goods and services produced in the region rose by $220.5 million, value added rose by $143.6 million, household income increased by $89.4 million, and 12,640 jobs were created. Tax revenues increased by $29.8 million, of which $19.5 million was added to the federal government and $10.3 million to state and local governments. JumpStart received awards from the State Science and Technology Institute, the International Economic Development Council, and the	From its inception, Innovation Works invested over $50 million in 150 companies, which raised more than $1.2 billion in follow-up financing. In 2011, IW invested $4.9 million in companies that created and retained 454 high-skilled jobs. IW assisted its portfolio companies to attract $218 million in follow-on investment from other sources. Many of the region's largest technology companies count IW among their earlier funders. AlphaLab assisted in the launching of 45 companies and was selected among the top 15 accelerators in the United States.	By the end of the fifth year managing the Michigan Pre-Seed Capital Fund, Ann Arbor SPARK has invested $15 million in technology startups that are just prior to the commercialization phase. SPARK incubator graduated several companies that moved to other locations within the region and hired new employees. Between 2006 and 2011, companies assisted by SPARK created nearly 11,000 jobs and received $1.3 billion in new follow-up investments. Ann Arbor was in the headlines of major media outlets. It received top rankings in job growth, education attainment, turnaround city within the Midwest, and among the best cities to find a job.

Economic Development
Administration of the U.S.
Department of Commerce.
JumpStart and its work were fea-
tured in many national media out-
lets, including *Parade Magazine*,
the *Chronicle of Philanthropy*,
VentureBeat, *Fast Company*, and the
New York Times.

SOURCE: Ann Arbor SPARK (2012); Austrian and Cloose (2012); Encyclopedia of Cleveland History (2012); Innovation Works (2012b).

encouraging risk taking in their localities. Due to their history, regional economies in the Midwest ranked lower on measures of innovation and entrepreneurship and experienced lower rates of growth. As a result, many bright and talented people worked for established companies or moved to the East or West Coasts, where innovation and starting a company were encouraged (Cortright 2005).

Over time, with the understanding that entrepreneurship is a critical element of economic growth, public policy has shifted from only investing in physical capital to also supporting risk capital, mentoring, and other support services that entrepreneurs need to foster job growth. In the 1990s and 2000s, more regional decision makers began to address the barriers to entrepreneurship caused by industrial history and the culture that discouraged risk taking and starting new businesses. Since the economies of the Midwest regions were lagging, state and local public policy intervened in the market in order to grow the entrepreneurship ecosystem. Many states, including those in the Midwest, instituted tax credits for early stage investments in order to create or increase the flow of available capital to invest in new companies.

In addition, many regions supported the formation of nonprofit intermediaries to promote and support innovative start-ups, providing them with access to capital as well as technical assistance and mentoring to help them accelerate the development of nascent ideas into successful companies. JumpStart and Innovation Works are both active seed-stage investors in start-up companies located in their respective regions. They offer similar programs, including technical assistance, mentoring, and talent attraction. JumpStart has a unique focus on inclusion that promotes funding and other services to women- and minority-owned businesses. Innovation Works has an accelerator that specializes in rapid product development and commercialization, working with a select group of individuals to launch the next generation of companies. Ann Arbor SPARK, also offers business accelerator services, but does not have its own seed fund. SPARK's funding activities are conducted as an administrator of several state-funded programs for start-up companies.

All three intermediaries affect their respective regions through the companies they mentor and the companies in which they invest, helping to overcome the legacy costs and economic history of their lagging industrial regions. The impacts include establishing new companies, creating and retaining jobs, raising follow-on funding from other sources, and generating revenues. Moreover, these organizations are changing their local entrepreneurial ecosystems by networking and referring, promoting new ideas and start-ups, increasing the availability of pre–seed capital, recruiting talent and creating a pool of individuals who can lead and work in start-up companies, and generally advocating for entrepreneurs. Direct impact is already observed, but future research will demonstrate whether these intermediaries have had lasting effect on their regions' economic growth.

Notes

1. The Leading MSAs include Baltimore-Towson, Maryland; Bridgeport-Stamford-Norwalk, Connecticut; Hartford-West Hartford-East Hartford, Connecticut; and Providence-New Bedford-Fall River, Rhode Island-Massachusetts. The selection of leading MSAs was based on several criteria, including minimum level of employment, rank in the top quartile in short-term and long-term growth, and improvement in ranking over time. The Midwest MSAs include Cincinnati-Middletown, Ohio-Kentucky-Indiana; Columbus, Ohio; Indianapolis-Carmel, Indiana; Kansas City, Missouri-Kansas; Milwaukee-Waukesha-West Allis, Wisconsin; Minneapolis-St. Paul-Bloomington, Minnesota-Wisconsin; Pittsburgh, Pennsylvania; and St. Louis, Missouri-Illinois. The northeast Ohio MSAs include Akron, Ohio; Canton-Massillon, Ohio; Cleveland-Elyria-Mentor, Ohio; and Youngstown-Warren-Boardman, Ohio-Pennsylvania.
2. People become angel investors for different reasons, including financial returns, supporting their community, creating and growing companies, making use of their expertise, and even for personal enjoyment.
3. Early stage investment tax credits are tax credits provided by state governments to private entities or investment firms for investing in early stage companies, early stage investment funds, angel investment funds, venture capital funds, or other investments toward businesses in the initial level. Each state has its own legal criteria on what it considers an "early stage investment" and each state has a set a cap on the dollar amount it will enumerate toward these investments.

References

Abramovitz, Moses. 1956. "Resource and Output Trends in the United States Since 1870." *American Economic Review* 46(2): 5–23.

Acs, Zolton J., and Catherine Armington. 2004. "Employment Growth and Entrepreneurial Activity in Cities." *Regional Studies* 38(8): 911–927.

Acs, Zoltan J., Pontus Brunerhjelm, David B. Audretsch, and Bo Carlsson. 2009. "The Knowledge Spillover Theory of Entrepreneurship." *Small Business Economics* 32(1): 15–30.

Acs, Zoltan J., Lawrence A. Plummer, and Ryan Sutter. 2009. "Penetrating the Knowledge Filter in 'Rust Belt' Economies." *Annals of Regional Science* 43(4): 989–1012.

Ann Arbor SPARK. 2012a. Ann Arbor SPARK. About Us. Ann Arbor, MI: Ann Arbor SPARK. http://www.annarborusa.org/about-us (accessed April 24, 2013).

———. 2012b. Ann Arbor SPARK 2011 Annual Report. Ann Arbor, MI: Ann Arbor SPARK. http://www.annarborusa.org/sites/default/files/content -documents/sparkannualreport2012.pdf (accessed September 24, 2013).

Audretsch, David B. 1995. *Innovation and Industry Evolution*. Cambridge, MA: MIT Press.

Audretsch, David B., Werner Bönte, and Max Keilbach. 2008. "Entrepreneurship Capital and Its Impact on Knowledge Diffusion and Economic Performance." *Journal of Business Venturing* 23(6): 687–698.

Audretsch, David B., and Max Keilbach. 2004. "Entrepreneurship and Regional Growth: An Evolutionary Interpretation." *Journal of Evolutionary Economics* 14(5): 605–616.

Audretsch, David B., and Erik E. Lehmann. 2005. "Does the Knowledge Spillover Theory of Entrepreneurship Hold for Regions?" *Research Policy* 34(8): 1191–1202.

Austrian, Ziona, and Candice Clouse. 2012. 2011 *Economic Impact of Jumpstart Inc. Portfolio and Client Companies*. Report prepared for JumpStart Inc. Cleveland, OH: Cleveland State University. http://www.jumpstartinc. org/results/~/media/JumpStartInc/Images/Results-Page/2011-Economic-Impact-Report.ashx (accessed April 24, 2013).

Austrian, Ziona, Afia Yamoah, and Candi Clouse. 2009. *Regional Dashboard of Economic Indicators 2009: Comparative Performance of Leading, Midwest, and Northeast Ohio Metropolitan Areas*. Report prepared for The Fund for Our Economic Future. Cleveland, OH: Cleveland State University. http:// urban.csuohio.edu/publications/center/center_for_economic_development/ final_indicators_report_08_10_09.pdf (accessed April 24, 2013).

Baptista, Rui, and Miguel Torres Preto. 2011. "New Firm Formation and Employment Growth: Regional and Business Dynamics." *Small Business Economics* 36(4): 419–442.

Booth, Douglas. 1986. "Long Waves and Uneven Regional Growth." *Southern Economic Journal* 53(2): 448-460.

Caree, Martin A., and A. Roy Thurik. 2010. "Impact of Entrepreneurship on Economic Growth." In *Handbook of Entrepreneurship Research: An Interdisciplinary Survey and Introduction*, 2nd ed., Zoltan J. Acs and David B. Audretsch, eds. New York: Springer, pp. 557–594.

Cortright, Joseph. 2005. *The Young and the Restless in the Knowlege Economy.* Chicago: CEO for Cities. http://www.ceosforcities.org/research/the-young-and-restless-in-a-knowledge-economy (accessed July 29, 2013).

Council on Competitiveness. 2007. *Where America Stands: Entrepreneurship Competitiveness Index.* Washington, DC: Council on Competitiveness.

Dejardin, Marcus. 2011. "Linking Net Entry to Regional Economic Growth." *Small Business Economics* 36(4): 443–460.

Elkins, David R. 2014. "Lost a Step: The Great Lakes Region and Entrenpreneurship." In *The Road through the Rust Belt: From Preeminence to Decline to Prosperity*, William M. Bowen, ed. Kalamazoo, MI: W.E. Upjohn Institute for Employment Research, pp. 277–306.

Encyclopedia of Cleveland History. 2012. JumpStart Inc.—The Encyclopedia of Cleveland History. Cleveland, OH: JumpStart Inc. http://ech.case.edu/cgi/article.pl?id=JI (accessed August 13, 2012).

Faberman, R. Jason. 2002. "Job Flows and Labor Dynamics in the U.S. Rust Belt." *Monthly Labor Review* 125(9): 3–10.

Fritsch, Michael. 2011. "The Role of New Businesses, Policy, and Regional Growth." In *Handbook of Research on Entrepreneurship and Regional Development: National and Regional Perspectives*, Michael Fritsch, ed. Cheltenham, UK: Edward Elgar, pp. 1–10.

Fritsch, Michael, and Alexandra Schroeter. 2011. "Why Does the Effect of New Business Formation Differ Across Regions?" *Small Business Economics* 36(4): 383–400.

Harris, Richard. 2011. "Models of Regional Growth: Past, Present, and Future." *Journal of Economic Surveys* 25(5): 913–951.

Holstein, William J. 2012. "Where is the Venture Capital?" *ChiefExecutive. Net*, July 11. http://chiefexecutive.net/wheres-the-venture (accessed July 20, 2012).

Innovation Works. 2012a. "About Us." Pittsburgh, PA: Innovation Works. http://www.innovationworks.org/AboutUs/tabid/86/Default.aspx (accessed April 24, 2013).

———. 2012b. 2011 Community Report: Seeds of Success. Pittsburgh, PA:

Innovation Works. http://www.innovationworks.org/Portals/1/documents/
IW 2011CommunityReport_lowres.pdf (accessed September 24, 2013).

JumpStart Inc. 2012. "About Us." Cleveland, OH: JumpStart Inc. http://www
.jumpstartinc.org/aboutus.aspx (accessed April 24, 2013).

Keuschnigga, Christian, and Soren Bo Nielsen. 2002. "Tax Policy, Venture Capital, and Entrepreneurship." *Journal of Public Economics* 87(1): 175–203.

Lerner, Josh. 2002. "When Bureaucrats Meet Entrepreneurs: The Design of Effective 'Public Venure Capital' Programmes." *Economic Journal* 112(477): F73–F84.

———. 2009. *Boulevard of Broken Dreams: Why Public Efforts to Boost Entrepreneurship and Venture Capital Have Failed—and What to Do About It*. Princeton, NJ: Princeton University Press.

Lucas, Jr., Robert E. 1988. "On the Mechanics of Economic Development." *Journal of Monetary Economics* 22(1): 3–42.

McQuaid, Ronald W. 2011. "The Entrepreneur in Economic Theory." In *New Directions in Regional Economic Development*, Sameeksha Desai, Peter Nijkamp, and Roger R. Stough, eds. Cheltenham, UK: Edward Elgar, pp. 13–26.

Moretti, Enrico. 2012. *The New Geography of Jobs*. Boston: Houghton Mifflin.

Mueller, Pamela. 2007. "Exploiting Entrepreneurial Opportunities: The Impact of Entrepreneurship on Economic Growth." *Small Business Economics* 28(4): 355–362.

Romer, Paul M. 1994. "The Origins of Endogenous Growth." *Journal of Economic Perspectives* 8(1): 3–22.

Rønning, Lars, Elisabet Ljunggren, and Johan Wiklund. 2010. "The Community Entrepreneur as a Facilitator of Local Economic Development." In *Entrepreneurship and Regional Development*, Charlie Karlsson, Börje Johansson, and Roger R. Stough, eds. Cheltenham, UK: Edward Elgar, pp. 195–237.

Schumpeter, Joseph M. 1934. *The Theory of Economic Development*. Cambridge, MA: Harvard University Press .

Slivinski, Stephen. 2012. *Increasing Entrepreneurship Is a Key to Lowering Poverty Rates*. Phoenix, AZ: Goldwater Institute.

Solow, Robert M. 1956. "A Contribution to the Theory of Economic Growth." *Quarterly Journal of Economics* 70(1): 65–94.

Stiglitz, Joseph, E. and Andrew Weiss. 1981. "Credit Rationing in Markets with Imperfect Information" *American Economic Review* 71 (3): 393–410.

Stough, Roger R., Sameeksha Desai, and Peter Nijkamp. 2011. "New Directions in Regional Economic Development: An Introduction." In *New Directions in Regional Economic Development*, Sameeksha Desai, Peter

Nijkamp, and Roger R. Stough, eds. Cheltenham, UK: Edward Elgar, pp. 3–12.

Taylor, Jill S. 2008. "What Makes A Region Entrepreneurial? A Review of the Literature." Cleveland, OH: Cleveland State University, Center for Economic Development. http://urban.csuohio.edu/publications/center/center_ for_economic_development/entrep_region0906.pdf (accessed April 24, 2013).

Thompson, Eric, and William Walstad. 2012. "State Entrepreneurship Index." *Business in Nebraska* 67(704). http://digitalcommons.unl.edu/bbrbin/67/ (accessed April 25, 2013).

Thurik, Roy. 2009. "Entreprenomics: Entrepreneurship, Economic Growth, and Policy." In *Entrepreneurship, Growth, and Public Policy*, Zoltan J. Acs, David B. Audretsch, and Robert J. Strom, eds. Cambridge: Cambridge University Press, pp. 219–249.

Tran, Van, Eric Thompson, and William Walstad. 2011. "Entrepreneurship in Nebraska." *Business in Nebraska* 66(700). http://digitalcommons.unl.edu/ bbrbin/68/ (accessed April 25, 2013).

U.S. Small Business Administration. 2005. *The Innovation-Entrepreneurship Nexus: A National Assessment of Entrepreneurship and Regional Economic Growth and Development*. Washington, DC: U.S. Small Business Administration.

10

Reasons for Misgivings about Local Economic Development Initiatives

William M. Bowen
Chang-Shik Song
Cleveland State University

Local and regional economic development efforts consisting of public subsidies for business and public support for promoting increased local consumption are based on the "market failure" approach. Such activities are attempts to correct the operation of nonfunctioning private markets. This approach, while still widely touted and utilized, also presents questions as to its effectiveness, especially in Rust Belt cities.

From the time of the Industrial Revolution through the middle of the twentieth century, the enormous capital investments made in cities such as Pittsburgh, Cleveland, Buffalo, Cincinnati, Milwaukee, St. Louis, and Detroit helped the industries within them to become pre-eminently competitive.[1] High levels of immigration, to supply their demands for largely blue-collar labor, were another contributing factor. As a result, these and similar cities became globally dominant industrial powerhouses. Fabulous wealth was created. But as the end of the twentieth century unfolded, knowledge and technology advanced, and the world economy changed.

Today these same places have earned reputations as lackluster, Rust Belt cities with serious problems. Large numbers of talented people have, for the past several decades, steadily out-migrated from them for better opportunities elsewhere, leaving behind obsolete production facilities built for early to mid twentieth century manufacturing, a public infrastructure in poor condition, relatively high taxes, and a strongly unionized workforce.[2] The large and now deteriorating investments in capital and infrastructure have become increasingly difficult to maintain with continuously declining populations and correspondingly smaller tax bases. Population loss has also brought reduced capacity for local and county government agencies to provide public services, as well as lessened representation in national-level political decision processes. Figure 10.1 shows the population decline over recent decades.

The public and to some degree nonprofit sectors in these cities have responded to the deterioration in part by enacting a range of local economic-development initiatives. These include public or quasi-public interventions into local markets through various forms of incentives and subsidies designed to change the respective city's local economic growth paths. They include industrial parks, tax abatements, enterprise zones, aquariums, artist incubators, river walks, casinos, festival marketplaces, and many others. There are many examples of these initiatives.

In Cuyahoga County, Ohio (home of Cleveland), for instance, the three county commissioners decided in 2007 to expend well in excess of $465 million of taxpayer money for a privately owned and operated "Medical Mart" (Nichols 2009). The decision was ostensibly predicated on the promise of a one-stop shop in which major medical vendors, such as GE, Phillips, and Siemens, would have floor space upon which to sell medical products to hospitals and doctors from around the world visiting Cleveland and looking to buy the latest in medical technology and cutting-edge equipment. A powerful local coalition of advocates alleged that this would attract a steady stream of conferences and conventions, bringing hundreds of thousands of physicians and hospital administrators to the city each year, creating a huge number of new jobs, generating major new local revenues, and otherwise revitalizing the region.

Insofar as public deliberation occurred at all, it was not widespread or robust. It did not include anything vaguely resembling judicious consideration of the expected value of returns to the public coffers from the expenditure, much less of the research showing that municipal outlays for purposes of attracting conventions in the past have not always yielded positive results for local economies (Fenich 1992; Hovinen 2002; Isler 2008; Laslo and Judd 2004; Noll and Zimbalist 1997; Sanders 2004, 2005). To support the mart, the county commissioners, in closed meetings purportedly held to protect the owner operator's trade secrets, without a vote of the county's citizens, and without a publicly available cost-benefit analysis, decided to fund the Medi-

Figure 10.1 Changing Population in Selected Rust Belt Cities, 1990–2010

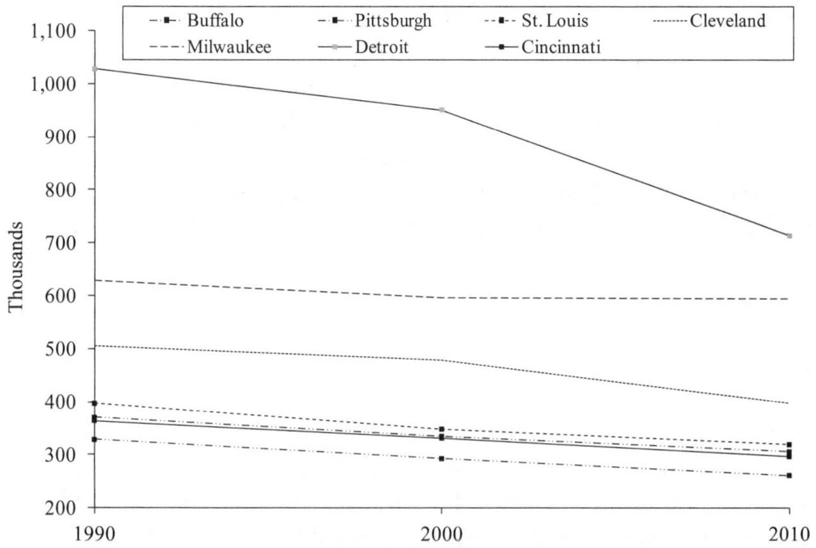

SOURCE: U.S. Census Bureau (1990, 2000, 2010).

cal Mart from a 20-year $0.0025 sales tax on every dollar spent in the county.

Similarly, throughout the industrial Midwest and beyond, elected and other urban authorities have supported and committed public funds to construct and operate major sports-related and other facilities that would supposedly raise the respective city's growth paths. Examples include stadiums, arenas, and training centers in Buffalo, Cincinnati, Cleveland, Detroit, Milwaukee, Pittsburgh, and St. Louis. Virtually all were designed and built using public funds, but privately owned and operated, ostensibly to stem decline and renew prosperity by creating jobs (Noll and Zimbalist 1997). The costs of constructing and running these facilities have been funded primarily through broad-based general taxes.[3] Specific illustrations of initiatives justified by local economic development objectives include the America's Center Convention Complex in St. Louis, the Detroit Creative Business Accelerator, the Detroit Economic Growth Corporation for Business Retention and Attraction, the Team Northeast Ohio (NEO) Minority Business Attraction Initiative in Cleveland, the National Underground Railroad Freedom Center and the Queensgate Terminals in Cincinnati, the Forest Hills Community Development Corporation in Pittsburgh, and the Niagara Convention Center in Buffalo, among many others.

Use of local economic development initiatives characteristically involves the exercise of public authority and the taxing power to claim some portion of the total local resource base for declared purposes of economic and job growth. The policies are supposed to affect consumer or firm behavior, or both. Generally, they involve tax abatements or public expenditures for the stated goals of providing public benefits within the urban or regional economic system.[4] They comprise a range of public subsidies and direct cash aid for businesses, such as financial incentives for branch plant recruitment, capital market programs, information and education, export assistance, and centers for business-related research. The approaches include property and income taxes that are reduced or credited to selected private interests. They also consist of public financial support for purposes of increasing levels of local consumption spending on items such as publicly financed tourism and art facilities, casinos, and outdoor recreation activities. All constitute one form or another of a "nonmarket allocation mechanism" (Arrow 1985).

In the following pages we focus specifically on the market failure rationale for these and similar local economic development initiatives (Bartik 1990). In this line of reasoning, economic development initiatives are justified in terms of standard neoclassical microeconomics by the effort to restore economic efficiency. The rationale for them assumes that they will have the effect of correcting impediments to the formation or operation of private markets. Such obstacles are widely considered to include external costs and benefits, imperfect information and the existence of various monopolies, such as public utilities. On Bartik's (1990) account, they also consist of involuntary unemployment and underemployment, imperfect capital markets attributable to suboptimal regulation, distorted fiscal benefits, improperly set social discount rates, underinvestment in human capital, imperfections in knowledge and information markets, and spillovers from research and development activities. Each of these forms of market failure has its own corresponding means of policy evaluation. The presence of any of them within a regional market could justify the use of an economic development initiative. Several forms of market failure may also occur simultaneously, in circumstances of multiple market failure.

We first consider some reasons to have reservations with this approach, specifically based on principles espoused by members of the Austrian school of economics (Hayek 1944; Ikeda 2004; O'Toole 2004; Sautet 2004). As the following pages describe, Austrian economic theory stipulates that competition in free markets is virtually the only real way to create local prosperity. Then we consider further reasons for such reservations based on the theory of the second best (Wolf 1979). The theory of the second best stipulates that, under conditions of multiple market failure, the outcomes of economic development initiatives are inherently unpredictable. Finally, we assess the implications of these considerations for the use of local economic development initiatives to renew prosperity in midwestern industrial cities today.

AUSTRIAN CRITIQUES OF LOCAL ECONOMIC DEVELOPMENT INITIATIVES

The Austrian critiques of local economic development initiatives differ markedly from popular knee-jerk misgivings about the growth in public spending and taxation that have occurred over the past decades (Tanzi and Schuknecht 2000). This is not to say that these popular concerns have no basis in fact. The growth in public spending and taxation is real, but the Austrian misgivings are in no way knee-jerk. One way to look at the trends within Rust Belt cities is in terms of change in per-capita locally generated general revenue.[5] Figures 10.2 and 10.3 illustrate these trends for the final decades of the twentieth century vis-a-vis selected cities from this group. Figure 10.2 indicates that per-capita locally generated general revenues incrementally have increased for time period 1977–2002. Figure 10.3 shows similar trends on a constant income basis, adjusted for the cost of living.[6] It may be noted that while Detroit is out of sync with the trends in the other cities, it is the only one that has recently gone bankrupt.

The Austrian critiques also differ from scholarly misgivings about local economic development initiatives that stem from the mixed and largely inconclusive results of analysis from the applied social science

Figure 10.2 Locally Generated General General Revenue per Capita in Selected Rust Belt Cities, 1977–2002

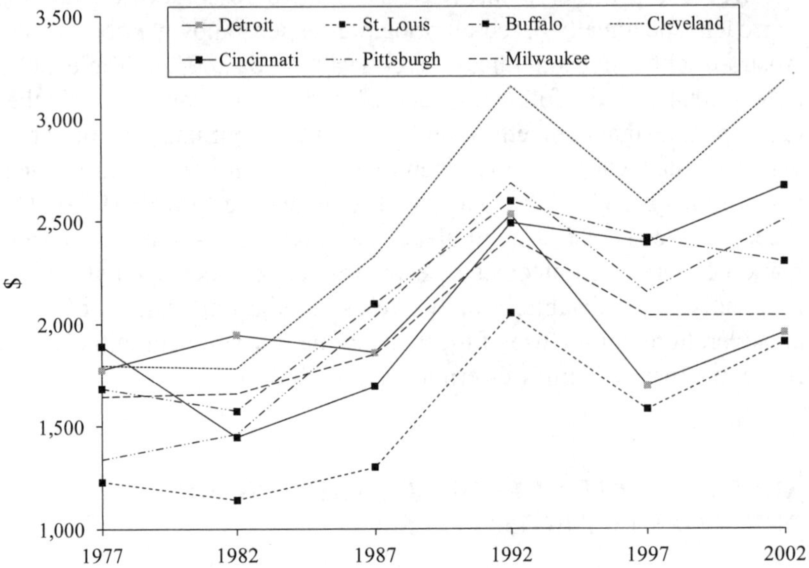

NOTE: Tax revenues are shown in 2002 dollars, which are adjusted at a constantly inflated rate of base year 2002. Data for all cities are based on county-level information for the county containing the central city. A linear regression through these data fit well and have positive slopes. The slopes and R^2 statistics are ($290.09, 0.7612), ($215.19, 0.6771), ($244.23, 0.7116), ($174.69, 0.6378), ($23.53, 0.0219), ($105.03, 0.4520), and ($156.33, 0.6015) for Cleveland, Cincinnati, Pittsburgh, Buffalo, Detroit, Milwaukee, and St. Louis, respectively.

SOURCE: Population numbers are from the U.S. Census Bureau for 1977, 1982, 1987, 1992, 1997, and 2002; locally generated general tax revenues are from Annual Survey of Governments of the U.S. Census Bureau, which are produced by Inter-university Consortium for Political and Social Research (ICPSR) and available at http://www .icpsr.umich.edu.

research community. Some of this social science research shows that local economic development initiatives have had at least some short-term positive effects (Bartik 1991; Reese and Ye 2011). Other studies find that economic development initiatives have either not induced the promised improvements, did not have any discernible effects at all, or led to less economic prosperity (Hissong 2003; Ikeda and Staley 2004; Peters and Fisher 2003, 2004; Reese and Ye 2011; Swetkis 2009).

**Figure 10.3 Locally Generated General Revenue per Thousand Dollars
of Personal Income in Selected Rust Belt Cities, 1977–2002**

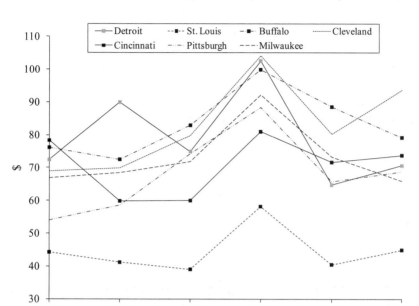

NOTE: General revenues and personal income are all adjusted to constant 2002 dollars using the Consumer Price Index (CPI). All cities are based on county-level data for the county containing the central city. Locally generated general revenues per $1,000 of personal income represent the financial burden of county residents to pay taxes. Though the regression lines in Figure 10.3 do not all fit as well as do the lines in Figure 10.2, with the exception of Detroit the slopes on the regression lines for all of the cities remain positive. The slopes and R^2 statistics are ($5.10, 0.4835), ($0.96, 0.0398), ($3.13, 0.2303), ($2.30, 0.1895), (−$1.62, 0.0453), ($0.84, 0.0254), and ($0.59, 0.0246) for Cleveland, Cincinnati, Pittsburgh, Buffalo, Detroit, Milwaukee, and St. Louis, respectively.

SOURCE: Locally generated general revenues are from the Annual Survey of Governments of the U.S. Census Bureau produced by ICPSR, which is available at http://www.icpsr.umich.edu); personal income is from the Bureau of Economic Analysis for time period 1977–2002 and is available at http://www.bea.gov/regional/index.htm.

The Austrian critiques instead are based conceptually in disputes over the realism of the assumptions made in neoclassical microeconomics, particularly the supposition that decision makers are rational and in possession of complete information (Caplan 1999). Austrian economic theorists specifically reject the realism of any assumption that market decision makers can ever act on the basis of anything remotely similar to omniscience about their situations. Instead, these theorists maintain that all decisions that create wealth and prosperity, or not, including those involving local economic development initiatives, are made by ordinary people. Accordingly, these people are fallible. They possess imperfect knowledge, and seldom if ever make fully rational choices. Their characteristics are those of Homo sapiens, not homo economicus. When in positions of authority to make public initiative decisions, they are at times seriously threatened by moral hazards, misaligned incentives, special interest groups, and political influences.

The Concept of Catallaxy

Much of the Austrian critique centers on the concept of catallaxy. This term describes the origin of wealth and prosperity, stipulating specifically that they must emanate at least in part from spontaneously arising circumstances beyond the capacity of any given finite set of human decision makers to design. The concept is rooted in Frederick Hayek's philosophy of social order (Hayek 1944, 1945, 1976a,b).

Hayek assumed the order that we as humans find in the world is given to it at least in part by our own minds (Gray 1982). Humans, he thought, are active and organic, albeit "constrained" choosers of purposes and means to achieve them (Sowell 1987). We make our choices and earn our living in the world not so much on the basis of primarily abstract or theoretical knowledge as on the basis of practical knowledge. Hayek used "special knowledge of circumstances" to refer to the knowledge with which we do this. Accordingly, special knowledge of circumstances is the understanding of concrete situations, local conditions, people, and opportunities. It has both abstract and practical dimensions. It is abstract in that all of it is explicitly or otherwise predicated upon assumptions, some of which are explicit but most are tacit, for instance, about human nature, language, and reasoning, through the relationships among elements of sensory perceptions. At the same time, such knowledge is practical in that it is embodied in habits of thought, perception, and behavior that allow us to act so as to survive, adapt to our ever-changing circumstances, and achieve our purposes.[7] At its best, this knowledge allows us to act so as to create wealth and prosperity, primarily through market exchanges.

The Limitations of Decision Makers

Because special knowledge of circumstances is always at least in part attributable to the active ordering structures of our own minds, it is at best limited and idiographic. Social and economic reality, Hayek contended, is far too complex to be comprehended by a single mind. While any one person or group may possess enough knowledge to successfully provide answers for the full range of questions that can be asked within the context of a given set of assumptions, only a limited range of questions may be asked from within that same set. The knowledge required to make sound decisions about how to improve prosperity for an entire urban economic system exists only in widely disbursed form among all of the members of that system, each of whom knows his or her own situation and purposes better than does anyone else. This information greatly exceeds that available to any single political authority or business leader, economic development planning committee, or government agency.

Accordingly, no decision maker, group of decision makers, or agency involved with a local economic development initiative can possibly be sufficiently well informed and rational to be able to calculate and coordinate all the variables that contribute to the creation of wealth and prosperity in an urban economic system. Therefore, it is not feasible for them to reliably predict the full range of outcomes from any such initiative. When social norms nevertheless routinely accept the use of local economic development initiatives as substitutes for market decisions, the likely effects include excessively large and unaccountable local governments, untrustworthy urban governance processes, waste of resources, retardation of the creation of wealth and the renewal of prosperity, and disrespect for the preferences, if not individual liberties, of those who are either unwilling or unable to exert political influence on the allocation decisions.

The Importance of the Market

The concept of catallaxy suggests that, in capitalistic markets, social and economic order and prosperity emerge from the chaos of myriads of human decisions in "the mutual adjustment of many individual economies in a market" (Hayek 1976b, pp. 108–109). Prosperity arises spontaneously through the coordinated interactions and mutual adjustments of multitudes of unfettered market exchanges, each of which occurs on the basis of price signals and the partial knowledge of the participants, not as a result of economic development initiatives. To be sure, some participants are more knowledgeable than others, and some are more resourceful. But none conduct their exchanges within the context of a fully integrated and orchestrated social system known as "the market," especially not one that produces any sort of definable public interest or overall product that local economic development authorities might optimize in the manner of a linear program. The idea that the purpose of an urban economy is to maximize one form or another of a social objective function or total social product, such as the number of new jobs, and that local economic development decision makers can make reliable decisions to improve or increase it is simply a misconception.

Following this line of reasoning, the idea that economic development decision makers know enough to somehow maximize a social objective function for the whole of an urban economy, or even at the margin to nudge things in their intended direction, is little more than hubris. The limitations on their knowledge imply that they could never conceive, much less design and orchestrate, the array of exchange most conducive to prosperity within a city of any size with anywhere near the degree of balance and nuance as can the market. Instead, the greatest feasible degree of decentralized, bottom-up decision making will lead to the greatest increases in prosperity. To reliably design and deliver a mechanism for changing a midwestern industrial city's economic path, authorities would have to know not only the entire range of relevant facts and relations, but also how all individuals would mutually accommodate each other as a result of its implementation. Even the very best theories of social planning, human behavior, and economics are not adequate for the requisite tasks.

Implications for the Role of Government

The concept of catallaxy also has implications for the institutions used to govern local market behavior, especially in terms of democratic values and individual rights. Hayek, in particular, was concerned about the reach of governmental power into economic affairs. He maintained that, when governmental power is held and exercised by those who do not recognize or care about the limitations of their own knowledge, or by those who are intent primarily on further enhancing their own power and authority, one of the likely effects is to unduly restrict individual freedoms and effectively violate the rights of others. The use of local economic development initiatives to change urban economic growth paths may thus at times conflict with the core values of freedom, equality, and private property on which the potential renewal of prosperity must be judged. Anyone who has gone before a zoning commission or an architectural review board, or who has attempted to change the mind of a determined county commissioner understands and knows that local governments can wield sweeping and at times even seemingly tyrannical powers.[8]

In the case of Cleveland's Medical Mart, by 2011, after project cost escalations of over $150 million, and after construction had started, it became evident that the concept had failed to attract large, multinational or national vendors who wanted to display their products. Instead, it was announced that the mart would house primarily local vendors, including hospitals, universities, and firms in the information technology, security system, and aromatherapy business (Campbell 2011). The stated purpose also morphed from the attraction of hundreds of thousands of doctors and hospital administrators from outside the region, looking to purchase high-tech medical devices, to a largely locally oriented center for continuing medical education (Campbell 2011; Gomez 2011). Rather than housing major national medical supply firms, the main tenants were local and included small medical businesses, universities, and other medical interests from the area, not outside vendors that would attract a steady stream of medical conventions.

In summary, the Austrian critiques argue that local economic development initiatives are no substitute for the verdicts of unfettered capitalist markets. There is moreover every reason to believe that private investors placing their own money at risk will make better decisions than will economic development authorities. Thus, if a medical mart, convention center, stadium, or other local initiative is predicted to generate net positive revenues for an urban economy, let private markets make the full investment and reap the full profits, or take the full losses it brings. Only unfettered markets can rationally coordinate the demand and supply of land, labor, capital, and technology so as to create widespread prosperity. Had the $465 million or more tax dollars spent on the Cleveland Medical Mart otherwise not been taxed, and had the funds instead remained in free markets, those dollars would have been used in other ways, some of which might have generated genuine prosperity for a range of the region's citizens.

LOCAL ECONOMIC DEVELOPMENT INITIATIVES AND THE THEORY OF THE SECOND BEST

On these conceptual foundations, Austrian economic theorists argue that, of all feasible alternatives thus far conceived, the activity of voluntary exchange in unfettered capitalist markets alone has the greatest potential to generate widespread wealth and prosperity. This process is hampered by substituting the purposes and conceptions of imperfectly informed and cognitively limited economic development authorities for those of the vastly larger number of firms and individuals who would otherwise participate with the same resources in free markets. Insofar as such policies are rationalized by market failures attributable to imperfect knowledge and information, they may not be so much a solution to economic decline as a contributing cause of it.

Markets fail for reasons other than imperfect information and sometimes for more than one reason at a time. Monopolies, for instance, are widely considered to constitute a source of market failure, as are nonrival and nonexcludable goods and services, market transactions involving costs and benefits that accrue to third parties not directly involved in the transaction, and transactions costs that are so high that markets are not economically viable and therefore do not exist (Arrow 1985; Bator 1985). Setting aside for the moment all considerations about imperfect knowledge, it is widely recognized that when instances of any one of these other forms of market failure occur, increases in prosperity cannot be properly incentivized by unfettered capitalist market activity alone. The concept of catallaxy as a basis for a critique of local economic development initiatives applies only to those market failures caused specifically by imperfect knowledge and information; it has very little if any direct bearing upon any of these other sources of market failure.

Less widely acknowledged, however, is that in instances when more than one market failure occurs simultaneously, actions taken to improve some of the conditions will not necessarily improve the efficiency of the urban economy as a whole. Indeed, exactly this point—that under conditions of multiple market failure the use of any sort of public policy intervention will not necessarily improve the efficiency of an economic system as a whole—was made formally in the general theory of the second best (Lipsey and Lancaster 1956; Wolf 1988).

The theory of the second best stipulates that the existence of an efficient market is not possible in the absence of the simultaneous fulfillment of a set of preconditions, all of which are jointly required to ensure that every participant in the market is a price taker. These preconditions specifically include zero entry and exit barriers, perfect information, perfect factor mobility, zero transactions cost, nonincreasing returns to scale, and homogeneous products across suppliers (Stigler 1957). Each precondition is necessary, because for a market to be efficient it must be impossible for any given participant to influence prices in the market. If any one of the preconditions is not fulfilled, some market participants are apt to become price makers, and market failure is likely to occur. Moreover, if in any given market more than one of the preconditions is not fulfilled, multiple market failure occurs. In turn, when the existence of an efficient market is not possible, the best remaining outcome is the "second best."

The theory of the second best has the important negative corollary that the public policy implications of multiple market failure are inherently ambiguous (Wolf 1979). That is, under conditions of multiple market failure it cannot be determined a priori exactly what the second-best outcome would look like or how to attain it. Moreover, a situation in which more, but not all, of the preconditions necessary for fully efficient markets are satisfied is not necessarily better than one in which fewer are satisfied. The removal of any one of the constituent failures through a local economic development initiative may affect overall urban economic efficiency by raising it, lowering it, or leaving it unchanged. But according to the theory of the second best there is no theoretically sound and reliable way to tell which. The only thing certain is that the result will vary on a situation-by-situation basis. Local economic development initiatives under multiple market failure conditions may be as likely to have a deleterious effect on the efficiency of the overall urban economy as they are to have a positive one.

This line of reasoning begs the question: do midwestern industrial urban economic systems contain multiple market failures? Certainly, pioneering urban economist Wilbur Thompson (1968) thought so, as have numerous subsequent urban scholars.[9] As an illustration, land use decisions in any given urban market are apt to be subject to a combination of market failures. Some of these failures are attributable to collective action problems (Foster 2011).[10] Others are due to discrimination in local housing markets (Herbert and Belsky 2008) and labor markets (Brueckner and Zenou 2003), to externalities in local housing markets (Dietz and Haurin 2003; Ewing 2008; Odland 1985), to capital market imperfections and positive external effects on the local educational systems (De Fraja 2002), to congestion on nearby roads (Arnott and Small 1994; Downs 1962; Timilsina and Dulal 2011), to urban air pollution (Kahn 2006), and to high information and transactions costs in financial systems (Levine 1997), among countless other challenges.

Both the concept of catallaxy and the theory of the second best thus lead to a similar general conclusion: the existence of market failure does not guarantee that local economic development initiatives designed and implemented to correct such a problem will succeed. Decisions to use local economic development initiatives in midwestern industrial cities may or may not lead to outcomes that include greater prosperity. The outcomes of using any given local economic development initiative can be assessed only approximately and ideographically on the basis of each individual case, and only using carefully designed and analyzed empirical evidence.

THE GOVERNMENT-FAILURE APPROACH TO LOCAL ECONOMIC DEVELOPMENT

Uncertainty and unpredictability are not only basic characteristics of markets but also fundamental aspects of government failure. By definition, this failure occurs in situations in which government has "created inefficiencies because it should not have intervened in the first place or when it could have solved a given problem or set of problems more efficiently" (Winston 2006, pp. 2–3). Government failure has to our knowledge not been widely considered in the local economic development literature. With this type of failure, the goal of increased prosperity would have been better served by analysis and application of fundamental economic principles of free markets rather than by leaving decisions to the tacit knowledge of circumstance possessed by local economic development authorities.

Both Austrian economic theory and the theory of the second best lead to the inference that local economic development initiatives cannot as a rule be counted upon to reduce waste or to stimulate wealth creation for average citizens. Nor can they be relied on to improve efficiency in the allocation of resources beyond the level that would otherwise have been feasible had the resources remained circulating in the market. Accordingly, this provides a theoretical framework within which misgivings about these initiatives are rational, logical, and consistent with evidence. The basic consideration is that the full range of outcomes is and must remain uncertain and unpredictable until well after the go-no-go decision is made with respect to any given local economic development initiative.

Intervention May Not Be the Answer

It is of significance to note that in any situation in which a market failure is shown to exist, its presence alone does not necessarily imply that intervention into the market can improve the situation. For one reason, market failures may correct themselves. For another reason, governments can fail, too. This could occur, for instance, in circumstances in which the decision to use a nonmarket allocation mechanism is based upon flawed or incomplete knowledge and shortsightedness, or when the relevant economic development authority, regardless of any conscious intentions, is subjected to the influences of local growth coalitions or other powerful special interests.

Logically, to be consistent with the market failure approach to economic development, decision makers deliberating a proposed initiative must first establish that a market failure exists. But this is not enough to rationally justify the use of a proposed local economic development initiative. The decision makers must also ensure that all expected benefits of the proposal are at least equal to all the expected costs.

The existence of a market failure means that properly functioning price signals are absent. In this situation, markets left alone will not yield the most efficient use of resources, and therefore will not generate the greatest feasible levels of prosperity. Demonstration of the existence of a market failure is necessary for a local economic development initiative to be rational, because in situations in which there is no market failure, reliance upon the unfettered market without government intervention is the most likely way to create new wealth or prosperity. At the same time, the existence of market failure is not a sufficient condition for such an initiative to be rationally justified because of government failure. Much as the absence of the preconditions for an efficient market accounts for market failure, so the absence of the preconditions for sound public sector decision making accounts for government failure. These preconditions include knowledge and information necessary for economic calculation on behalf of economic development authorities, appropriate incentives, adequately conceptualized decision processes, no unanticipated behavioral responses, and no abuses of political power.[11]

If while considering a local economic development initiative decision makers fail to thoroughly consider both market failure and government failure, they cannot possibly tell in advance of its implementation whether or not the costs of the initiative will or will not exceed the corresponding benefits (Bartik 1997; Peters and Fisher 2004).

The Need for Benefit-Cost Analysis

One of the best known ways to protect against situations in which the costs of an initiative exceed the benefits is through careful benefit-cost analysis. Benefit-cost analysis is an underutilized framework for the planning and appraisal of policies and projects (Little and Mirrlees 1996). While there is little doubt that this type of analysis is imperfect, if it is done properly it nevertheless makes the bases for decisions systematic and explicit. It thus forces decision makers to think clearly and carefully about their choices and to make the rationale for them transparent and subject to wide public scrutiny and discussion. This occurs through prescribing a set of steps by which decision makers carefully consider all of the possible consequences or outcomes of a decision, evaluate them, and determine whether the total benefits promise to outweigh the total costs, and for whom.

Decision makers would, for example, explicitly define the objectives of a proposed local economic development initiative, specify the alternative approaches to achieving the growth objectives, and estimate the costs associated with the entire range of outcomes from each of the alternative approaches, including all of the capital, operating, and intangible factors, such as dislocations, aesthetic alterations, etc. The benefits would include any improvements in the efficiency of the urban economic system, as well as changes in valuation of existing facilities or businesses due to shifts in markets. A proposed initiative would be undertaken only if its benefits are at least as great as its costs.

In this light it is notable that neither massive out-migration from cities nor the presence of too few jobs to support a population within a city in and of itself constitutes evidence of market failure. Rather, even in the presence of out-migration, markets may be working perfectly. People and firms may simply be moving to avail themselves of greater satisfactions, opportunities, or profits at other locations. People tend to migrate their residences to places at which, all else equal, the amenities are better, the quality of life is higher, or the present value of increased income in the new region is greater than the increased cost of living in that area. Similarly, firms may migrate out of an urban core area to avail themselves of greater potential profits attributable to changes in production, communication, or transportation technology; relative prices of factor inputs; or large-scale shifts in the location of service-consuming populations. Observed out-migration only constitutes evidence of market failure when it can be shown that in its absence some people would be better off without anyone else being made worse off, and that this is not happening on its own. Thus, Pfister (1985) labeled the use of local public policy to stem urban out-migration "pathological."

UNFATHOMABLE AND UNCERTAIN ASPECTS OF LOCAL ECONOMIC DEVELOPMENT INITIATIVES

Some of the decline in twentieth-century midwestern industrial cities has undoubtedly been attributable to macro-scale economic and geographical change, driven by recent advances in technologies and over which urban policymakers have little or no control. Insofar as these large-scale shifts were the primary cause of such decline, there is no apparent a priori reason to suppose that market failures exist. And insofar as no market failures exist, there is no good, theoretically sound reason to think that the use of economic development initiatives will in any significant way stem further decline. Indeed, two causes of decline that cannot be altered through local economic development initiatives come immediately to mind.

Changing Preferences Enabled by Technology

The first is that technological progress has made it increasingly possible for people to realize their seemingly innate preferences for living in places with relatively mild winters and under more satisfactory conditions. As noted by Andrew Thomas in Chapter 7, beginning shortly after air conditioning became widely accessible, the population of the United States has been steadily migrating from the Northeast and Midwest to the South and West (Rappaport 2003). These preferences, and the associated large-scale migration, have also been enabled by the changing composition of industry from heavy manufacturing to services, since service industries are freer than manufacturing to locate throughout the country. Also, the preferences of relatively affluent residents to live under more satisfactory conditions, in conjunction with comparatively inexpensive transportation, have led them to suburbs and beyond, where the infrastructure and schools are in better condition, commercial corridors are available, housing stock is adequate, and many of the problems of the inner city can be left behind. At least insofar as the recent decline of twentieth-century midwestern industrial cities has been driven by behaviors based on innate preferences and enabled by technology, the use of local economic development initiatives is not likely to make much difference.

Globalization

The second is globalization. Technological advancements, together with relaxation of legal and other institutional restrictions on international trade, have forced firms in midwestern industrial cities to compete today as never before with businesses in other cities around the country and the world (Amendola and Gaffard 1988; Antonelli 2001, 2003; Atkinson and Stiglitz 1969; Geroski 1995; North 1991; Scotchmer 2004; Searle 2005). First and foremost among these cities are those in China, as is described by Chieh-Chen Bowen earlier in this book. Among other things, newly globalized competition means that midwestern industrial cities are inextricably affected by inclusion in or exclusion from global networks of information and financial control (Cohen 1981; Friedmann 1986; Friedmann and Wolff 1982; Neal 2011; Sassen 1996). The levels of wealth and prosperity within these cities have thus arguably become closely linked to, if not completely determined by, their positions in these networks.[12]

Moreover, firms in these cities must vie with companies in places that have lower labor, energy, environmental compliance, and other costs of production. They must thus compete within the context of vast worldwide disparities in factors such as savings rates and rates of return on capital investments, population size, wages, levels of migration, natural endowments, regulatory environments, and investment in research, development and education, all of which in part determine the success of rivals. Firms in midwestern industrial cities are in many ways at a competitive disadvantage relative to similar businesses located in other areas around the world. To the extent that the relative decline in the preeminence of these cities has been attributable to globalization, the use of local economic development initiatives cannot be reasonably expected to significantly ameliorate the corresponding urban problems.

It is somewhat easy to recognize and accept that historical and geographical drivers of change are of a scale that goes beyond anyone's complete comprehension. But we also tend to think that, even when focusing only on events within local urban economic systems in the Midwest, complete knowledge of the effects of many local economic development initiatives is beyond the capacity of the human mind. This argument is not only intuitive but it is consistent with considerable research on human psychological limitations and capacities (Kahneman, Slovic, and Tversky 1982; Miller 1956; Simon 1974; Warfield 1988). Thus, we find ourselves inclined to suppose that the full range of the causes of some of the perceived problems in Rust Belt cities is simply unfathomable. Local economic development initiatives responding to these issues would, upon closer examination, be found to be attributable not so much to market failure as to the interests of political and economic regimes, in combination with cultural and institutional traditions in which the intrinsic limitations on human knowledge are not recognized. A moment's reflection will reveal that this is not trivial. It implies that problems of renewing prosperity are inseparable from political and economic aspects of society as well as from human psychological incapacities and biases that characterize virtually all other choices made under uncertainty. Decisions to use economic development policies are thus tied to the possibility of human error, not to mention undue political influence.

The Nature and Incidence of Benefits

Do local economic development initiatives lead to a greater abundance of resources and a fuller life for average people and whole urban populations, or only for a relatively small and exceptionally fortunate segment thereof? Given that public revenues are used to fund nonmarket allocation mechanisms, one might reasonably suppose that the taxpayers who bear the costs would have some legitimate claim to a commensurate portion of the rewards. What constitutes the basis upon which legitimate claims to these benefits does and should rest? What is the minimally tolerable share of the gains due to any given taxpayer? These and similar questions seem to us to be among the most difficult and complex in any serious consideration about using these mechanisms. Especially when the levels of public funding for economic development initiatives are relatively large, they will have positive effects on at least some segment of the local taxpaying population. But what if this includes primarily or only a relatively limited subset of the relevant taxpaying population, composed of, for instance, local landholders, real estate firms, and companies with business and other financial linkages to the particular funding channels through which the public expenditures are provided?

It is not always clear exactly who the beneficiaries of local economic development initiatives are and whether the incidence of the benefits reflects the incidence of costs. Proponents predictably assert that the initiatives are conducive to the renewal of prosperity, but it is rarely made clear how the validity of their assertions can be determined, and it is rarer still that net benefits over costs are actually demonstrated in a thorough and impartial manner through an independent benefit-cost analysis. Seldom are clear and compelling arguments made that the policies will lead to a greater abundance of resources and a fuller life for average people within an urban system. Moreover, use of local economic development initiatives is not always consistent with the spirit and principles of democratic governance, in which individual freedoms and rights are core values and great weight is placed on local institutions that exercise public authority, leadership, and representation of the interests of all citizens rather than only some (Selznick 1957, 1984).

Probably the most viable way to renew prosperity in midwestern industrial cities is to rely as fully as possible on capitalist markets to make allocation decisions. This is not to say that this approach would always be wise or equitable. Rather it is to say that such reliance draws to the greatest feasible extent on the use of prices for making allocations, puts the information in the hands of the dispersed individuals most directly impacted by the decisions, and puts the proper incentives on innovators and entrepreneurs competing in markets. It also provides feedback about success and failure. These are all powerful systemic factors in renewing prosperity. Moreover, it also puts individuals in situations in which their choices to participate or not in market exchanges are voluntary.

At times, uncritical use of local economic development initiatives has incurred huge costs in situations where no market failure has been demonstrated. At other times, when market failures have clearly existed, different approaches might have improved resource allocation in a much more efficient manner. This raises the practical difficulty of both identifying circumstances in which the use of local economic development initiatives will improve efficiency and distinguishing them from those in which it will not. Indeed, it may raise this difficulty beyond analytical tractability. Nevertheless, because resource allocations must be decided in some manner, and because the ways they are decided will with virtual certainty affect the renewal of prosperity in these cities, there is no choice but to exercise a value judgment on the matter. Accordingly, our preference would be for less uncritical and unevaluated reliance on local economic development initiatives, and more performance of careful benefit-cost analysis. Our suspicion is that given such scrutiny, many of the policies would be very difficult to justify.

In light of these considerations we would propose that prosperity in midwestern industrial cities would be renewed most effectively by establishing local rules and institutional arrangements whereby all proposed new local economic development initiatives must be accompanied by statements indicating their purpose, evidence that their design will lead to the fulfillment of this purpose at acceptable cost, and a clear rationale for why such a policy should be employed. Rather than placing excessive reliance on local economic development initiatives to renew prosperity in midwestern industrial cities, we would generally favor directing public funds primarily toward efficiently supplying public goods and services and protecting the rights of individuals. Local governments should, in our view, consider investing fewer resources in economic development initiatives and more in areas such as establishing appropriate levels of centralization of authority in the public sector, achieving an adequate degree of collective trust in public authority, and defining and enforcing functional ownership arrangements and property markets. Efforts to renew prosperity in these cities should be directed toward creating and sustaining institutions that encourage the fullest possible range of initiative and responsibility on behalf of private economic agents acting in pursuit of their own individual purposes. Appropriate goals include developing and implementing institutional arrangements that provide individuals with the greatest possible discretion about how they will use their private property (and to hold them accountable for their choices), incentivizing the formation of competitive markets, ensuring low tax rates, and setting appropriate limitations on the use of nonmarket allocation mechanisms.

Insofar as local governments get involved in renewing prosperity past this point, the guiding principle should be to establish the conditions necessary for the operation of efficient markets. These conditions notably include adequate schools. Markets alone will not provide for the lower strata of society to acquire sufficient levels of the essential skills of reading, writing, and arithmetic. Without these competencies, a segment of the population in any urban economy will not be educated enough to make sound political judgments as participants in local democratic governance processes. In turn, without a suitably functioning democratic system, autonomy, benevolence, trust, and free exchanges are more likely to cease; human relations are more apt to assume the sort of dominance/subordination relationships that characterize serfdom or slavery; and overall prosperity is more likely to decrease than to increase.

CONCLUSION

Both theory and empirical evidence indicate that markets can fail and that sometimes local economic development initiatives conceived and implemented in the name of correcting the malfunction actually improve efficiency. This poses a practical difficulty of evaluation in that, while the list of market failures is long, the roster of successful government interventions taken to correct them is somewhat shorter. Moreover, while the difference between these inventories can be discussed in abstract terms, the effect of government action taken in response to a market failure in any given situation can only be assessed with empirical evidence.

But data and evidence alone will not resolve some of the basic public policy issues raised in this chapter. On the one hand is a popular and widely accepted perspective that local fiscal policy should take an active role in renewing prosperity, such as through efforts to reverse out-migration from central cities, lower unemployment rates, stabilize economies, and generally to intervene in markets when doing so arguably leads to improved collective welfare. On the other is an Austrian economic perspective in which public fiscal policy cannot and should not as a rule intervene in the market, and the theory of the second best, according to which, under conditions of multiple market failure, the outcomes of such intervention are unpredictable. These divergent perspectives are not resolvable on the basis of available empirical evidence alone, due in large measure to the conceptual and theoretical nature of the differences between them. At the same time, until these disagreements are satisfactorily resolved, no a posteriori ways will be available to answer the question: what mix of public and private activities is most likely to lead to renewed prosperity in midwestern industrial cities? The only remaining viable option is one of trial, error, data acquisition, analysis, and adjustment.

If the use of economic development initiatives is to be consistent with the spirit and principles of democratic governance, in which local institutions exercise public authority, leadership, and representation of the interests of all citizens rather than only some, these questions must be considered seriously and at length in public discourse. Decisions to use local economic development initiatives are thus not only about production and consumption, but also about ethics and values. Is the increment to economic output generated by a local economic development initiative worth more to society than what it displaces? How greatly does the population value democratic governance? These are but a couple of the wide range of ethical questions indissolubly tied up with the use of these policies. Thus, in our view, the problems involved are far too important and complex to be left only to economists of any ilk, largely because they involve a great deal more than what is typically considered to be "economic."

Notes

1. While Buffalo may not be a midwestern city, it is clearly a Rust Belt city and is thus included in the chapter.
2. Walters (2010) argues that any satisfactory explanation of the decline of U.S. cities must start with the treatment of capital and the security of property rights within them, with particular emphasis on labor unions that reduce the returns to capital.
3. Considerable evidence indicates that the lion's share of the benefits inure to the highly paid players and team owners, concession suppliers, some nearby local businesses, and businesses that buy season tickets as a means of increasing their own ticket sales. Despite gross overestimates of newly created job numbers contained in promotional studies heavily funded by affected cities or teams, such facilities are evidently built only with substantial net economic cost to the public (Zimbalist 2006).
4. Many tax incentives are really public spending in disguise (Toder 2002, p. 66), but it is easier to enact ineffective or unnecessary programs in the form of tax incentives than in the form of direct spending.
5. According to the definition used by the Census of Governments (2002), locally generated general revenues are divided into three categories: 1) local taxes, 2) charges, and 3) miscellaneous general revenues. Local taxes contain property, individual income, general sales and use, motor fuel, corporate income, other

selected sales, vehicle license, utility, and other taxes. Current charges include higher education, hospital, sewerage, and other current charges. Miscellaneous revenues include interest and other miscellaneous revenues. All were used for this study. We did not include taxes on utility revenues such as electricity, water, and other utility revenues, and insurance trust revenues. We calculated per-capita revenues by dividing locally generated total revenue in a county by that county's total population. Locally generated general revenue per $1,000 of county personal income was calculated by dividing locally generated total revenues by total county personal income and multiplying that value by $1,000. The data were from the U.S. Census Bureau and the Bureau of Economic Analysis.

6. According to U.S. Census Bureau data, the 31 percent population loss in Detroit between 1990 and 2010 was relatively greater than the population loss in any of the other cities (Buffalo, 17 percent; Pittsburgh, 17 percent; St. Louis, 20 percent; Cleveland, 22 percent; and Cincinnati, 18 percent). To the extent that this translated into correspondingly greater losses of property values and other components of locally generated general revenues in Detroit vis-à-vis these other cities, this would contribute to, if not completely account for, the slightly negative slope in Detroit's trend.

7. Hayek's conception of knowledge in its practical aspect is much akin to what we have variously heard referred to as "know how," "tacit knowledge," or "traditional knowledge."

8. The circumstances that reflect this concern are clearly illustrated in Bolick's (1993) description of the ways both liberals and conservatives miss the central point about individual liberties that the framers of the U.S. Constitution had in mind in the Bill of Rights as well as in the 9th and 14th Amendments. In providing this description he cites specific examples in which actions of local governments have wasted or misused tax dollars, imposed a particular set of social values on people who do not subscribe to those values, interfered with voluntary, nonharmful economic activities, violated private property rights, and rearranged "opportunities for the benefit of some and to the detriment of others" (p. 97).

9. Thompson (1968) argues that urban markets are in many ways profoundly distorted by widespread failure to rely sufficiently on price signals. He primarily considered collectively consumed public goods, merit goods, and payments to redistribute income.

10. Collective action problems occur when an individual's contribution to the attainment of a common interest is unlikely to have sufficient impact on the advancement of that interest to warrant the costs of political engagement. These problems tend to give way on the demand side to the capture of the governance process by special interests or rent seekers. On the supply side, they are associated with short-termism and the monopoly characteristics of the political market.

11. The logic of government failure from a decision-making point of view is spelled out clearly by Dörner (1996). It stems largely from unintended consequences that tend to occur as a result of failure or neglect on behalf of government decision makers to fully recognize and adequately consider the complexity involved in their decision situations. The general set of circumstances may be described as

follows. If two aspects of a given decision situation are interdependent, this means that they are correlated. So let us suppose aspects A and B within a given city's economic system are correlated. Let us further suppose that an economic development authority wants to alter B to change a city's growth path. B and C are known to have a causal relationship, and B can be manipulated and changed at will. This means that by altering the level of B, the official can alter the level of C, thereby changing the growth path. But if the decision maker is not aware of the correlation between A and B, in manipulating B to alter C she will also unknowingly alter A. The change in A is indirect, and may not be recognized until much later, if ever. However, the change in A is an unintended consequence of manipulating B to alter C. If the consequences of changing A are significant in some other aspect of the urban economic system, and perhaps even deleterious, the actions taken to change the growth path in one way may unintentionally create other, new problems, some of which are as serious if not more serious than the original one.

12. Neal (2011) finds that the direction of the causal relationship between a city's position in the global urban hierarchy and levels of employment goes from the position in the hierarchy to urban employment growth, not vice versa.

References

Amendola, Mario, and Jean-Luc Gaffard. 1988. *The Innovative Choice: An Economic Analysis of the Dynamics of Technology.* Oxford: Basil Blackwell.

Antonelli, Cristiano. 2001. *The Microeconomics of Technological Systems.* Oxford: Oxford University Press.

———. 2003. *The Economics of Innovation, New Technologies, and Structural Change.* London: Routledge.

Arnott, Richard, and Kenneth Small. 1994. "The Economics of Traffic Congestion." *American Scientist* 82(5): 446–455.

Arrow, Kenneth J. 1985. "The Organization of Economic Activity: Issues Pertinent to the Choice of Market versus Nonmarket Allocation." In *Microeconomics: Selected Readings*, 5th ed., Edwin Mansfield, ed. New York: W.W. Norton and Company, pp. 500–518.

Atkinson, Anthony Barnes, and Joseph E. Stiglitz. 1969. "A New View of Technological Change." *Economic Journal* 79(315): 573–578.

Bartik, Timothy J. 1990. "The Market Failure Approach to Regional Economic Development Initiative." *Economic Development Quarterly* 4(4): 361–370.

———. 1991. *Who Benefits From State and Local Economic Development Initiatives?* Kalamazoo, MI: W.E. Upjohn Institute for Employment Research.

———. 1997. "Can Economic Development Programs Be Evaluated?" In *Dilemmas of Urban Economic Development: Issues in Theory and Practice*, Richard D. Bingham and Robert Mier, eds. Thousand Oaks, CA: Sage Publications, pp. 246–277.

Bator, Francis M. 1985. "The Anatomy of Market Failure." In *Microeconomics: Selected Readings*, 5th ed., Edwin Mansfield, ed. New York: W.W. Norton and Company, pp. 474–499.

Bolick, Clint. 1993. *Grassroots Tyranny: The Limits of Federalism.* Washington, DC: Cato Institute.

Brueckner, Jan K., and Yves Zenou. 2003. "Space and Unemployment: The Labor-Market Effects of Spatial Mismatch." *Journal of Labor Economics* 21(1): 242–262.

Bureau of Economic Analysis. Local Area Personal Income, 1977–2002. Washington, DC: U.S. Bureau of Economic Analysis. http://www.bea.gov/regional/index.htm (accessed August 19, 2013).

Campbell, Maude L. 2011. "Med Mart Version 2.0: The Original Plan Isn't Going to Work. What about the Latest One?" *Scene Magazine*, September 28. http://www.clevescene.com/cleveland/med-mart-version-20/Content?oid =2737315 (accessed April 25, 2013).

Caplan, Bryan. 1999. "The Austrian Search for Realistic Foundations." *Southern Economic Journal* 64(4): 823–838.

Cohen, Robert B. 1981. "The New International Division of Labor, Multinational Corporations, and Urban Hierarchy." In *Urbanization and Urban Planning in Capitalist Societies*, Michael Dear and Allen.J. Scott, eds. London: Methuen & Co. Ltd., pp. 287–315.

De Fraja, Gianni. 2002. "The Design of Optimal Education Policies." *Review of Economic Studies* 69(2): 437–466.

Dietz, Robert D., and Donald R. Haurin. 2003. "The Social and Private Micro-Level Consequences of Homeownership." *Journal of Urban Economics* 54(3): 401–450.

Dörner, Deitrich. 1996. *The Logic of Failure: Recognizing and Avoiding Error in Complex Situations.* New York: Basic Books.

Downs, Anthony. 1962. "The Law of Peak-Hour Expressway Congestion." *Traffic Quarterly* 16(3): 393–409.

Ewing, Reid H. 2008. "Characteristics, Causes, and Effects of Sprawl: A Literature Review." In *Urban Ecology: An International Perspective on the Interaction Between Humans and Nature*, John M. Marzluff, Eric Shulenberger, Wilfried Endlicher, Marina Alberti, Gordon Bradley, Clare Ryan, Ute Simon, and Craig ZumBrunnen, eds. New York: Springer, pp. 519–535.

Fenich, George. 1992. "Convention Center Development: Pros, Cons, and Unanswered Questions." *International Journal of Hospitality Management* 11(3): 183–196.

Foster, Shelia R. 2011. "Collective Action and the Urban Commons." *Notre Dame Law Review* 87(1): 57–133.

Friedmann, John. 1986. "The World City Hypothesis." *Development and Change* 17(1): 69–83.

Friedmann, John, and Goetz Wolff. 1982. "World City Formation: An Agenda for Research and Action." *International Journal of Urban and Regional Research* 6(3): 309–344.

Geroski, Paul. 1995. "Markets for Technology: Knowledge, Innovation, and Appropriability." In *Handbook of the Economics of Innovation and Technological Change*, Paul Stoneman, ed. Oxford: Basil Blackwell, pp. 90–131.

Gomez, Henry J. 2011. "Changeup in Medical Mart Plans Surprises Longtime Supporters, Raises Questions about Viability." *Cleveland Today*, October 8. http://blog.cleveland.com/metro/2011/10/changeup_in_medical_mart_plans.html (accessed April 25, 2013).

Gray, John N. 1982. "F. A. Hayek and the Rebirth of Classical Liberalism." *Literature of Liberty* 5(4): 19–101.

Hayek, Frederick A. 1944. *The Road to Serfdom*. Chicago: University of Chicago Press.

———. 1945. "The Use of Knowledge in Society." *American Economic Review* 35(4): 519–530.

———. 1976a. *Individualism and Economic Order*. London: Routledge.

———. 1976b. *Law, Legislation, and Liberty, Vol. 2: The Mirage of Social Justice*. Chicago: University of Chicago Press.

Herbert, Christopher E., and Eric S. Belsky. 2008. "The Homeownership Experience of Low-Income and Minority Families: A Review and Synthesis of the Literature." Washington, DC: U.S Department of Housing and Urban Development, Office of Policy Development and Research.

Hissong, Ron. 2003. "The Efficacy of Local Economic Development Incentives." In *Financing Economic Development in the 21st Century*, Sammis B. White, Richard D. Bingham, and Edward W. Hill, eds. Armonk, NY: M.E. Sharp, pp. 131–144.

Hovinen, Gary. 2002. "Revisiting the Destination Lifecycle Model." *Annals of Tourism Research* 29(1): 209–230.

Ikeda, Sanford. 2004. "Urban Interventionism and Local Knowledge." *Review of Austrian Economics* 17(2/3): 247–264.

Ikeda, Sanford, and Sam Staley. 2004. "Introductory Essay for a Symposium on 'Urban Interventionism.'" *Review of Austrian Economics* 17(2/3): 151–154.

Isler, Tom. 2008. "Convention Center Performance Review." *Meetings & Conventions* 43(3): 64–80.

Kahn, Matthew E. 2006. "Air Pollution in Cities." In *A Companion to Urban Economics*, Richard J. Arnott and Daniel P. McMillen, eds. Malden, MA: Blackwell Publishing Ltd., pp. 502–514.

Kahneman, Daniel, Paul Slovic, and Amos Tversky. 1982. *Judgment Under*

Uncertainty: Heuristics and Biases. Cambridge: Cambridge University Press.

Laslo, David, and Dennis Judd. 2004. "Convention Center Wars and the Decline of Local Democracy." *Journal of Convention & Event Tourism* 6(1/2): 81–98.

Levine, Ross. 1997. "Financial Development and Economic Growth: Views and Agenda." *Journal of Economic Literature* 35(2): 688–726.

Lipsey, R.G., and Kelvin Lancaster. 1956. "The General Theory of Second Best." *Review of Economic Studies* 24(1): 11–32.

Little, I.M.D., and James A. Mirrlees. 1996. "The Costs and Benefits of Analysis: Project Appraisal and Planning Twenty Years On." In *Cost-Benefit Analysis*, 2nd ed., Richard Layard and Stephen Glaister, eds. Cambridge: Cambridge University Press, pp. 199–231.

Miller, George A. 1956. "The Magical Number Seven, Plus or Minus Two: Some Limitations on Our Capacity for Processing Information." *Psychology Review* 63(2): 81–97.

Neal, Zachary P. 2011. "The Causal Relationship between Employment and Business Networks in U.S. Cities." *Journal of Urban Affairs* 33(2): 167–184.

Nichols, Jim. 2009. "Why Wouldn't Taxpayers Own the Medical Mart?" *cleveland.com*, February 11. http://blog.cleveland.com/metro/2009/02/_the_ publicprivate_partnership.html (accessed April 25, 2013).

Noll, Roger G., and Andrew Zimbalist. 1997. "Sports, Jobs, and Taxes: The Real Connection." In *Sports, Jobs and Taxes: The Economic Impact of Sports Teams and Stadiums*, Roger G. Noll and Andrew Zimbalist, eds. Washington, DC: Brookings Institution Press, pp. 494–508.

North, Douglass C. 1991. "Institutions." *Journal of Economic Perspectives* 5(1): 97–112.

Odland, John. 1985. "Interdependence and Deterioration in the Housing Stock of an American City." In *Pathologies of Urban Processes*, Kingsley E. Haynes, Antoni Kuklinski, and Olli Kultalahti, eds. Tampere, Finland: Finnpublishers Oy, pp. 323–340.

O'Toole, Randal. 2004. "A Portlander's View of Smart Growth." *Review of Austrian Economics* 17(2/3): 203–212.

Peters, Alan, and Peter Fisher. 2003. "Enterprise Zone Incentives: How Effective Are They?" In *Financing Economic Development in the 21st Century*, Sammis B. White, Richard D. Bingham, and Edward W. Hill, eds. Armonk, New York: M.E. Sharp, pp. 113–130.

———. 2004. "The Failures of Economic Development Initiatives." *Journal of the American Planning Association* 70(1): 27–37.

Pfister, Richard L. 1985. "Inappropriate Policy Responses to Urban Change in the United States: A New Pathology." In *Pathologies of Urban Processes*, Kingsley E. Haynes, Antoni Kuklinski, and Olli Kultalahti, eds. Tampere, Finland: Finnpublishers Oy, pp. 425–436.

Rappaport, Jordon. 2003. "U.S. Urban Decline and Growth, 1950 to 2000." *Economic Review* (3rd Quarter): 15–44. http://www.kc.frb.org/Publicat/ECONREV/Pdf/3q03rapp.pdf (accessed April 26, 2013).

Reese, Laura A., and Minting Ye. 2011. "Policy Versus Place Luck: Achieving Local Economic Prosperity." *Economic Development Quarterly* 25(3): 221–236.

Sassen, Saskia. 1996. *Losing Control: Sovereignty in an Age of Globalization*. New York: Columbia University Press.

Sanders, Heywood. 2004. "Convention Mythology." *Journal of Convention & Event Tourism* 6(1/2): 99–143.

———. 2005. "Space Available: The Realities of Convention Centers as Economic Development Strategy." Research Brief. Washington, DC: Brookings Institution. http://www.brookings.edu/~/media/research/files/reports/2005/1/01cities%20sanders/20050117_conventioncenters (accessed April 26, 2013).

Sautet, Frederic. 2004. "Cluster-Based Economic Strategy, Facilitation Policy and the Market Process." *Review of Austrian Economics* 17(2/3): 233–245.

Scotchmer, Suzanne. 2004. *Innovation and Incentives*. Cambridge, MA: MIT Press.

Searle, John R. 2005. "What Is an Institution?" *Journal of Institutional Economics* 1(1): 1–22.

Selznick, Philip. 1957. *Leadership in Administration: A Sociological Interpretation*. New York: Harper & Row, Publishers, Inc.

———. 1984. *Leadership in Administration: A Sociological Interpretation*. Berkeley, CA: University of California Press.

Simon, Herbert A. 1974. "How Big is a Chunk?" *Science* 183(4124): 482–488.

Sowell, Thomas. 1987. *A Conflict of Visions. Ideological Origins of Political Struggles*. New York: William Morrow and Company.

Stigler, George J. 1957. "Perfect Competition, Historically Contemplated." *Journal of Political Economy* 65(1): 1–17.

Swetkis, Doreen. 2009. Residential Property Tax Abatement: Testing a Model of Neighborhood Impact. Unpublished Doctoral Dissertation. Cleveland, OH: Cleveland State University.

Tanzi, Vito, and Ludger Schuknecht. 2000. *Public Spending in the 20th Century*. Cambridge, MA: Cambridge University Press.

Thompson, Wilbur R. 1968. "The City as a Distorted Price System." In *The*

City Reader, 4th ed., Richard T. LeGates and Frederic Stout, eds. New York: Routledge, pp. 266–274.

Timilsina, Govinda R., and Hari B. Dulal. 2011. "Urban Road Transportation Externalities: Costs and Choice of Policy Instruments." *World Bank Research Observer* 26(1): 162–191.

Toder, Eric. 2002. "Evaluating Tax Incentives as a Tool for Social and Economic Policy." In *Bad Breaks All Around*. New York: The Century Foundation Press, pp. 3–77.

U.S. Census Bureau. Census 1990 (SF1 and SF3), Census 2000 (SF1 and SF3), and Census 2010 (SF1 and SF3). Washington, DC: U.S. Census Bureau. http://factfinder2.census.gov/faces/nav/jsf/pages/index.xhtml (accessed August 19, 2013).

————. Annual Survey of Governments, 1977, 1982, 1987, 1992, 1997 and 2002: Government Employment and Finance Files. Ann Arbor, MI: Interuniversity Consortium for Political and Social Research. http://www.icpsr.umich.edu (accessed August 19, 2013).

————. 2002. Census of Governments: Finances of County Governments. Washington, DC: U.S. Census Bureau. http://www.census.gov/govs/cog/historical_data_2002.html (accessed August 19, 2013).

Walters, Stephen J. K. 2010. "Unions and the Decline of U.S. Cities." *Cato Journal* 30(1): 117–135.

Warfield, John N. 1988. "The Magical Number Three—Plus or Minus Zero." *Cybernetics and Systems* 19(4): 339–358.

Winston, Clifford. 2006. *Government Failure versus Market Failure: Microeconomics Policy Research and Government Performance*. Washington, DC: AEI-Brookings Joint Center for Regulatory Studies.

Wolf Jr., Charles. 1979. "A Theory of Nonmarket Failure." *Journal of Law and Economics* 22(1): 107–140.

————. 1988. *Markets or Governments: Choosing between Imperfect Alternatives*. Cambridge, MA: The MIT Press.

Zimbalist, Andrew S. 2006. *The Bottom Line: Observations and Arguments on the Sports Business*. Philadelphia: Temple University Press.

11
Lost a Step

The Great Lakes Region and Entrepreneurship

David R. Elkins
Cleveland State University

The Great Lakes region is often synonymous with the Rust Belt. Those tracking the vitality of cities such as Buffalo, Chicago, Cleveland, Detroit, and Milwaukee see economies and populations that are now just fractions of what they once were. But is this really the case? During the Second Industrial Revolution, the Great Lakes region was the focus of intense entrepreneurial activity. Today, while it has lost some of that earlier dynamism, entrepreneurs remain a part of the region's economy. With aggresive and thoughtful policy actions, the region may reclaim some of its former stature as a region attractive to entrepreneurs.

"Lost a step" is an adage directed at the older football player who misses a well-thrown pass, the tennis player who fails to return a serve with the ball just short of her racquet, the athlete who just doesn't appear to be the star he or she once was. A *New York Times Magazine* article ruminated on the nature of the aging athlete, sports, and the New York Yankees shortstop Derek Jeter. The article concluded with a quote from the Yankees general manager, Brian Cashman, "'He's not the same player he used to be,' Cashman said. 'But I think he's above average at that position, despite his age'" (Sokolove 2011).

"Lost a step" is apropos to the issue of entrepreneurialism in the Great Lakes region, which once produced some of the major industries and fortunes that fueled the Gilded Age. Today that entrepreneurial energy and dynamism appear to have drifted to other regions of the United States and the world. For instance, in the high-technology field the most lionized entrepreneurial activities are associated with the West

Coast and not with the industrial Midwest. Today, the entrepreneurial image of the Great Lakes region, to the extent it has one, appears worn and tattered. Is it an empirical reality that the Great Lakes region lacks an entrepreneurial dynamic?

This is the central research question posed by this chapter, which will first explore the nature of entrepreneurship and what it means for an economy. Next, it will present descriptive evidence tackling the issue of whether the Great Lakes region has lost its entrepreneurial vigor. Finally, statistical tests are performed to examine whether, controlling for critical variables, the Great Lakes region has lost a step. The short answer to this final question is that it largely depends on how entrepreneurialism is measured. In one sense, the Great Lakes region has, indeed, lost a step. However, like many seasoned athletes, it remains in the game and competitive.

ENTREPRENEURS AND THE ECONOMY

Who is an entrepreneur and what does the entrepreneur do? Joseph Schumpeter (1939) defined the entrepreneur as an individual who carries out innovations. He suggested that an entrepreneur is neither a profession nor a social class (p. 104; 1949, p. 78). Schumpeter argued that "entrepreneurs come from all classes which at the time of their emergence happen to exist" (p. 104). He also contended that entrepreneurs do not assume financial risk; the entrepreneur risks reputation but "loses other people's money" (p. 104). By contrast, Knight (1921) suggested that the assumption of risk and uncertainty was one of the defining features of the entrepreneur. In fact, Schumpeter's notion that entrepreneurs do not assume risk has been one of the most frequently challenged of his contentions (Hébert and Link 1982, pp. 82–84).

Multiple streams of scholarship have developed in this area, typically contrasting entrepreneurs with nonentrepreneurs (Lundstrom and Stevenson 2005). While at least one scholar suggests that entrepreneurs share distinct personality pathology (Gartner 2005), another stream of literature submits that "special types of individuals create entrepreneurship" (Thornton 1999, p. 22). Scholars have found that entrepreneurs are motivated by a desire to achieve (McCelland 1961) and by other nonpecuniary benefits of entrepreneurial activity (Evans and Leighton 1989; Hamilton 2000) and that they have higher tolerances for risk (Brockhaus 1982; Lazear 2004, 2005; Van Praag and Cramer 2001). In general, entrepreneurs start their ventures at the point at which they have reached maturity in both their careers and their lives. Entrepreneurs with professional and educational training opt for such training that reflects a managerial generalist approach (Lazear 2004, 2005). Access to capital is important for entrepreneurs, and research has shown that individuals with greater access to funding are more likely to be not only entrepreneurs but successful ones (Holtz-Eakin, Joulfaian, and Rosen 1994). Some work suggests that inheritances are an important source of entrepreneurial capital (Branchflower and Oswald 1998), while other research implies that inherited wealth has a limited effect on entrepreneurship (Hurst and Lusardi 2004). Additional exploration indicates that, although parental wealth has a positive impact on entrepreneurial self-employment, it is the parent's self-employment, particularly successful parental self-employment, that may be the defining feature associated with the adult child's trend toward entrepreneurial self-employment (Dunn and Holtz-Eakin 2000).

What do entrepreneurs do? The Schumpeterian notion is that the entrepreneur is an innovator who brings ideas to markets. However, after a lengthy survey of economic literature, economic historians Robert F. Hébert and Albert N. Link suggest in their book *The Entrepreneur* (1982) that the entrepreneur varies by the theoretical context into which that individual is thrust (Hébert and Link 1982, pp. 107–110). At its basic level, the entrepreneur is engaged in both the assumption of risk and innovation. Stated more simply, Shackle, in his introduction to Hébert and Link's book, notes, "the entrepreneur is a man whose characteristic act is a gamble on his imagination" (Shackle 1982, p. viii). Acs and Armington (2006) suggest that entrepreneurship is "what happens at the intersection of history and new technology" (p. 7). Baumol (2010) underscores this idea by noting that there are innovators and replicators. He defines the innovative entrepreneur as one fitting the Schumpeterian model, whose job is "to locate new ideas and to put them into effect" (p. 18). The role of the entrepreneur in the economic system is that of a destabilizing catalyst for economic growth, who "sparks" the economic system and thereby generates economic expansion. The entrepreneur thus acts to transform knowledge into "economic knowledge that otherwise would have remained uncommercialized" (Audretsch and Keilbach 2004, p. 608).

ENTREPRENEURSHIP AND THE GREAT LAKES REGION

During the Second Industrial Revolution roughly between the 1840s and the early part of the twentieth century, the Great Lakes region was filled with entrepreneurial activity. Landes (1969) characterizes this period as having been shaped by "electric power and motors; organic chemistry and synthetics, the internal-combustion engine and automotive devices, precision manufacture and assembly-line production—a cluster of innovations that have earned the name of the Second Industrial Revolution" (p. 235). Schmookler (1966) argues that invention and innovation are not the mere happenstance of noneconomic actors but that they are central to economic enterprise. Further supporting Schumpeter's (1939) argument, Shane's (1996) empirical analysis prompts him to observe that "rates of technological change drive rates of entrepreneurship" (p. 773). Figure 11.1 illustrates the rapid expansion of technological innovation, as shown by the number of U.S. patents per 100,000 population for each year between 1840 and 20000.[1] Around 1850, coinciding with the start of the Second Industrial Revolution, there was a sharp increase in the number of patents, and this level of innovative activity remained high for nearly 100 years. While drawing firm conclusions about economic activity from patent data is problematic (Schmookler 1966; Worgman and Nunn 2002), the statistics are suggestive of the economic expansion taking place in the United States. It just so happens that this surge in invention and innovation coincided with a rapid expansion of the population of the Great Lakes region.[2]

Figure 11.2 illustrates the scope of the Great Lakes regional population expansion. The solid line indicates the decade-to-decade percentage change of the total U.S. population, and the dashed line depicts the decade-to-decade percentage change in the population for the counties containing five major Great Lakes cities.[3] For many decades the decennial growth of these counties far exceeded the growth of the United States. According to U.S. Census figures, these five counties had fewer than 250,000 persons combined in 1840, but by 1930 they had well over

Figure 11.1 Patent Rate, 1840–2000

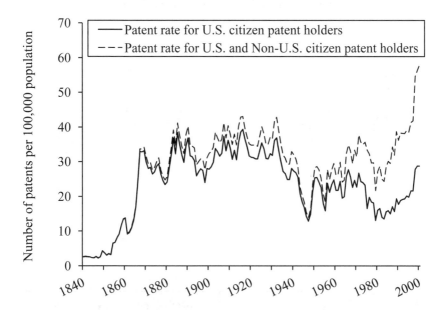

SOURCE: Wright (2006).

8 million, accounting for over 7 percent of the total U.S. population. It is worth noting that prior to 1860, no Great Lakes city was ranked in the nation's top 10 by population. However, beginning in 1860 and for decades thereafter, Great Lakes cities would emerge as some of the largest in the country (Gibson 1998). McClelland (1961) finds that the surge in his measure of "achievement motivation" coincided with the jump in patent issuances. It seems plausible that the growth in population, invention and innovation, and the desire to achieve found fertile entrepreneurial ground in the Great Lakes region. Certainly, between 1840 and the start of the Great Depression, cities in the area thrived, as did the entrepreneurs who called these places home. Indeed, some scholars have compared the dynamism of the Great Lakes region to that which occurred during California's high technology boom (Klepper 2009; Lamoreaux, Levenstein, and Sokoloff 2006).

In recent years, this area has been viewed as home to old manufacturing centers enduring steep declines in production and employment

Figure 11.2 Percentage Change in Population for the United States and Selected Great Lakes Counties, 1850–2000

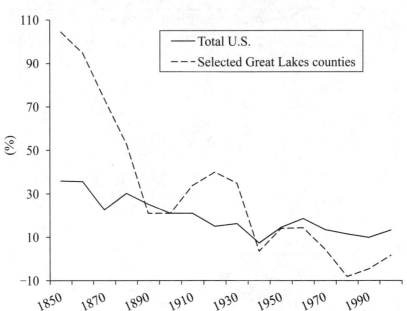

SOURCE: U.S. Census Bureau (1996).

(Hill and Negrey 1987). As depicted in Figure 11.2, the decennial percentage growth for the region either kept pace with or exceeded that of the nation for nearly a century. However, since 1960 the trend shows a region lagging substantially behind the rest of the nation in population growth, a phenomenon that has led some to describe the area as decaying and abandoned. For instance, in 1985 the Federal Reserve Bank of Chicago (FRBC) (1985) suggested that too many observers think of the Great Lakes states as the "sick old man" of the United States (p. v). Still, the FRBC underscored that this was not an entirely accurate image. Later, for instance, Negrey and Zickel (1994) noted that the region is home to metropolitan areas that are both "stable transition centers" and "innovation centers" (p. 35). More recently, Acs and Armington (2006) have commented, "The South and the West have the strongest new firm start-up rates, while the Northeast and the Midwest, which were formerly characterized by large-scale manufacturing, generally continue to lag behind the rest of the country" (p. 53). Clearly, the region trails in many areas. Its population is growing more slowly than is that of much of the United States. Many of its central cities have lost significant population due to out-migration to either nearby suburban areas or other parts of the country. The nature of this long-term decline raises the chief question for this chapter: Relative to other regions of the United States, is entrepreneurship lagging in the Great Lakes region?

DATA AND METHODS

Proximity to the Great Lakes directly affects the region and its population. From commerce to leisure, this connection is fundamental. For the purposes of this chapter, the Great Lakes region is inclusive of both urbanized and rural areas and is defined here as any county that is contiguous to one of the Great Lakes and any county bordering that county. For example, Wayne County, Michigan, adjoins Lake Erie. Wayne County is defined as part of the Great Lakes region, along with its two neighboring counties, Oakland County and Washtenaw County. In addition, the National Oceanic and Atmospheric Administration provides a list of counties that are relevant to this list.[4] According to the definition used in this chapter, the Great Lakes region consists of 178 counties across 8 states. For this analysis, however, because of missing or otherwise unreported data, only 146 of these 178 counties are included in this designation.[5]

This regional definition is unambiguously narrow. It is used to identify the core of the region and to exclude those areas that are geographically peripheral. This approach avoids some of the pitfalls of defining regions by the states that they contain. For instance, if all of New York State were included in a definition of the Great Lakes region, the region would include New York City and Buffalo.

Three measurements of entrepreneurial activity will be used: 1) business establishments per 1,000 labor force (business density); 2) percent self-employed individuals (percent self-employed; Branchflower and Oswald [1998]); and 3) business establishment "births" per 1,000 labor force (business birth rate; Acs and Armington [2004, 2006]). Each method covers some feature of the conceptual notion of entrepreneurship. For instance, business density provides a generalized notion of commercial activity and, perhaps, reflects the idea that members of the business community perceive opportunity. The number of business establishment births provides a direct indicator of entrepreneurial activity. The ratio of business births to business deaths is not included in this analysis because the key issue is an examination of entrepreneurial business starts and not entrepreneurial success. Stated another way, this chapter explores whether entrepreneurialism occurs and not whether it is successful. Finally, percent self-employed provides a measure of the degree to which individuals alone are engaged in entrepreneurial activity. The data for business density and business establishment births are derived from the U.S. Census Bureau's County Business Patterns, and the data for self-employed individuals are derived from the U.S. Social Security Administration (2011).

Table 11.1 provides the means and standard deviations for each of the three indicators of entrepreneurship. Several points are established in the table. First, the regions vary in entrepreneurial activity. For instance, the Great Lakes region's business density has a mean of 4.71 (standard deviation [sd] = 1.09), which means 4.71 business establishments per 1,000 members of the labor force. This places the business density of the counties of the Great Lakes region above that of the counties in the South but below that of every other region. Second, the variation among the regions for each of these variables is statistically significant.[6] Third, a pattern emerges that places the counties of the Great Lakes region at or near the bottom among these measures and the West's counties at either the top or near the top. Finally, the Great Lakes' counties, for every measure, fall below the average for all the counties. For example, the Great Lakes' counties mean for percent self-employed is 10.5 (sd = 0.04); however the total for all counties, including the Great Lakes' counties, is 12.4 (sd = 0.05). This snapshot of the nature of the Great Lakes region depicts an area that, while still engaged in entrepreneurial activity, lags behind the nation as a whole and most all other regions. Despite these apparent regional differences, it is important to determine, once controlling for variables linked to entrepreneurship, whether the Great Lakes region lacks the same degree of entrepreneurship as do other regions in the United States.

**Table 11.1 County Business Density, Percent Self-Employed, and
Business Birth Rate by Region, 2008**

Region	Business density	% self-employed	Business birth rate
Great Lakes[a]	4.71	10.49	3.99
(n = 146)	(1.09)	(0.04)	(1.19)
Northeast[b]	5.03	11.32	4.14
(n = 183)	(1.25)	(0.04)	(1.28)
Midwest[c]	4.80	13.06	3.66
(n = 509)	(1.07)	(0.06)	(1.06)
South[d]	4.60	12.41	4.15
(n = 884)	(1.37)	(0.04)	(1.40)
West[e]	5.71	13.03	5.74
(n = 249)	(1.92)	(0.05)	(2.31)
Total	4.83	12.41	4.21
(N = 1,971)	(1.40)	(0.05)	(1.57)

NOTE: Means are reported, with standard deviations in parentheses.
[a] Includes all counties bordering the Great Lakes and their contiguous counties across
eight states: Illinois, Indiana, Michigan, Minnesota, New York, Ohio, Pennsylvania,
and Wisconsin.
[b] Includes all counties in Connecticut, Massachusetts, Maine, New Hampshire, New
Jersey, Rhode Island, and Vermont. New York and Pennsylvania counties not defined
as Great Lakes counties are defined as Northeast region counties.
[c] Includes all counties in Iowa, Kansas, Missouri, North Dakota, Nebraska, and South
Dakota. Illinois, Indiana, Michigan, Minnesota, Ohio, and Wisconsin counties not
defined as Great Lakes counties are defined as Midwest region counties.
[d] Includes all counties in the states of Alabama, Arkansas, Delaware, Florida, Georgia, Kentucky, Louisiana, Maryland, Mississippi, North Carolina, Oklahoma, South
Carolina, Tennessee, Texas, Virginia, and West Virginia.
[e] Includes all counties in the states of Alaska, Arizona, California, Colorado, Hawaii,
Idaho, Montana, New Mexico, Nevada, Oregon, Utah, Washington, and Wyoming.
SOURCE: U.S. Census Bureau (2008); U.S. Social Security Administration (2011).

Analysis of Entrepreneurship

Scholars have found a number of variables associated with entrepreneurship. Age is one of these factors. The notion behind entrepreneur's age is that over time individuals develop knowledge (both formal and experiential), reputations within their fields, and a degree of
communication acumen. At a point in life, a person may view a propi-
tious moment to leverage these traits and go into an entrepreneurial

venture. By contrast, as individuals become older they are less willing to bear risk: "[A]ge has a curvilinear relationship with the exploitation of opportunity," as noted by Shane (2003, p. 95). For the purposes of this analysis, it is anticipated that there will be a positive relationship between the median age of a county's population and entrepreneurial activity.

Secondly, most empirical research on entrepreneurs finds that they have relatively extensive formal education. While formal schooling is not required to engage in entrepreneurial efforts, those entrepreneurs who are successful frequently have higher levels of education (Brüderl, Preisendörfer, and Ziegler 1992; Van Praag and Cramer 2001). As part of a theoretical approach advocating the importance of human capital, education has been linked empirically with measures of U.S. economic growth (Hoyman and Faricy 2008). I expect that the proportion of a county's population that is college educated is positively associated with entrepreneurial activity and measure the college-educated population as the percentage of people aged 25 years or older in a county who have at least a bachelor's degree.[7]

A third variable is immigration. A number of scholars have noted that some immigrant groups trend toward entrepreneurial self-employment and that this is a significant feature of the immigrant experience (Borjas 1986). Researchers suggest several reasons immigrants are involved in entrepreneurial self-employment. For instance, they may do so because of their lack of adequate English language skills, the possibility to reduce labor costs by recruiting family members as employees, the potential absence of host-country recognition for their educational credentials, and a more generalized host-country hostility (Bonacich 1973; Evans 1989; Portes and Jensen 1989; Sanders and Nee 1996; Wilson and Portes 1980). While some immigrant groups may be drawn toward self-employment, it may also be that as self-selected migrants they have a greater degree of entrepreneurial spirit than others. For example, Saxenian (2002) finds that immigrant labor is a vital component of the Silicon Valley's entrepreneurial success. Also, it is not clear that immigrants are prompting greater entrepreneurship; immigrants' location decisions may be driven by a desire to locate in areas of the country where they believe they will have the most economic opportunity. Unlike native-born residents, who may have familial obligations and attachments that increase domestic relocation costs, immigrants may have comparatively lower costs and be freer to select where to live. I anticipate that the percentage of foreign-born population in a county will be positively associated with entrepreneurship.[8]

Another variable associated with entrepreneurship is taxation. There is a debate in the literature regarding taxation's role in entrepreneurial behavior. One stream of research suggests that a higher marginal tax rate in a progressive tax system depresses entrepreneurialism (Gentry and Hubbard 2000; Shane 2003). Shane (2003) suggests, "Higher marginal tax rates make people less willing to accept variable earning, thus decreasing the likelihood of self-employment" and they "reduce people's perception of the profitability of exploiting opportunities" (p. 153). Additional scholars have found that tax rates affect other features of entrepreneurial behavior. For instance, one study suggests that when the marginal tax rates of self-employed entrepreneurs increase, they are less likely to hire more employees (Carroll et al. 2000, p. 349). Bartik (1985) finds that higher marginal corporate tax rates are linked with a slight decline in new manufacturing plants among the states.

By contrast, a separate stream of literature suggests that higher marginal tax rates compel individuals toward self-employment, a measure of entrepreneurship, to avoid tax obligations (Blau 1987; Bruce 2000; Schuetze 2000). As Blau (1987) states, "The main effect of higher tax rates is expected to be an increase in self-employment due to the increased attractiveness of underreporting income at higher tax rates and the presumed greater ease of underreporting self-employment income relative to wage-salary income" (p. 457). Clearly, to the extent that entrepreneurs are less risk averse, pursuing tax avoidance represents a risk-taking venture. For the purposes of this analysis, no position is taken on the underlying theoretical motivations of entrepreneurs and taxation. However, the expectation is that taxation will have some influence on the degree of a county's entrepreneurship. Taxation will be measured as a statewide variable of per-capita individual income tax as of 2008 (Council of State Governments 2010).[9]

An economically related variable is unemployment. Some suggest that joblessness may prompt individuals toward self-employment. The argument is that should an individual become unemployed, a reasonable response might be to form a new business (Reynolds 1994). To that extent, it is anticipated that counties with higher levels of unemployment will see higher levels of entrepreneurial behavior. Still, other research has strongly indicated that capital is a critical element of the entrepreneurial effort. To the extent that unemployment suggests a lagging economy, there may simply be less start-up capital available to initiate an entrepreneurial venture, no matter how much a potential entrepreneur may desire to do so. To that end, an alternative expectation is that unemployment will be inversely associated with entrepreneurialism. The variable used here is the county's unemployment rate for 2008, derived from the U.S. Bureau of Labor Statistics Local Area Unemployment Statistics.

Because many counties have varying degrees of an urban-rural split, I include a variable depicting the percentage of rural population for each county. The reasoning is that in more rural areas one may find entrepreneurialism captured by self-ownership of family farms and other enterprises. The variable is an eight-year extrapolation between the census counts of the years 2000 and 2010 for the percentage of urban population.

Finally, region is measured as a dichotomous dummy variable. For instance, the analysis will identify those counties defined as part of the Great Lakes region as 1 and all others as 0. This method will be used for all other regions as well (Northeast, Midwest, South, and West). The following ordinary least squares (OLS) estimations examine each region separately. If the assumption that the Great Lakes region is lagging in its entrepreneurial activity is correct, it is expected that each of the following OLS estimates will be both statistically significant and negative. Before proceeding to that feature of this analysis, a brief examination of the descriptive statistics is in order.

Reported in Table 11.2 are the summary statistics for the control variables by the five regions. Among the control variables, the Northeast counties have the highest mean value for median age and the West has the lowest value. By contrast, the Northeast counties, on average, have a high proportion of their populations with bachelor's degrees. For example, among the valid data used for this analysis, nearly one-quarter (24.6 percent, n = 45) of Northeast counties have populations where one-third has bachelor's degrees. In comparison, only nine of the Great Lakes counties report such a statistic. The counties of the West show populations that are nearly as well educated.

Counties of the West and the Northeast have the greatest proportion of foreign-born population, while the Midwest and the Great Lakes

Table 11.2 Descriptive Statistics for Key Variables by Regional Counties

Variables	Great Lakes N = 146	Northeast N = 183	Midwest N = 509	South N = 884	West N = 249
Median age, 2008 (est.)	39.20	40.14	38.54	37.41	36.89
	(3.14)	(2.73)	(3.85)	(3.69)	(4.91)
Percent bachelor's degree,	21.04	26.97	20.18	19.21	25.15
2006–2010	(7.74)	(9.73)	(7.90)	(9.10)	(10.37)
Percent foreign born,	3.55	7.26	2.86	4.95	9.74
2006–2010	(3.41)	(8.18)	(3.08)	(5.29)	(7.80)
Unemployment rate, 2008	7.29	5.49	5.47	5.87	6.09
	(1.76)	(1.05)	(1.59)	(1.80)	(2.54)
State-level per-capita	1,009.95	1,256.39	930.60	648.75	848.58
income tax, 2008 ($)	(416.77)	(531.17)	(289.66)	(449.32)	(551.97)
Percent rural, 2008 (est.)	51.40	41.70	50.81	50.34	35.42
	(26.89)	(29.80)	(25.55)	(27.48)	(25.89)

NOTE: Means are reported with standard deviation (in parentheses).
SOURCE: Council of State Governments (2010); U.S. Census Bureau (2009, 2011a, 2012); U.S. Department of Labor (2008).

counties have the lowest values. To provide some further perspective, this variable is divided into three categories. According to 2010 census figures, 12.9 percent of the population is foreign born (Grieco et al. 2012). Using the 12.9 percent figure, three foreign-born population categories were created: 1) 6.5 percent and less (half the 12.9 percent figure); 2) between 6.5 and 12.9 percent; and 3) 12.9 percent and greater. More than 9 out of 10 Midwest counties (90.0 percent, n = 458) have less than half the U.S. average for foreign-born population. The proportions are nearly identical for Great Lakes region counties (88.4 percent, n = 129). However, over a quarter (26.9 percent, n = 67) of the West region counties have proportions of foreign-born populations above the national average.

Turning to economic variables, this cross-sectional analysis depicts the Great Lakes region with the highest mean unemployment rate at 7.28 percent (sd = 1.75). By contrast, the Midwest and Northeast counties have the lowest mean unemployment rates. Finally, the per-capita personal income tax is greatest in the Northeast counties and lowest in the South.

Regression Findings

In Tables 11.3, 11.4, and 11.5 the OLS results are presented for each of the dependent variables. Table 11.3 depicts the OLS outcomes for business density with the control variables and the regional dummy variables, which confirm many of the findings of previous scholars studying entrepreneurship. The data indicate that counties with higher median ages and larger proportions of their populations with bachelor's degrees are positively associated with business density. In addition, the analysis suggests that unemployment is inversely associated with the business density variable. This offers some support for the notion that economic challenges depress entrepreneurship rather than inspiring it. Among the regional variables, the Northeast, the South, and the West show statistically significant results. The Northeast and the South regions report inverse relationships with the business density variable, −0.537 and −0.183, respectively. This suggests that these regions' counties have lower business densities than other regions' counties, all other things being equal. By contrast, the West regional variable shows a positive, statistically significant result (0.937), indicating that this region's counties have greater business density. Finally, in the Great Lakes region the estimate is negative, but it is not statistically significant.

Table 11.4 illustrates the regression data for the percent self-employed. As with the business density variable from the previous table, the results depicted in Table 11.4 provide support for much of the previous scholarship in this field. Across most categories depicted in Table 11.4, the control variables are statistically significant. Age and percent foreign born are positively associated with percent self-employed. By contrast, the unemployment rate and a state's tax burden are inversely associated with percent self-employment. The percent of population with bachelor's degree fails to attain statistical significance. According to these findings, a county's percent self-employed is independent of its population proportion of college educated. Finally, the percent rural variable has a positive, statistically significant result, indicating that the greater the rural proportion of a county, the greater the proportion of self-employed residents.

Table 11.4 indicates that counties in both the Great Lakes and Northeast regions have statistically significant, inverse associations with percent self-employed. These results suggest that, in general, a county in

Table 11.3 Multivariate Linear Regression Results for Business Density, 2008

		Regional analysis				
Variables	Control variables	Great Lakes	Northeast	Midwest	South	West
Constant	-0.828***	-0.889***	-1.209***	-0.807**	-0.537	-0.798***
	(0.320)	(0.322)	(0.325)	(0.322)	(0.333)	(0.310)
Median age, 2008	0.123***	0.124***	0.131***	0.123***	0.120***	0.124***
(est.)	(0.007)	(0.007)	(0.008)	(0.007)	(0.008)	(0.007)
Percent bachelor's	0.062**	0.062***	0.064***	0.062***	0.060***	0.059***
degree, 2006–2010	(0.004)	(0.004)	(0.004)	(0.004)	(0.004)	(0.004)
Percent foreign born,	0.009	0.008	0.011**	0.008	0.010	-0.005
2006–2010	(0.006)	(0.006)	(0.006)	(0.006)	(0.006)	(0.006)
Unemployment rate,	-0.045***	-0.039**	-0.046***	-0.046***	-0.048***	-0.061***
2008	(0.016)	(0.017)	(0.016)	(0.016)	(0.016)	(0.016)
State-level income	-0.106	-0.099	0.030	-0.101	-0.163***	-0.093
tax, 2008	(0.059)	(0.059)	(0.060)	(0.060)	(0.062)	(0.057)
Percent rural, 2008	-0.028	-0.031	-0.035	-0.031	-0.003	-0.005
(est.)	(0.122)	(0.122)	(0.121)	(0.122)	(0.122)	(0.118)
Great Lakes		-0.157				
		(0.108)				
Northeast			-0.537***			
			(0.101)			
Midwest				-0.039		
				(0.065)		
South					-0.183***	
					(0.059)	
West						0.937***
						(0.083)
Adjusted R^2	0.258	0.259	0.269	0.258	0.262	0.303
N	1,971	1,971	1,971	1,971	1,971	1,971

NOTE: Standard errors are in parentheses. * significant at the 0.10 level; ** significant at the 0.05 level; *** significant at the 0.01 level.
SOURCE: Council of State Governments (2010); U.S. Census Bureau (2008, 2009, 2011a,b, 2012); U.S. Department of Labor (2008).

either the Northeast or Great Lakes regions will report nearly 2 percent fewer self-employed. By contrast, positive coefficients are associated with both the Midwest and West dummy variables. This indicates that counties in the Midwest and the West regions are likely to have moderately greater levels of self-employment than are those counties not in these regions. While the West dummy variable's positive coefficient is as anticipated, the Midwest variable's positive relationship is unex-

Table 11.4 Multivariate Linear Regression Results for Percent Self-Employed, 2008

Variables	Control variables	Regional analysis				
		Great Lakes	Northeast	Midwest	South	West
Constant	−0.015	−0.023*	−0.029**	−0.020	−0.011	−0.015
	(0.011)	(0.011)	(0.011)	(0.011)	(0.011)	(0.011)
Median age, 2008	0.003***	0.003***	0.003***	0.003***	0.003***	0.003***
(est.)	(0.000)	(0.000)	(0.000)	(0.000)	(0.000)	(0.000)
Percent bachelor's	0.000	0.000	0.000	0.000	0.000	0.000
degree, 2006–2010	(0.000)	(0.000)	(0.000)	(0.000)	(0.000)	(0.000)
Percent foreign born,	0.002***	0.002***	0.002***	0.002***	0.002***	0.001***
2006–2010	(0.000)	(0.000)	(0.000)	(0.000)	(0.000)	(0.000)
Unemployment rate,	−0.003***	−0.002***	−0.003***	−0.003***	−0.003***	−0.003***
2008	(0.001)	(0.001)	(0.001)	(0.001)	(0.001)	(0.001)
State-level income	−0.009***	−0.008***	−0.006***	−0.010***	−0.009***	−0.008***
tax, 2008	(0.002)	(0.002)	(0.002)	(0.002)	(0.002)	(0.002)
Percent rural, 2008	0.074***	0.074***	0.074***	0.075***	0.075***	0.075***
(est.)	(0.004)	(0.004)	(0.004)	(0.004)	(0.004)	(0.004)
Great Lakes		−0.020***				
		(0.004)				
Northeast			−0.019***			
			(0.003)			
Midwest				0.009***		
				(0.002)		
South					−0.003	
					(0.002)	
West						0.015***
						(0.003)
Adjusted R^2	0.257	0.266	0.266	0.261	0.255	0.265
N	1,971	1,971	1,971	1,971	1,971	1,971

NOTE: Standard errors are in parentheses. * significant at the 0.10 level; ** significant at the 0.05 level; *** significant at the 0.01 level.
SOURCE: Council of State Governments (2010); U.S. Census Bureau (2008, 2009, 2011a,b, 2012); U.S. Department of Labor (2008).

pected. To some degree, the prevailing stereotype is that this region is not associated with exceptional entrepreneurial activity. Part of this result may be explained by the way the Great Lakes dummy variable has been created. That is to say, other definitions of the Midwest region frequently include counties of the Great Lakes. The definition used in this chapter creates a discrete Great Lakes counties variable. By excluding those counties from the Midwest variable designation, the Midwest dummy variable's results suggest that the drag on the Midwest's economic dynamism may be associated with those counties in and around the Great Lakes. The result of the Great Lakes dummy variable does support the notion that the counties of this region are lagging in entrepreneurial activity.

Table 11.5 depicts the OLS results for the final dependent variable, the business birth rate. Among the control variables, age, education, and foreign-born population are statistically significant and positively associated with the business birth rate. While the unemployment rate is not statistically significant in these results, the variable representing the tax burden is statistically significant with across-the-board negative coefficients. As with the percent self-employment dependent variable, the percent rural variable's positive coefficient indicates that the less urbanized a county is, the more business births that county is likely to experience. The regional variables depict results consistent with previous analyses. First, the Northeast dummy variable has a negative coefficient with the business birth rate. Second, the West dummy variable has a positive coefficient with the business birth rate. Unlike the Midwest dummy variable's positive association with percent self-employment, the variable has a statistically significant negative coefficient with the business birth rate. By contrast, the South and the Great Lakes dummy variables do not achieve statistical significance with the dependent variable. The South dummy variable has a positive but not statistically significant coefficient. The Great Lakes dummy variable is negative, but it is not a statistically significant result.

Table 11.6 provides a summary of the various statistical tests for each of the dependent variables. In general, the results depicted in these statistical tests confirm much of the scholarship examining entrepreneurial activity. The consistent or near-consistent outcomes for many of the control variables suggest that in counties with relatively better educated and older populations there is greater probability of entrepreneurial activity. A relatively larger foreign-born population is also associated with entrepreneurial activity, and rural areas report consistent degrees of entrepreneurial activity. By contrast, the economic and tax burdens can, according to this cross-sectional analysis, depress entrepreneurial activity.

Turning to the regional analysis, there are some consistent results that comport with both previous research and conventional wisdom.

**Table 11.5 Multivariate Linear Regression Results for Business Birth
Rate, 2008**

Variables	Control variables	Great Lakes	Northeast	Midwest	South	West
			Regional analysis			
Constant	−0.728**	−0.805**	−1.257***	−0.425	−0.881**	−0.682**
	(0.352)	(0.355)	(0.357)	(0.349)	(0.367)	(0.331)
Median age, 2008	0.086***	0.087***	0.098***	0.087***	0.088***	0.088***
(est.)	(0.008)	(0.008)	(0.008)	(0.008)	(0.008)	(0.008)
Percent bachelor's	0.083***	0.084***	0.087***	0.081***	0.084***	0.079***
degree, 2006–2010	(0.004)	(0.004)	(0.004)	(0.004)	(0.004)	(0.004)
Percent foreign born,	0.042***	0.041***	0.046***	0.032***	0.042***	0.021***
2006–2010	(0.006)	(0.006)	(0.006)	(0.006)	(0.006)	(0.006)
Unemployment rate,	0.002	0.009	0.000	−0.019	0.003	−0.022
2008	(0.018)	(0.018)	(0.018)	(0.018)	(0.018)	(0.017)
State-level income	−0.557***	−0.548***	−0.451***	−0.476***	−0.527***	−0.536***
tax, 2008	(0.065)	(0.065)	(0.066)	(0.065)	(0.068)	(0.061)
Percent rural, 2008	0.291**	0.287***	0.281**	0.244	0.277**	0.326***
(est.)	(0.134)	(0.134)	(0.133)	(0.132)	(0.134)	(0.126)
Great Lakes		−0.198				
		(0.119)				
Northeast			−0.744***			
			(0.110)			
Midwest				−0.567***		
				(0.070)		
South					0.096	
					(0.066)	
West						1.445***
						(0.089)
Adjusted R^2	0.285	0.286	0.308	0.308	0.286	0.369
N	1,971	1,971	1,971	1,971	1,971	1,971

NOTE: Standard errors are in parentheses. * significant at the 0.10 level; ** significant
at the 0.05 level; *** significant at the 0.01 level.
SOURCE: Council of State Governments (2010); U.S. Census Bureau (2008, 2009,
2011a,b, 2012); U.S. Department of Labor (2008).

Across all three dependent variables, counties of the West are positively
associated with business density, self-employment, and business births.
To the extent that the three dependent variables represent features of
entrepreneurship, the strong impression is that the West is leading in
entrepreneurial efforts. By contrast, a different result is apparent for
Northeast counties. For the Northeast, the evidence indicates that business density, self-employment, and business births are relatively lower

Table 11.6 Summary Results of Statistical Tests for Business Density Rate, Percent Self-Employed, and Business Birth Rate

Variables	Business density rate	Percent self-employed	Business birth rate
Median age, 2008 (est.)	+	+	+
Percent bachelor's degree, 2006–2010	+		+
Percent foreign born, 2006–2010		+	+
Unemployment rate, 2008	−	−	
State-level individual income tax, 2008		−	−
Percent rural, 2008 (est.)		+	+
Great Lakes		−	
Northeast	−	−	−
Midwest		+	−
South	−		
West	+	+	+

SOURCE: Tables 11.3, 11.4, and 11.5.

than found in non-Northeast counties. However, the interpretation of the results for the counties of the Great Lakes must be guarded. In only one of the dependent variables, percent self-employed, does this regional variable report statistical significance.

ENTREPRENEURIAL POLICY AND THE GREAT LAKES

What strategies may be offered given the mixed empirical results for the Great Lakes region? As stated by Eisinger (1995), entrepreneurial policies, particularly state-based ones, are "designed to foster indigenous firms and local entrepreneurial capabilities" (p. 147). Eisinger (1988) once argued that entrepreneurial economic development policies were emerging as an important feature of a state's overall portfolio of developmental initiatives and as a movement away from the strategy of industrial relocation policies. However, a few years after making that claim, Eisinger (1995) suggested that as policy learning took place, state development policy evolved in other directions. Saiz (2001) argues that the underlying motive for this policy shift was one of context. He suggests that states strategically retreated from entrepreneurial policies once confronted with the possibility of losing business to neighboring states competing for industrial relocation.

Another reason for this shift among state policymakers is that they have few tangible incentives to initiate entrepreneurial policies. As Hart (2008) observes,

> [T]he puzzle for political scientists is why entrepreneurial state ED [economic development] strategies have caught on. Their economic and programmatic promise notwithstanding, their political logic seems to contain neither rent seeking nor credit claiming. At least at first glance, the direct beneficiaries of entrepreneurial strategies appear to be far more widely diffused and poorly organized than those of locational strategies. In fact, in the case of future start-ups, the individual beneficiaries are unknown and the corporate beneficiaries, nonexistent. Most of the economic gains that these beneficiaries produce will emerge long after those who instigated the policies have left office. The credit for this economic success, if it can be claimed by any policy makers at all, will not accrue to the instigators of the strategy, but rather their successors in office. (p. 154)

A full examination of state-based entrepreneurial policies is beyond the scope of this chapter. However, one place to start would be to analyze the degree to which the variables empirically associated with entrepreneurship may be used to capture some features of the regions, an approach that may help policymakers identify strengths and weaknesses they may wish to address. Logistic regression is used, with each region defined as a binomial dependent variable. A county is assigned to its constituent region, coded one if it is in a region and otherwise a zero. Next, each independent variable associated with entrepreneurship regression analysis is used to detect regional features.

As depicted in Table 11.7, the Great Lakes region, in the first column, indicates with its positive coefficients for median age and education that it is presumably well positioned for entrepreneurship. However, the Great Lakes region is also defined by its unemployment, and to that extent unemployment may act as a drag on entrepreneurial activities. For policymakers, the inverse coefficient with percent foreign born strongly suggests that the region's public and private sector leaders should attempt to find ways to make the area more attractive to immigrants. It is clear that some of the region's leaders are moving to address this issue.

Recently, the city of Chicago passed what its officials call a "Welcoming City" ordinance. In addition, Mayor Rahm Emanuel declared his desire to make Chicago the most immigrant-friendly city in the United States (City of Chicago 2012). The largely symbolic ordinance was seen as a response to the anti-immigrant measures being adopted in some states (Huffington Post 2012). Still, the underlying desire on the part of officials in the Great Lakes region to attract immigrants is to be encouraged. For example, the National League of Cities identifies a number of proposals to assist with immigrant integration (Gambetta and Gedrimaite 2010). Many of the strategies focus on administrative coordination between and among federal, state, and local authorities. More concrete recommendations are targeted toward the creation of mayoral

Table 11.7 Logistic Regression Results for Regional Variables

Variables	Great Lakes	Northeast	Midwest	South	West
Constant	−11.180***	−13.490***	1.294	5.409***	−2.838***
	(1.210)	(1.194)	(0.700)	(0.611)	(0.785)
Median age, 2008 (est.)	0.071***	0.221***	−0.008	−0.091***	−0.022
	(0.014)	(0.027)	(0.016)	(0.014)	(0.18)
Percent bachelor's degree, 2006–2010	0.092***	0.044***	−0.005	−0.042***	0.031***
	(0.014)	(0.011)	(0.009)	(0.007)	(0.009)
Percent foreign born, 2006–2010	−0.195***	0.010	−0.254***	0.019	0.079***
	(0.034)	(0.017)	(0.026)	(0.011)	(0.012)
Unemployment rate, 2008	0.609***	−0.053	−0.252***	−0.077***	0.147***
	(0.057	(0.062)	(0.037)	(0.029)	(0.042)
State-level income tax, 2008	1.169***	2.085***	0.934***	−1.512***	−0.184
	(0.231)	(0.212)	(0.140)	(0.119)	(0.143)
Percent rural, 2008 (est.)	−0.581	−0.686	−0.678***	0.644***	−0.467
	(0.413)	(0.365)	(0.253)	(0.225)	(0.318)
−2 log likelihood	855.592	935.928	1,974.009	2,373.771	1,343.403
Cox and Snell adjusted R^2	0.087	0.134	0.130	0.157	0.076
N	1,971	1,971	1,971	1,971	1,971

NOTE: The values in the table represent logistic regression coefficients, with the standard errors are in parentheses. * significant at the 0.10 level; ** significant at the 0.05 level; *** significant at the 0.01 level.
SOURCE: Council of State Governments (2010); U.S. Census Bureau (2008, 2009, 2011a,b, 2012); U.S. Department of Labor (2008).

advisory boards and addressing language issues. The National League of Cities report identified 20 cities engaged in meeting the challenges of immigrant populations. To be globally competitive in an entrepreneurial world, the Great Lakes region must more vigorously engage in immigration outreach and support.

Separately, policymakers may need to address issues related to their region's less-than-competitive tax burden. The statistically significant positive coefficient in Table 11.7 indicates that the counties of the Great Lakes region are characterized, relative to the counties of most other regions, as having a relatively higher tax burden. Recently, many of the region's policymakers, most notably led by recently elected conservative Republican governors, have been moving to adjust their state's tax structures. From the perspective of stimulating entrepreneurial development, the challenge for these officials is to find the means to provide appropriate entrepreneur-oriented tax relief while not undermining the region's educational advantage. The analysis depicted here clearly links an educated population with some forms of entrepreneurial activity. Cutting state education budgets to provide tax relief may not work in the long-term interest of developing an entrepreneurial environment. Still, as Hart (2008) observes, providing for a future long-term developmental payoff may be less compelling than a more immediate political one.

Beyond the central focus of this chapter, it is worth briefly commenting on the nature of the results relative to the other regional designations. The counties of the Northeast region are distinctly urban and defined by their relatively low rates of unemployment, older populations, and high percent of foreign born. They are also defined by state-level tax burdens that may depress entrepreneurialism. The Midwest region benefits from its relatively low levels of unemployment, but is defined by its very low rates of immigration and its state-level tax burden, which is greater than either the West or South. Indeed, perhaps the signature characteristic of the Midwest counties is the low levels of foreign born. The Southern counties can be identified by their relatively low tax burdens. However, this region is also defined by its youth and relative lack of college-educated adult citizens. Southern policymakers continue to struggle with their education systems and making them competitive in a global economy. To the extent that education plays a significant role in entrepreneurship, that region's policymakers will need to address these issues. Finally, the counties of the West are defined by their relatively higher degrees of education and large foreign-born populations. Still, the counties of the West lead in entrepreneurialism. The challenge public and private actors may need to address is that it remains defined by a degree of unemployment.

CONCLUSION

Entrepreneurialism is a driver of economic growth. Historically, the Great Lakes region has been linked with the entrepreneurial development of many major companies in the United States. However, today there is a strong sense that this region, like an aging star athlete, has lost a step in its entrepreneurial dynamism. The results depicted in this analysis support elements of that assumption. To be clear, this analysis is a snapshot of a time prior to the enduring economic slump beginning in the fall of 2008. The region is still productive and competitive in a number of ways, but, in several factors related to self-employment, all things being equal, it lags behind other U.S. regions. In addition, this analysis is consistent with the current and widely held view of the western United States as a driver of U.S. entrepreneurial activity.

For policymakers in the Great Lakes region, some features of their locales are signs of hope. They are advantaged by the degree to which they have an educated population relative to other places. Given the notion that entrepreneurialism links innovation to the market, an educated workforce is an important asset, particularly in a digital information age. However, to the extent that the region is also defined by its relatively high tax burdens and its relatively low proportion of foreign born, these elements need to be addressed. In the Great Lakes states, recently elected Republican governors and Republican-controlled state legislatures have made it part of their agenda to address noncompetitive features of their states' tax codes. For the purpose of entrepreneurial economic stimulation, this is a worthwhile endeavor. However, these groups must use caution not to undermine the quality of their states' educational institutions. In addition, some regional leaders are making strides in finding methods to make the Great Lakes area a magnet for highly educated immigrants. This is important. During the region's boom years it was a major destination for many migrants and immigrants. They brought their energy and inventiveness and spurred unprecedented industrial development.

To the cities and counties that comprise the Great Lakes region, this is a marketing opportunity to showcase the advantages of the area's many unique and shared attributes, such as direct access to a stable, natural fresh-water resource. The communities of this region may wish to shape their appeals to educated potential immigrant populations. Such a campaign may wish to express that this region offers, for the right entrepreneurs, an overlooked opportunity.

Notes

1. Figure 11.1 includes data illustrating patents issued to both domestic and foreign patent holders. While the potential implications of the growing disparity between domestic and foreign patent holders are interesting, they are beyond the scope of this chapter to explore more fully.
2. By contrast, Wilken (1972) places the surge of U.S. economic growth between 1810 and 1880.
3. The counties include Cook County (Chicago, Illinois), Cuyahoga County (Cleveland, Ohio), Erie County (Buffalo, New York), Milwaukee County (Milwaukee, Wisconsin), and Wayne County (Detroit, Michigan). The data for Figure 11.2 are derived from U.S. Census Bureau (1996).
4. The National Oceanic and Atmospheric Administration coastal counties are identified in U.S. Census Bureau (2011c).
5. Missing data occur among all of the regions, with the Northeast and the Great Lakes regions having the most valid observations and the Midwest, South, and West having many more counties not reporting self-employment data. There are 3,140 counties among the 50 American states, but because of missing or otherwise unreported data among the Social Security figures, the valid number is 1,971 counties. The vast majority of the missing data come from sparsely populated rural counties. For example, the counties with missing self-employment figures have mean estimated 2008 populations of 10,380 persons, with nearly four-fifths of their 2000 population defined as rural (mean = 0.79). By contrast, the valid data's 2008 estimated population is 147,735 persons, with over half of these counties' populations defined as urbanized (mean = 0.52).
6. Business establishment rate: $F = 35.796$, significant at the 0.001 level [MSBW= 65.594 (df=4), MSWI= 1.832 (df=1967)]; percent self-employed: $F = 12.42$, significant at the 0.001 level [MSBW= 0.026 (df=4), MSWI= 0.026 (df=1967)]; business birth rate: $F = 89.515$, significant at the 0.001 level [MSBW= 187.695 (df=4), MSWI= 2.097 (df=1967)].
7. This variable is derived from data from the U.S. Census Bureau (2011a).

8. The data for this variable are derived from the U.S. Census Bureau (2011b).
9. It should be stressed that much of the literature relating to taxation and entrepreneurial behavior is about the effect the marginal rate has on behavior. This analysis uses a far less sensitive measure related to the tax burden.

References

Acs, Zoltan J., and Catherine Armington. 2004. "Employment Growth and Entrepreneurial Activity in Cities." *Regional Studies* 38(8): 911–927.

———. 2006. *Entrepreneurship, Geography, and American Economic Growth*. New York: Cambridge University Press.

Audretsch, David B., and Max Keilbach. 2004. "Entrepreneurship and Regional Growth: An Evolutionary Interpretation." *Journal of Evolutionary Economics* 14(5): 605–616.

Bartik, Timothy J. 1985. "Business Location Decisions in the United States: Estimation of the Effects of Unionization, Taxes, and Other Characteristics of States." *Journal of Business and Economic Statistics* 3(1): 14–22.

Baumol, William J. 2010. *The Microtheory of Innovative Entrepreneurship*. Princeton, NJ: Princeton University Press.

Blau, David M. 1987. "A Time-Series Analysis of Self-Employment in the United States." *Journal of Political Economy* 95 (3): 445–467.

Bonacich, Edna. 1973. "A Theory of Middleman Minorities." *American Sociological Review* 38(5): 583–894.

Borjas, George J. 1986. "The Self-Employment Experience of Immigrants." *Journal of Human Resources* 21(4): 485–506.

Branchflower, David G., and Andrew J. Oswald. 1998. "What Makes an Entrepreneur?" *Journal of Labor Economics* 16(1): 26–60.

Brockhaus, Robert H. 1982. "The Psychology of the Entrepreneur." In *Encyclopedia of Entrepreneurs*, Calvin A. Kent, Donald L. Sexton, and Karl H. Vesper, eds. Englewood Cliffs, NJ: Prentice-Hall, pp. 39–57.

Bruce, Donald. 2000. "Effects of the United States Tax System on Transitions into Self-Employment," *Labour Economics* 7(5): 545–574.

Brüderl, Josef, Peter Preisendörfer, and Rolf Ziegler. 1992. "Survival Chances of Newly Founded Business Organizations." *American Sociological Review* 57(2): 227–242.

Carroll, Robert, Douglas Holtz-Eakin, Mark Rider, Harvey S. Rosen. 2000. "Income Taxes and Entrepreneurs' Use of Labor." *Journal of Labor Economics* 18(2): 324–351.

City of Chicago. 2012. "Mayor Mayor Emanuel Announces Creation of Office of New Americans to Support Chicago's Immigrant Communites and

Enhance Their Contributions to Chicago's Economic, Civic, and Cultural Life." News release, July 19. Chicago: City of Chicago, Mayor's Press Office. http://www.cityofchicago.org/city/en/depts/mayor/provdrs/office_of_new_americans/news/2011/jul/mayor_emanuel_announcescreation ofofficeofnewamericanstosupportch.html (accessed April 29, 2013).

Council of State Governments. 2010. *Book of the States, 2010*. Table 7.21 State General Revenue, By Source and By State: 2008. Lexington, KY: Council of State Governments. http://knowledgecenter.csg.org/drupal/content/book-states-2010-chapter-7-state-finance (accessed July 29, 2011).

Dunn, Thomas, and Douglas Holtz-Eakin. 2000. "Financial Capital, Human Capital, and the Transition to Self-Employment: Evidence from Intergenerational Links." *Journal of Labor Economics* 18(2): 282–305.

Eisinger, Peter K. 1988. *The Entrepreneurial State: State and Local Economic Development Policies in the United States*. Madison, WI: University of Wisconsin Press.

———. 1995. "State Economic Development in the 1990s: Politics and Policy Learning." *Economic Development Quarterly* 9(2): 146–158.

Evans, David S., and Linda S. Leighton. 1989. "Some Empirical Aspects of Entrepreneurship." *American Economic Review* 79(3): 519–535.

Evans, M.D.R. 1989. "Immigrant Entrepreneurship: Effects of Ethnic Market Size and Isolated Labor Pool." *American Sociological Review* 54(6): 950–962.

Federal Reserve Bank of Chicago. 1985. *The Great Lakes Economy: A Resource and Industry Profile of the Great Lakes States*. Boyne City, MI: Harbor House Publishers.

Gambetta, Ricardo, and Zivile Gedrimaite. 2010. *Municipal Innovations in Immigrant Integration: 20 Cities, 20 Good Practices*. Washington, DC: National League of Cities.

Gartner, John. 2005. "America's Manic Entrepreneurs." *American Enterprise* 16(5): 18–21.

Gentry, William M., and R. Glenn Hubbard. 2000. "Tax Policy and Entrepreneurial Entry." *American Economic Review* 90 (2): 283–287.

Gibson, Campbell. 1998. "Population of the 100 Largest Cities and Other Urban Places in the United States: 1790 to 1990." Population Division Working Paper No. 27. Washington, DC: U.S. Census Bureau, Population Division. http://www.census.gov/population/www/documentation/twps0027/twps0027.html (accessed September 22, 2011).

Grieco, Elizabeth M., Yesenia D. Acosta, G. Patricia de la Cruz, Christine Gambino, Thomas Gryn, Luke J. Larsen, Edward N. Trevelyan, and Nathan P. Walters. 2012. "The Foreign Born Population in the United States: 2010." American Community Survey Reports, May. Washington, DC: U.S. Census

Bureau. http://www.census.gov/prod/2012pubs/acs-19.pdf (accessed September 18, 2012).

Hamilton, Barton H. 2000. "Does Entrepreneurship Pay? An Empirical Analysis of the Returns to Self-Employment." *Journal of Political Economy* 108(3): 604–631.

Hart, David M. 2008. "The Politics of 'Entrepreneurial' Economic Development Policy of States in the U.S." *Review of Policy Research* 25(2): 149–168.

Hébert, Robert F., and Albert N. Link. 1982. *The Entrepreneur: Mainstream Views and Radical Critiques*. New York: Praeger.

Hill, Richard Child, and Cynthia Negrey. 1987. "Deindustrialization in the Great Lakes." *Urban Affairs Quarterly* 22(4): 580–597.

Holtz-Eakin, Douglas, David Joulfaian, and Harvey S. Rosen. 1994. "Sticking It Out: Entrepreneurial Survival and Liquidity Constraints." *Journal of Political Economy* 102(1): 53–75.

Hoyman, Michele, and Christopher Faricy. 2008. "It Takes a Village: A Test of the Creative Class, Social Capital, and Human Capital Theories." *Urban Affairs Review* 44(3): 311–333.

Huffington Post. 2012. "Chicago City Council Passes 'Welcoming City Ordinance' to Protect Undocumented Immigrants." Huffington Post: Latino Voices, September 13. http://www.huffingtonpost.com/2012/09/13/chicago-welcoming-city-ordinance_n_1882115.html (accessed September 24, 2011).

Hurst, Erik, and Annamaria Lusardi. 2004. "Liquidity Constraints, Household Wealth, and Entrepreneurship." *Journal of Political Economy* 112(2): 319–347.

Klepper, Steven. 2009. "Silicon Valley, a Chip off the Old Detroit Bloc." In *Entrepreneurship, Growth, and Public Policy*, Zoltan J. Acs, David B. Audretsch, and Robert J. Strom, eds. Cambridge, UK: Cambridge University Press, pp. 79–115.

Knight, Frank H. 1921. *Risk, Uncertainty, and Profit*. Boston: Houghton.

Lamoreaux, Naomi R., Margaret Levenstein, and Kenneth L. Sokoloff. 2006. "Mobilizing Venture Capital during the Second Industrial Revolution: Cleveland, Ohio, 1870–1920." *Capitalism and Society* 1(3): 1–61.

Landes, David S. 1969. *The Unbound Prometheus: Technological Change 1750 to the Present*. Cambridge, UK: Cambridge University Press.

Lazear, Edward P. 2004. "Balanced Skills and Entrepreneurship." *American Economic Review* 94 (2): 208–211.

———. 2005. "Entrepreneurship." *Journal of Labor Economics* 23(4): 649–680.

Lundstrom, Anders, and Lois A. Stevenson. 2005. *Entrepreneurship Policy: Theory and Practice*. New York: Kluwer Academic Publishers.

McClelland, David C. 1961. *The Achieving Society*. Princeton, NJ: D. Van Nostrand Company, Inc.

Negrey, Cynthia, and Mary Beth Zickel. 1994. "Industrial Shifts and Uneven Development: Patterns of Growth and Decline in U.S. Metropolitan Areas." *Urban Affairs Review* 30(1): 27–47.

Portes, Alejandro, and Leif Jensen. 1989. "The Enclave and the Entrants: Patterns of Ethnic Enterprise in Miami Before and After Mariel." *American Sociological Review* 54(6): 929–949.

Reynolds, Paul. 1994. "Autonomous Firm Dynamics and Economic Growth in the United States, 1986–1990." *Regional Studies* 28(4): 429–442.

Saiz, Martin. 2001. "Politics and Economic Development: Why Governments Adopt Different Strategies to Induce Economic Growth." *Policies Studies Journal* 29(2): 203–214.

Sanders, Jimy M., and Victor Nee. 1996. "Immigrant Self-Employment: The Family as Social Capital and the Value of Human Capital." *American Sociological Review* 61(2): 231–249.

Saxenian, AnnaLee. 2002. "Silicon Valley's New Immigrant High-Growth Entrepreneurs." *Economic Development Quarterly* 16(1): 20–31.

Schmookler. Jacob. 1966. *Invention and Economic Growth*. Cambridge, MA: Harvard University Press.

Schuetze, Herb J. 2000. "Taxes, Economic Conditions, and Recent Trends in Male Self-Employment: A Canada-U.S. Comparison." *Labour Economics* 7(5): 507–544.

Schumpeter, Joseph A. 1939. *Business Cycles: A Theoretical, Historical, and Statistical Analysis of the Capitalist Process*. New York: McGraw-Hill Book Company.

———. 1949. *The Theory of Economic Development: An Inquiry into Profits, Capital, Credit, Interest, and the Business Cycle*. Cambridge, MA: Harvard University Press.

Shackle, G. L. S. 1982. Foreword to *The Entrepreneur: Mainstream Views and Radical Critiques*, by Robert F. Hébert and Albert N. Link. New York: Praeger.

Shane, Scott. 1996. "Explaining Variations in Rates of Entrepreneurship in the United States." *Journal of Management* 22: 747–781.

———. 2003. *A General Theory of Entrepreneurship: The Individual-Opportunity Nexus*. Cheltenham, UK: Edward Elgar.

Sokolove, Michael. 2011. "For Derek Jeter, on His 37th Birthday." *New York Times Magazine*, June 23. http://www.nytimes.com/2011/06/26/magazine/for-derek-jeter-on-his-37th-birthday.html?pagewanted=all (accessed April 29, 2013).

Thornton, Patricia H. 1999. "The Sociology of Entrepreneurship." *Annual Review of Sociology* (25): 19–46.

U.S. Census Bureau. 1996. Population of the States and Counties of the United States: 1790–1990. Washington, DC: U.S. Census Bureau. http://www .census.gov/population/www/censusdata/pop1790-1990.html   (accessed October 2011).

———. 2008 County Business Patterns. Washington, DC: U.S. Census Bureau. http://www.census.gov/econ/cbp/index.html (accessed July 2011).

———. 2009. Age and Sex, 2006–2008 American Community Survey. Washington, DC: U.S. Census Bureau.

———. 2011a. American Community Survey 5-Year Estimates, GCT1502 - Percent Of People 25 Years And Over Who Have Completed A Bachelor's Degree, United States—County by State; and for Puerto Rico (2006–2010). Washington, DC: U.S. Census Bureau.

———. 2011b. American Community Survey 5-Year Estimates, GCT0501- Geography-United States: Percent Of People Who Are Foreign Born, United States—County by State; and for Puerto Rico, Universe: Total population (2006–2010). Washington, DC: U.S. Census Bureau.

———. 2011c. NOAA's List of Coastal Counties for the Bureau of the Census. Statistical Abstract Series. Washington, DC: U.S. Census Bureau. http:// www.census.gov/geo/landview/lv6help/coastal_cty.pdf (accessed August 15, 2011).

———. 2012. "2010 Census Urban Lists Record Layouts, Percent Urban and and Rural by County," Washington, D.C.: U.S. Census Bureau, (accessed September 4, 2012).

U.S. Department of Labor. 2008. Local Area Unemployment Statistics. Washington, DC: U.S. Department of Labor, Bureau of Labor Statistics. http:// www.bls.gov/lau/#data (accessed April 29, 2013).

U.S. Social Security Administration. 2011. "Earnings and Employment Data for Workers Covered under Social Security and Medicare, by State and County, 2008." Research, Statistics, and Policy Analysis. Washington, DC: U.S. Social Security Administration. http://www.ssa.gov/policy/docs/ statcomps/eedata_sc/2008/index.html (accessed April 29, 2013).

Van Praag, C. M., and J. S. Cramer. 2001. "The Roots of Entrepreneurship and Labour Demand: Individual Ability and Low Risk Aversion." *Economica* 68(269): 45–62.

Wilken, Paul H. 1972. *Entrepreneurship: A Comparative and Historical Study.* Norwood, NJ: ABLEX Publishing Corporation.

Worgman, Amy, and Samuel Nunn. 2002. "Exploring a Complicated Labyrinth: Some Tips on Using Patent Data to Measure Urban and Regional Innovation." *Economic Development Quarterly* 16(3): 229–236.

Wright, Gavin. 2006. "Patent Applications Filed and Patents Issued, by Type of Patent and Patentee: 1790–2000." Table Cg27-37. In *Historical Statistics of the United States, Earliest Times to the Present: Millennial Edition*, Susan B. Carter, Scott Sigmund Gartner, Michael R. Haines, Alan L. Olmstead, Richard Sutch, and Gavin Wright, eds. New York: Cambridge University Press. http://dx.doi.org/10.1017/ISBN-9780511132971.Cg1-109 (accessed August 24, 2011).

Authors

Ziona Austrian is director of the Center for Economic Development and a college fellow at the Maxine Goodman Levin College of Urban Affairs at Cleveland State University. Her focus is on urban and regional economics, industrial clusters, the high-tech economy, entrepreneurship, and evaluation of economic development initiatives. Austrian received her PhD in economics from Case Western Reserve University.

Chieh-Chen Bowen is associate professor of psychology and director, Consumer and Industrial Research Program, College of Sciences and Health Professions, at Cleveland State University. Her work focuses on applying psychological principles in the workplace to improve organizational efficiency and employees' wellbeing. Bowen is an industrial and organizational psychologist with a PhD from Penn State University.

William M. Bowen is a native of Cleveland and attended the University of North Carolina-Chapel Hill, the College of Charleston, and the University of South Carolina, and Indiana University. He has published four books and nearly 50 peer-reviewed articles in a wide range of fields including public policy and administration, geography, psychology, regional science, operations research, demography, expert systems, economic development, and urban studies. He earned his PhD in regional analysis and planning in 1990.

Joan Chase holds a master's in urban studies with a concentration in economic development from the Levin School of Urban Affairs at Cleveland State University. Joan is a member of the grant-making committee of the Cleveland Foundation's Neighborhood Connections program and a member of the board of directors at Cogswell Hall, a residence for adults facing critical life challenges. She also works in economic development finance in northeast Ohio.

Benjamin Y. Clark is assistant professor of public administration in the Levin College of Urban Affairs at Cleveland State University. His research focuses on collaboration, public budgeting and finance, and reducing health disparities. Dr. Clark received his PhD in public administration from the University of Georgia.

David R. Elkins is associate professor of political science in the College of Liberal Arts and Social Sciences at Cleveland State University. His interests include public policy in urban communities, urban economic development, conflicts and coalition building, and taxation policy. Elkins received his PhD from the University of Kansas. Joel Elvery is an economist at the Federal Reserve Bank of Cleveland and does applied urban and labor economics research. Elvery earned his PhD in economics from the University of Maryland and received the Upjohn Institute 2005 Dissertation Award Honorable Mention.

Edward W. (Ned) Hill is the Dean of the Maxine Goodman Levin College of Urban Affairs at Cleveland State University. He is also a Nonresident Senior Fellow of the Metropolitan Policy Program at The Brookings Institution and a Nonresident Visiting Fellow of the Institute of Government Studies at the University of California at Berkeley though his membership in the MacArthur Foundation's Research Network on Building Resilient Regions. He earned his PhD in both economics and urban and regional planning from the Massachusetts Institute of Technology.

Kelly Kinahan is a doctoral candidate in urban policy and development in the Maxine Goodman Levin College of Urban Affairs, Cleveland State University. Her research focus is community and economic development, with specific interests in urban revitalization and historic preservation. Kinahan holds a Master of Urban and Regional Planning degree from Virginia Commonwealth University.

Merissa C. Piazza is a research associate in the Center for Economic Development at the Maxine Goodman Levin College of Urban Affairs at Cleveland State University. Merissa has a Master of Public and International Affairs from the University of Pittsburgh. In addition to working full time as a researcher, she is a doctoral student in urban studies and public policy at Cleveland State University.

Haifeng Qian is assistant professor of economic development in the Maxine Goodman Levin College of Urban Affairs at Cleveland State University. His research interests include economic development, economic geography, innovation and entrepreneurship, and public policy. Qian received his PhD in public policy from George Mason University.

Gregory M. Sadlek is the founding dean of the College of Liberal Arts and Social Sciences, a college that includes departments in the fine arts, at Cleveland State University. He received his PhD in English language and literature from Northern Illinois University and has been affiliated with urban/metropolitan universities since 1989.

Chang-Shik Song is a visiting research scholar in the Maxine Goodman Levin College of Urban Affairs at Cleveland State University. His research interests focus on the interactions between human activities and the environment, particularly in the fields of urban and regional economic development, air pollution, climate change, energy, and land use planning. He received his PhD in urban studies and public affairs from Cleveland State University.

Andrew R. Thomas is executive in residence at the Energy Policy Center in the Levin Urban College at Cleveland State University. He has many years of experience as a geophysicist for an oil company and as a lawyer in the energy sector. Thomas has a JD from Loyola University in New Orleans. He teaches courses in energy law and policy at Cleveland State University and at various venues around the world.

Index

Note: The italic letters *b, f, n,* and *t* following page numbers indicate a box, figure, note, or table on that page. Double italics mean more than one such item.

About the Institute

The W.E. Upjohn Institute for Employment Research is a nonprofit research organization devoted to finding and promoting solutions to employment-related problems at the national, state, and local levels. It is an activity of the W.E. Upjohn Unemployment Trustee Corporation, which was established in 1932 to administer a fund set aside by Dr. W.E. Upjohn, founder of The Upjohn Company, to seek ways to counteract the loss of employment income during economic downturns.

The Institute is funded largely by income from the W.E. Upjohn Unemployment Trust, supplemented by outside grants, contracts, and sales of publications. Activities of the Institute comprise the following elements: 1) a research program conducted by a resident staff of professional social scientists; 2) a competitive grant program, which expands and complements the internal research program by providing financial support to researchers outside the Institute; 3) a publications program, which provides the major vehicle for disseminating the research of staff and grantees, as well as other selected works in the field; and 4) an Employment Management Services division, which manages most of the publicly funded employment and training programs in the local area.

The broad objectives of the Institute's research, grant, and publication programs are to 1) promote scholarship and experimentation on issues of public and private employment and unemployment policy, and 2) make knowledge and scholarship relevant and useful to policymakers in their pursuit of solutions to employment and unemployment problems.

Current areas of concentration for these programs include causes, consequences, and measures to alleviate unemployment; social insurance and income maintenance programs; compensation; workforce quality; work arrangements; family labor issues; labor-management relations; and regional economic development and local labor markets.